The Big Book of
BABY
NAMES

The Big Book of
BABY
NAMES

*Every parent's inspirational
guide to naming their new child*

Marissa Charles

**SELECT
EDITIONS**

This edition printed in 2005

Selectabook Ltd
Folly Road, Roundway, Devizes,
Wiltshire SN10 2HT

Copyright © 2004, Arcturus Publishing Limited
26/27 Bickels Yard, 151–153 Bermondsey Street,
London SE1 3HA

Cover design by Alex Ingr
Layout by Metro Media Limited
With thanks to Andrew Adamides, Lee Coventry

ISBN 1-84193-283-3

Printed in India

Contents

Introduction

Introduction

Naming your newborn can be a daunting task. With thousands of names to choose from, it is easy to become overwhelmed. Should you opt for the traditional – Victoria, Mary or John – or the 'out-there': Moon Unit or Stardust? Should you choose a name that reflects your religious beliefs or one that has been used in your family for generations?

Does the name of a celebrity or current storybook hero appeal, or do you want to preserve your child's individuality by being creative and inventing something truly original? The options are seemingly endless, but leaf through the pages of this book and you will find answers to these questions which plague all parents. There are handy tips on the best way to choose a name for your child and the pitfalls to avoid.

If you want a name that reflects your ethnic or cultural background, we have separate sections highlighting those that are popular in the African, Celtic, Muslim and Native American communities. You can also read up on naming fashions and trends that have influenced parents through the ages. Having said that, the main aim of this book is dedicated to answering the basic question: what does the name mean and where does it come from?

Obviously, a name is much more than just a label. It is a gift from you to your children, and one that you hope they will love enough to carry with them for the rest of their lives. It is also the first step towards building their unique personal identity.

In years to come your child may be interested to know how you chose his or her name – the story behind it, the history and meaning. What language does the name come from? With which culture is it associated? Which historical figures bore the name and what was their contribution to society?

However, the very thing that makes choosing a name interesting can also make it confusing. A single name may have come from more than one language, each one seemingly unrelated. It is perfectly possible for one name to boast Latin, Old French, Old English and German roots simultaneously. In some cases it is because the exact meaning or origin of the name is unknown and research has thrown up more than one possible

Introduction

source. However, another factor lies in the history of Europe and the development of the English language.

When the Romans first invaded Britain in 54 BC they found a land largely inhabited by Celtic-speaking peoples. The invading forces left their own cultural imprint on the area – Latin – and subsequent armies did the same. West Germanic invaders such as the Jutes, Angles and Saxons all contributed linguistic marks. The result was that, from around AD 500 onwards, Anglo-Saxon – or Old English – became the dominant language in England.

Later, the arrival of the Danish and Norwegian Vikings injected Old Norse elements, and, after the Battle of Hastings in 1066, the Normans brought with them their French dialect, which was also imbued with Old Norse by the way.

These three elements – Anglo-Saxon, Old Norse and Norman French – developed into Middle English and later, Modern English. Add the fact that the Latin the Romans brought with them borrowed from Greek and it is clear that the languages of Europe are multi-layered and interrelated.

The ebb and flow of history, the changing fortunes of different rulers and invaders also explains why some names are popular and others are not, why some survived throughout the centuries but others did not. For example, after William the Conqueror and his followers arrived in England in the mid-11th century, many Anglo-Saxon names were replaced by Norman French ones. It was the Victorians who, fuelled by their fascination with Old English and Medieval names, reintroduced Alfred and Edwin into society. The renewed interest in the legend of King Arthur and his Knights of the Round Table also contributed to the hunger for names associated with early English folklore.

Similarly, as Christianity spread throughout Europe, efforts were made to break ties with the pagan past. Names from the classical world – especially those associated with Greek and Roman mythology – were replaced with ones belonging to characters from the Bible. Adam and Eve, Mary and Sarah, Rebecca and Joseph, the

Introduction

names of Christ's Apostles, especially Andrew, John and Peter, were all favoured by parents wanting to reflect their faith.

Equally popular were the names of Christian martyrs, saints and missionaries, such as St Francis of Assisi and St Christopher. It was not until the English Renaissance that classical names like Penelope were plucked from the past and bestowed upon children.

This pattern is repeated throughout the annals of history. During the Reformation, English parents shied away from names associated with the Roman Catholic Church. In the 17th century the Puritans sought out obscure Old Testament names such as Malachy, Zillah and Beulah or ordinary words that reflected a quality they would like their child to possess, like Hope, Faith and Patience.

In the modern age no such rules or social mores apply. Of course there are names that parents may avoid because of the current or historical figures associated with them. Adolph conjures up images of the Austrian-born German dictator Adolf Hitler. However, there are also names that mothers and fathers warm to because of a well-known personality. In the last 20 years Kylie, Madonna and Britney have found favour because of the influence of popular culture.

It is this, the influence of the arts (literature, plays, music, film and television), that has guided many of the definitions in this book. While the works of Shakespeare and other classical writers have long been a source of inspiration for parents, it is wrong to underestimate the powerful force of the mass media in today's world. In the golden age of Hollywood, films like *Gone with the Wind* and *High Society* inspired parents to name their children after leading characters like Scarlett and Tracy. But in the 21st century, soap operas, sitcoms, pop music and even the Internet have a role. Parents today truly have a wealth of information at their fingertips.

We have tried to offer some guidance within the pages of this book, as well as provide thousands of suggestions that may appeal to you – see the Index on page 367 for a full listing. Naming your baby should be entertaining, educational and fun. We hope you enjoy the journey. ■

How to choose a name

The process of choosing a baby name is a straightforward process for those who are already decided, particularly if there is a favourite name selected years in advance of giving birth. However, there are plenty of parents who are not at all decided and don't even know to start. Here are a few tips to help kickstart the process.

Meaning

Look at names that have meaning for you and/or your family, perhaps naming the baby after a favourite relative or relatives. Alternatively, if you don't have a preference for your relatives, names, or want the baby to be more individual without being entirely different, look for derivatives or feminine/masculine versions of relatives' names.

Avoid teasing

Bear in mind the different stages of life your child will go through with their name, and try to avoid picking something which could lead to teasing in the classroom and playground. Look at your baby's physical characteristics (or those that tend to run in your family) and if there are any which generate teasing, avoid names that can exacerbate this.

Syllables

Look at the length of each name and the number of syllables. Very long names can be difficult to fit on forms, while very short ones may look odd. In terms of syllables, try to vary the number of syllables in the first name and surname, and avoid first names that stress the same syllable as the last name.

Rhyme and rhythm

Think of the rhythm of the name in combination with your last name. Try and avoid repeated sounds, as in Herman Wyman, for example. Also try and avoid rhyming names like Jane Vane and names that repeat part of the surname (e.g. John Johnson).

How to choose a name

Pronunciation
Think about pronunciation. Going through life with a name that is difficult to pronounce – or that is pronounced very differently to how it is spelt – can lead to frustration. The same goes for anything spelt in an overly-exotic way.

Middle names
Middle names are a means of including relatives who might otherwise feel excluded from the baby-naming process – as long as the names all work together. The syllable rule also applies when picking out a middle name, so do check how all three sound together.

Anne, Lynne and Marie are popular girls names due to the number of syllables they contain. Most first and last names have two syllables and the emphasis is placed on the first, so these names change this and make for a comfortable rhythm. There are, however, plenty of other names accented differently that can be used instead, like Alexandra, Fiona, Evelyn and Valerie.

Middle names for boys can be trickier, as most male names follow the same pattern of having two syllables, with the accent on the first. There are, however, plenty which differ, like Adrian, Anthony and Xavier. ∎

Top 10 first names

ENGLAND & WALES

BOYS

1800		1900		2000	
1	William	1	William	1	Jack
2	John	2	John	2	Thomas
3	Thomas	3	George	3	James
4	James	4	Thomas	4	Joshua
5	George	5	Charles	5	Daniel
6	Joseph	6	Frederick	6	Harry
7	Richard	7	Arthur	7	Samuel
8	Henry	8	James	8	Joseph
9	Robert	9	Albert	9	Matthew
10	Charles	10	Ernest	10	Callum

1850		1950	
1	William	1	David
2	John	2	John
3	George	3	Peter
4	Thomas	4	Michael
5	James	5	Alan
6	Henry	6	Robert
7	Charles	7	Stephen
8	Joseph	8	Paul
9	Robert	9	Brian
10	Samuel	10	Graham

Top 10 first names

GIRLS

	1800		1900		2000
1	Mary	1	Florence	1	Chloe
2	Ann	2	Mary	2	Emily
3	Elizabeth	3	Alice	3	Megan
4	Sarah	4	Annie	4	Charlotte
5	Jane	5	Elsie	5	Jessica
6	Hannah	6	Edith	6	Lauren
7	Susan	7	Elizabeth	7	Sophie
8	Martha	8	Doris	8	Olivia
9	Margaret	9	Dorothy	9	Hannah
10	Charlotte	10	Ethel	10	Lucy

	1850		1950
1	Mary	1	Susan
2	Elizabeth	2	Linda
3	Sarah	3	Christine
4	Ann	4	Margaret
5	Eliza	5	Carol
6	Jane	6	Jennifer
7	Emma	7	Janet
8	Hannah	8	Patricia
9	Ellen	9	Barbara
10	Martha	10	Ann

Top 10 first names

USA

BOYS   GIRLS

1900		2000		1900	
1	John	1	Jacob	1	Mary
2	William	2	Michael	2	Ruth
3	Charles	3	Matthew	3	Helen
4	Robert	4	Joshua	4	Margaret
5	Joseph	5	Christopher	5	Elizabeth
6	James	6	Nicholas	6	Dorothy
7	George	7	Andrew	7	Catherine
8	Samuel	8	Joseph	8	Mildred
9	Thomas	9	Daniel	9	Frances
10	Arthur	10	Tyler	10=	Alice
				10=	Marion

1950				1950	
1	Robert			1	Linda
2	Michael			2	Mary
3	James			3	Patricia
4	John			4	Susan
5	David			5	Deborah
6	William			6	Kathleen
7	Thomas			7	Barbara
8	Richard			8	Nancy
9	Gary			9	Sharon
10	Charles			10	Karen

Top 10 first names

AUSTRALIA

	BOYS	GIRLS

2000
1 Emily
2 Hannah
3 Madison
4 Ashley
5 Sarah
6 Alexis
7 Samantha
8 Jessica
9 Taylor
10 Elizabeth

BOYS 1950	GIRLS 1950
1 John	1 Susan
2 Peter	2 Margaret
3 Michael	3 Ann(e)
4 David	4 Elizabeth
5 Robert	5 Christine
6 Stephen	6 Jennifer
7 Paul	7 Judith
8 Philip	8 Patricia
9 Christopher	9 Catherine
10 Ian	10 Helen

BOYS 2000	GIRLS 2000
1 Joshua	1 Jessica
2 Jack	2 Emily
3 Thomas	3 Sarah
4 Lachlan	4 Georgia
5 Matthew	5 Olivia
6 James	6 Emma
7 Daniel	7 Chloe
8 Nicholas	8 Sophie
9 Benjamin	9 Hannah
10 William	10 Isabella

Naming trends

Fads and fashions in names are nothing new – in fact they date way back into history, with favoured names coming in and going out of fashion as easily and as often as clothing styles do. Of late, however, one interesting factor has been noted – girls names tend to be subject to more trends than boys names, with the likes of David and Michael remaining popular, while Rose, Ruby and Emma come and go far more regularly. Here are a few trends from the last thousand years or so!

Upper Class Names (1066 onwards)
When the Normans invaded England, they became the higher members of society, and Norman names became trendy with the lower, and more aspirational classes. Prior to this, Anglo Saxon names had been altered from generation to generation, while Norman names stayed the same. Norman names include William, Brian, Robert, Alan, Alice, Laura and Emma.

Biblical Names (Medieval times)
As the Christian church took hold, it became all the rage to name your child after a character from the Bible. Saints' names in particular started to become extremely popular. By the 16th century, 28 per cent of boys were being named John, overtaking William as most popular boy's name somewhere around 1400. Other popular biblical names of the period include Matthew, Luke, Mary, Margaret and Agnes.

Puritan Names (16th – 17th century)
The Puritans brought with them their own favoured names. Catholic names went out of favour and names denoting qualities the Puritans thought were admirable became popular. Hence, the likes of Patience, Temperance, Mercy, Hope, Charity and Faith came to the fore. In addition to not liking Catholic names, the Puritans also avoided any Biblical names associated with anything less than savoury. Hence Eve, Cain, Bathsheba and Dinah all declined in popularity.

Literature and Fame (17th century onwards)
While it can be argued that naming children after the famous really starts when people took names from the Bible, this is one trend that has continued to this day, with many parents looking to both real-life figures and artistic movements for naming inspiration. The author JM Barrie created the name Wendy for his play *Peter Pan*. The romantic movement popularised romance names like Quentin, Nigel and Amy, and the pre-Raphaelite movement gave renewed popularity to medieval names like Mabel, Lancelot and Edith. In Victorian times, those who weren't too enamoured of the flower-name trend turned to the Gothic revival and picked Norman and Anglo-Saxon names from this, including Alfred, Emma and Matilda.

Flowers and Jewels (19th century)
From the 1850s onwards, flowers became hugely popular as names for girls, with Lily, Ivy, Hyacinth, Poppy, Rose and Daisy all cutting huge swathes into the public consciousness. Gemstones also started appearing as first names for the first time, such as: pearl, ruby, amber, jade and amethyst.

Flower Power (1960s)
The psychedelic 1960s saw a major breakout in the number of 'out-there' names chosen for children, with the rise of flower power, free love and the hippy movement. Names like Sun, Moon and Sky briefly became popular.

Unisex Names (1970s)
Unisex names became fashionable in the 1970s due to the influence of women's lib and the desire to erase the lines between the sexes. Girls' names such as Georgie, Nicola and Philippa all became popular during this time.

Welsh Names (20th century)
A recent trend has pushed Welsh names to the fore. Rhys, Rees, Lewis, Sian and Evan have all become popular. ■

Naming traditions

While most westerners simply pick a name they like for their child, or choose the name of a favourite friend or relative, other parts of the world have rather more rigid and unusual traditions for naming babies. Even other parts of Europe have customs and traditions which seem rather unusual by British standards.

France
In France, theoretically, a law passed in 1803 limits parents' choices to the names of saints or historical figures. While the law has been relaxed over the years, there have still been recent court cases where parents demanded the right to give their babies rather more unusual names.

Spain
In Spain, the child gets two last names – first the father's name, then the mother's maiden name. Hence, if Juan Perez Castillo marries Carmen Ramirez Polo, their child Ramon would be named Ramon Perez Ramirez.

Italy
Italian first names are never unisex. Boys' names generally end with the letter O, as in Enrico, Paulo, etc, while girls' names generally end with the letter A, as in Valeria, Anna, etc. Families often use both the male and female derivatives of names, so it is quite common to have a brother and sister called, for example, Ilario and Ilaria.

Austria and Germany
In Germany and Austria, the names of historical kings and other royals are extremely popular, with the likes of Wilhelm and Ludwig being used frequently.

India
Indians enjoy many different naming methods, with many citizens having several names; a first name, a name derived from

their father, a village name, a caste name etc. In different parts of the country these are used in different orders.

Hindu families will often call their children after one of their ancestors, as the Hindu religion believes in reincarnation and in this way the ancestor can be 'reborn' in the child.

Parents also often use words as names, choosing words which mean qualities they would like the children to possess. Kaushal, for example, means clever or skilled.

Another popular source of names are the Hindu gods, including Siva, Lakshmi, etc.

Israel
Israelis usually pick first names from the old testament of the bible. Even quite obscure Biblical names, like Eldad and Medad are popular. Many names end in the suffix 'el' as in Hebrew this refers to God. Israelis do not have middle names.

China and Japan
Due to the different way they use language the Chinese naming system is wholly different. All the characters in the Chinese alphabet can be used as first names, and as there are thousands of these, there is plenty of choice! The most common include Wen (culture, writing), Zhi (will, intention, emotions), Yi (cheerful), Ya (elegant), Ming (bright), Hui (smart, wise), Hong (great, wide). Boys' names are picked from a set of around 20 characters used in rotation by generations of the same family. Girls' names are far less rigidly governed – parents can pick anything they like.

Similarly, in Japan, Chinese characters are used as first names. Boys are often given names which indicate the order in which they were born. Neither use middle names. ∎

Popular culture and names

Since popular culture took over from – well, from pretty much everything else as the dominant force in peoples' lives, its no coincidence that more and more children have found themselves being named after TV and film characters, celebrities and, in a few cases, even the children of celebrities. In fact, numerous internet baby-naming sites now tell you what TV show character/famous person shares which particular name, along the lines of 'Daphne – featured character in *Frasier* and *Scooby Doo*.'

Probably the best-remembered case of TV-related naming obsession occurred in the late 1980s, when the proliferation of children named Kylie and Jason in the UK was attributed to the huge popularity of Australian TV soap *Neighbours* and its then-stars Kylie Minogue and Jason Donovan.

However, as far back as the thirties, parents were turning to celebs for name inspiration. A quick look at the statistics shows Greta (as in Garbo) peaked in popularity in the 1930s, while Marilyn (as in Monroe) held its popularity throughout the 1950s and 1960s, declining thereafter. Boys' names tend not to be quite so trend-driven, however, although Clark (as in Gable) was slightly more popular in the 1930s and 1940s than it is today. This may well be due to the fact that trends tend to affect female names more than male, as standards like James, which have been particularly popular in the 1950s and 1960s thanks to James Dean and James Bond, have stayed at an almost constant level of popularity for the past hundred years.

TV chef Jamie Oliver's use of the name Poppy for his daughter has been credited with the resurgence in popularity of a name last popular in the Victorian era. Elsewhere, the Beckhams' choice of Romeo as a name for their second son was also copied by numerous other parents. *Amelie* became more popular after the French film of the same name hit it big recently.

When considering a pop-culture name, however, do beware. TV shows date quickly, and while Kylie and Jason were everyone's favourites yesterday, the names swiftly went out of fashion. ■

Making up a name

The quest for a name that is unique is becoming increasingly difficult. Where once unusual names have now become commonplace, an option is to make up your own name for baby. Here are a few guidelines that can be used when making up a name.

Try combining names to come up with something new. You can try putting the baby's parents' names together, hence John and Eileen might have Joneen, or with the names of two or more relatives (this also dodges arguments about who the baby gets named after!). Alternately, it's a great way, if you are undecided between two names, just to try putting them together. Since most made-up names are combinations of some sort, try combining words you like either the sounds or the meanings of. This can apply to choosing names to combine as well, since you can create a new name with a combination meaning.

Try spelling another name or word or last name backwards, which can create a nice effect by giving the baby a 'mirror' effect name. For example, the last name Allen becomes a first name Nella.

Anagrams can also be very effective. Try re-arranging the letters in one or both parents' names. This can be a good option if you like the idea of combining the two names into one, but have names that don't work for this. This usually works better with longer names.

Alternately, you can combine any or all of the above or try random name generators, of which there are plenty online. ■

Embarrassing names – beware!

It is up to you to make sure whatever name is chosen is not going to cause embarrassment to your son or daughter.

Considerations include; initials, how does your first name combine with your surname, and how it could potentially be broken down into a diminutive or nickname.

When it comes to initials, write down the initials and make sure you don't end up with something like Roland Andrew Taylor, or Penelope Irene Grainger.

As for checking how names work together, just try saying the names out loud, and you will soon notice if there is something not quite right. Most of the following are urban legends, but you will want to avoid the likes of Paige Turner, Crystal Waters, Theresa Greene, Jay Walker and Ima Hogg. (Ms. Hogg actually existed – she was the daughter of a prominent Texas politician in the early 20th century).

Children can be incredibly cruel when it comes to nicknames as well, so try and think of these in advance. Richard can often be turned into Dick, so if your last name is Head, you may want to avoid using that as a first name. So probably best to jot down all options before making your final decision. ■

Named for greatness?

Many cultures do believe that your name affects your life-path, and giving a child the right name can influence what he/she does in life. Certainly, Hindu cultures choose names based on what qualities parents hope a child will possess as an adult.

Historically speaking, there are certain names which have been associated with those in positions of power, although it should be borne in mind that royalty and other powerful families tend to use the same names, but already have the connections and status in place to push their children on to success, so it is not really a coincidence that Henry and Elizabeth are popular.

Nevertheless, US academics have identified several names – including Anne, Joseph, Samuel, Henry and William – as being 'successful' names, based mostly on the track records of individuals with those names throughout US history (i.e. William Clinton being an example of success, having been US President for eight years.)

Numerology can also be applied to naming. Numbers are assigned to each letter of the alphabet (i.e. A is one, B is two etc), and all the letters in a first and last name are added together until one final number is found. This is then used to determine numerous things about the subject's life. There are many variations on how this is calculated, however, and the eventual meaning of this number. It should also be noted that in some cases numerology does also take into account nicknames and diminutives, which may not be known when the baby is named. Hence, you may name your baby Christopher, with no intention of referring to him as Chris, but he may then become known as such by his own demand or through interaction with peers. As this is his own chosen name, numerology would use that, rather than his full name.

So there are many facts that can be played around with in order to try and ensure success for your child. However, no amount of slaving over a numerology chart or the history books in search of a name guaranteeing fame will replace good parenting in terms of increasing your child's chances of success in life. ■

Celebrity name changes

Celebrities change their names for a variety of reasons, most commonly because their birth names just don't trip off the tongue easily enough. In a business where names have to be short, sharp, instantly recognisable, and project the right sort of image, it's doubtful whether Thomas Cruise Mapother IV would have got nearly as far had he not dropped the Mapother and shortened Thomas to Tom. In music, a single name makes even more of an impact, hence Madonna Ciccone dropping her last name all together, and Gordon Sumner opting to be called Sting.

In the early days of Hollywood, the studio system dictated stars' name changes, often running fan contests to come up with new names for up-and-coming actors. That was how Lucille LeSueur became Joan Crawford, a name she hated, in 1925. There was also often the question of ethnicity in rather less free-thinking times and this lead to many casting off their more exotic-sounding names. Besides which, foreign names were often harder to pronounce and hence easier to forget. Although in a few cases, performers have gone for more ethnic-sounding names, Lou Diamond Phillips, for example, was born Lou Upchurch.

In just as many cases, however, actors' union rules dictate that names must be changed because two performers can't have names that are too similar. In many name-change cases, whatever the reason, many have altered their original first/last name and swapped them around, Tammy Wynette, for example, was born Wynette Pugh, while veteran actor Karl Malden was born Mladen Sekulovich.

In some cases, celebs have changed names for religious reasons, most notably Cassius Clay who became Muhammad Ali. Others, meanwhile, have deliberately chosen a different name to avoid being accused of using family connections – hence the actor Nicholas Coppola became Nicholas Cage. Charlie Sheen, meanwhile, adopted for his father Martin's self-chosen last name (Martin was born Ramon Estevez, Charlie Carlos Estevez) while brother Emilio stuck with the family's original name. ■

Celebrity name changes – a few of the best:

Woody Allen — **Allen Stewart Konigsberg**
Lauren Bacall — **Betty Joan Perske**
Anne Bancroft — **Anna Maria Louisa Italiano**
David Bowie — **David Robert Hayward-Jones**
Richard Burton — **Richard Jenkins**
Nicholas Cage — **Nicholas Coppola**
Michael Caine — **Maurice J. Micklewhite**
Chevy Chase — **Cornelius Crane Chase**
Eric Clapton — **Eric Clapp**
Alice Cooper — **Vincent Damon Furnier**
Elvis Costello — **Declan Patrick McManus**
Bo Derek — **Mary Cathleen Collins**
Kirk Douglas — **Issur Danielovitch Demsky**
Jodie Foster — **Alicia Christian Foster**
Cary Grant — **Archibald Alexander Leach**
Jean Harlow — **Harlean Carpentier**
Rita Hayworth — **Margarita Cansino**
Hulk Hogan — **Terry Jean Bollette**
Bob Hope — **Leslie Townes Hope**
Rock Hudson — **Roy Scherer**
Engelbert Humperdinck — **Arnold Gerry Dorsey**
Michael Keaton — **Michael Douglas**
Ben Kingsley — **Krishna Bhanji**
Stan Laurel — **Arthur Stanley Jefferson**
Spike Lee — **Shelton Lee**
Sophia Loren — **Sophia Scicoloni**
Meat Loaf — **Marvin Lee Adair**
George Michael — **Georgios Panayiotou**
Joan Rivers — **Joan Sandra Molinsky**
Mickey Rooney — **Joe Yule, Jr.**
Dusty Springfield — **Mary Isobel Catherine O'Brien**
Donna Summer — **La Donna Andrea Gaines**
John Wayne — **Marion Michael Morrison**
Stevie Wonder — **Steveland Judkins**

Girls

Girls

Aaliyah
Both Arabic and Hebrew in origin, this name means 'to ascend', 'highly exalted' and 'tall or towering'. Aaliyah may have also been derived from the Biblical Aliya, which means 'defender'.

Abigail
In the Bible Abigail was one of King David's wives. In Hebrew the name Avigayil means 'father rejoiced', 'source of joy'. In Britain Abigail has been in use since the 16th century, but in the 17th century the name was used as a term for 'lady's maid' and fell out of favour. It regained its popularity in the 19th century and again in the 20th century.
Variants: Abbie, Abby, Abagael, Abigael, Abigayle

Abira
This Hebrew name means 'strong' and 'heroic'.
Variants: Adira, Amiza

Abra
A female form of the Biblical name Abraham, Abra means 'mother of multitudes' and 'mother of the earth'. It was a popular name in the 17th century.

Ada
There are two main theories about the origin of this name. One belief suggests Ada is the Latin version of the Biblical name Adah, which means 'lovely ornament' in Hebrew. In the Old Testament Adah was the wife of Lamech, a direct descendant of Adam and Eve.

But another theory suggests Ada comes from the Old English for 'happy' and the Old German for 'noble and kind'. Either way it has been used in English-speaking countries since the 16th century and, in 1815, the poet Lord Byron gave the name to his daughter.
Variants: Adah, Adda, Addie, Addy, Aeda, Aida, Eada, Eda, Etta

Adelaide

Of Germanic origin, Adelaide is the French form of the Old German for 'noble' and 'sort'. At the beginning of the 10th century the name held some currency because of the wife of the Holy Roman Emperor, Otto the Great. She bore the name and was known for her beauty and goodness.

In Britain Queen Adelaide, the wife of William IV, increased its popularity in the 19th century. In 1836, an Australian city was named in her honour.

Variants: Ada, Adalhaide, Adalia, Adda, Addi, Addison, Adélaïde, Adelina, Heidi

Adelpha

This name comes from the feminine form of the Greek for 'brother' or 'brotherhood'. Therefore, it means 'sisterly' or 'sister to mankind'.

Adesina

Families from the Yoruba tribe in West Africa give this name to the first baby of a previously childless couple. It means 'my arrival opens the way for more'.

Adiel

In Hebrew this name means 'ornament of the Lord'.
Variants: Adie, Adiell, Adiella

Aditi

'Free abundance' or 'unbounded creativity' is what this name stands for in Sanskrit. Aditi was the mother of the Hindu deities.

Adrienne

The origin of Adrienne and its male counterpart Adrian could be the place name, Adria – a city and port in northern Italy close to the Adriatic Sea. Distinctive because of its dark water and sand, it may explain the eventual Latin meaning of the name – 'dark one' or 'black, mysterious one'. In Greek, Adrienne means 'rich'.

Girls

Adria is also the family name of the Roman Emperor Hadrian.
Variants: Adrea, Adria, Adriana, Adrianna, Adriane, Adrien, Adrienne, Hadria, Riana

Afina
Romanian in origin, this name means 'blueberry'.

Agatha
This name is the feminine form of the Greek word agathos, which means 'good' and 'honourable'. It can also mean 'good, kind woman'.

In the 3rd century the veil of St Agatha was supposed to have saved her from the lava of Mount Etna. Hence, she is the patron saint of fire fighters.

The name was first introduced to Britain by a Norman conqueror who bestowed it upon his daughter. Its popularity increased in the 19th century.
Variants: Ag, Aga, Agathe, Agg, Aggi, Aggie, Atka

Agnes
Another name of Greek origin, the adjective hagnos ('pure' and 'holy') led to the name Hagne, the Latin form of which is Agnes. The first saint to bear this name was a child who, refusing to marry, offered herself for martyrdom in 3rd century Rome. Her story made the name popular during the Middle Ages and the Old English forms – Annis, Annes and Annot – reflect the pronunciation of the time. It is especially popular in Scotland.
Variants: Aggie, Aggy, Annais, Annice, Anis, Ina, Inez, Nesta

Aida
Aida is the feminine form of Aidan and the title of Giuseppe Verdi's 1871 opera. The heroine, who bears the name, is an Ethiopian princess who is enslaved in Egypt.

But the origins of this name do not lie in Africa. In Latin and Old French Aida comes from words meaning 'to help, assist'. When taken from Greek it means 'modesty', and in

Arabic it means 'reward' and the Old English interpretation is 'happy'.
Variants: Aidan, Iraida, Zaida, Zenaida, Zoraida

Aine
According to Irish mythology Aine was the queen of the fairies. The name is of Irish Gaelic origin and means 'little fire' or 'brightness, splendour and delight'.

Aisha
The favourite wife of the Prophet Mohammed was called Aisha. It was also the name of Pharaoh's wife, who Aisha drowned in the Red Sea when the Children of Israel fled Egypt. In Arabic the name means 'woman', 'prospering' or 'alive and well'.
Variants: Aesha, Asha, Ayasha, Ayesha, Aysha, Aishali, Asia

Alberta
The 19th century trend of calling girls Alberta may have something to do with Queen Victoria's husband, Prince Albert, and their daughter, Princess (Louise) Alberta.

Like Albert, this name is of Germanic origin. It stems from the elements: adal 'noble' and bertht which means 'bright and famous'. Brought to England by the Normans, the name died out until its Victorian revival.
Variants: Albertha, Albertina

Alcina
Alcina, the feminine version of Alcander, was the name of King Arthur's half sister. The origin of the name stems from Greek meaning 'strong-willed' and 'determined'.
Variants: Alcie, Alcine, Alzina, Elsie

Alexandra
Like Albert, Elizabeth and Victoria this name has long been associated with royalty. According to Greek mythology the first

person to be called Alexander – the male version – was the Trojan, Paris, Helen of Troy's lover. A group of shepherds gave him the nickname Alexander because he protected their flock from thieves. Hence the name means 'defender'.

The female variant, Alexandra, has been popular among European royalty for many generations. It was the name of the last Tsarina of Russia. The Danish princess who married Edward VII, and went on to become Queen Alexandra, revived its use in 19th century Britain.

Variants: Alexandria, Alexandrina, Alexandrine, Alexia, Alessandra, Lexie, Xandra

Alice

An independent name in its own right, Alice started life as a pet form of the German name Adelaide, which means 'noble'. It first appeared in England – via the French shortened variant Adaliz – as Aliz and Alys.

The popularity of the name in English-speaking countries grew in the 19th century following the success of Lewis Carroll's children's books – *Alice's Adventures in Wonderland (1865)* and *Through the Looking Glass (1872)*.

Variants: Alicia, Allie, Alli, Allis, Alix, Alys

Alicia

A variant of Alice, this name is a modern Latinate form of the same name.

Variants: Alissa, Alyssa

Alison

This name, like Alicia, is a pet form of Alice that is now an independent name in its own right. Although it was popular in the 20th century it has long had currency in Europe. It was a common medieval name that died out in England in the 15th century, only surviving in the UK in Scotland.

Like Alice and Adelaide, Alison means 'noble'.

Variants: Allie, Allison, Ally

Alma

The name Alma has several roots. In Hebrew it comes from the word for 'maiden'. In Italian it means 'soul' and in Spanish, 'warm-hearted'. 'Apple' is the Turkish interpretation and to the Celts it is 'all good'.

But in Latin it comes from the word almus, which means 'nourishing, kind'. From this is derived the term for one's university – 'alma mater' or 'fostering mother'.

When Britain and her allies defeated the Russians in the Crimean War at the Battle of Alma in the mid-19th century, the name grew in popularity in the UK.
Variants: Aluma, Alumit, Elma

Almita

Of Latin origin, this name means 'benign' or 'kindly behaviour'.

Alvina

The roots of this name are firmly entrenched in Old English. It is derived from words that mean 'noble', 'sharp' and 'friend'. Thus the name Alvina has been interpreted to mean 'strong, wise woman'.
Variants: Alvinia, Vina, Vinni, Vinnie, Vinny

Amalia

A variant of the name Amelia, Amalia comes from the Latin for 'toil' and 'hard work'. It is also derived from the Hebrew for 'God's labour'.
Variants: Amalie, Amaliah, Amalthea, Amelia

Amanda

British dramatist John Vanbrugh may have invented the name Amanda for his 1697 work *The Relapse*, where it was the name of his heroine. However, if he did, he derived it from the Latin for 'worthy of love' or 'loveable'. He may have also devised it as a feminine equivalent of Amandus, which was borne by a number of saints from the 4th to the 7th century.
Variants: Amandine, Amata, Manda, Mandi, Mandie, Mandy

Amarinda
Of Greek origin, Amarinda means 'long-lived'.
Variants: Amara, Amargo, Mara

Amaryllis
A favourite of the poets Theocritus, Virgil and Ovid, who often used it in their works, Amaryllis comes from the Greek word amarullis meaning 'refreshing' and 'sparkling' and refers to eyes that were either sparkling or giving quick glances.

Milton also used the name in his poem *Lycidas.*

Amber
Both a colour and a gemstone Amber was a fashionable name for girls in the 1960s. It comes from the Arabic ambar, which means 'jewel' and obviously refers to the precious stone that is used to make jewellery and ornaments.

First used as a given name in the late 19th century its popularity grew in North America during the 1980s and 1990s.
Variants: Amberlea, Amberlee, Amberline, Amberly, Ambur, Amby

Ambrosia
The Greek word ambrosios means 'immortality' and 'elixir of life' and was often used in reference to the food of the gods. Thus it came to be associated with delicious foods and smells.
Variants: Ambrosina, Ambrosine

Amelia
The Latin meaning of Amelia is 'industrious'. In the 20th century Amelia Earhart, the American aviator, was the embodiment of the qualities of her first name. She toiled and worked hard for her success.

But the name Amelia may have come from another Latin word, aemilia, which meant 'persuasive and flattering'. This version of the name, Aemilia, was used by Shakespeare in his 16th century play *The Comedy of Errors.*
Variants: Amalea, Amalia, Amalie, Ameline, Emelita, Emil, Emilia, Emily

Amethyst

Also the name of a violet-coloured gemstone, Amethyst comes from the Greek word for 'intoxicated'. This jewel was thought to prevent intoxication from alcohol. Leonardo Da Vinci wrote that amethyst was able to dissipate evil thoughts and quicken the intelligence.

Amina

The female form of Amin, Amina, has its roots in both Arabic and Hebrew. It means 'truth, certainty' and 'affirmation'.

Aminta

The origin of this name is uncertain but it is thought to come from the Latin word amintas, which means 'protector'. One theory suggests that Aminta is a derivative of the Greek masculine name Amyntas, which was used by the country's royal family from the 4th century onwards.

But another theory puts the creation of Aminta in the 17th century during the Restoration, when it was often used by the poets of the day.

Variants: Amynta, Arminta, Minty

Amorette

Amorette comes from the Latin for 'beloved, sweetheart' and 'little dear'. It may have been an invention of the poet Spenser who used it for a character in *Faerie Queene* in 1590.

Variant: Amorita

Amy

Amor is Latin for 'love'. Aimée is the French interpretation of this word as a girl's name and Amy is the Anglicised version. A direct descendant of Esmée – the early French form of this name – is Esme, the Scottish variant.

The name enjoyed popularity during the 1600s and was revived in the 19th century.

Variants: Aimee, Aimée, Amata, Ame, Ami, Esme, Esmee, Ismay

Anaïs

This is a French name, taken from the Greek for 'fruitful'.

Anastasia

The Russian name Anastasia comes from the Greek for 'resurrection' or 'one who will rise again'.
Variants: Ana, Anastas, Anstis, Annestas, Anstes, Nastia, Stasa, Tansy, Tasya

Andrea

Andrea is thought to be the feminine form of the name Andrew, which comes from the Greek word 'andreia' ('manliness' or 'virility').

An Italian variant of this name is Andreana, while in France it becomes Andrée.

Scotland has produced numerous variants of this name including Andrina, Andrene, Andreena, Dreena and Rena.

Andrea has been in use since the 17th century.
Variants: Andreana, Andrée, Andreena, Andrene, Andrina, Dreena, Rena

Anemone

According to Greek mythology this is the name of a nymph who was transformed into a flower by the wind. Hence, it comes from the Greek for 'wind flower'.

Another Grecian tale suggests that the anemone flower is so named because it sprang from the blood of the god Adonis who was killed while out hunting.

Angel

The word angel comes from the Greek for 'a messenger from God'. It is more frequently given to children as a name in Spanish-speaking countries and then mostly to boys. However, it is sometimes given to girls born on the festival of St Michael and the Angels which falls on 29 September.

As a girl's name it is popular among African-Americans.
Variants: Angela, Angeles, Angelica, Angelina, Angelique

Angela

Like Angel this name comes from the Greek word for 'messenger'. But it is also the female version of the Latin name Angelus. It has been in use in America and Britain since the 18th century.

It is also the name of the 16th century saint from northern Italy, who founded the first teaching order of nuns.

Variants: Ange, Angeles, Angelica, Angelina, Angelique, Angy

Angelique

This is another member of the Angel/Angela family of names. Angelique comes from the Latin (via French) angelicus, which means 'like an angel'.

Variants: Angeliki, Angelita

Annabel

Common in Scotland since the 12th century, Annabel is thought to be an elaborate form of the name Anna, which itself is derived from the Biblical name Hannah. According to that theory Annabel is a compound of Anna (Hebrew for 'God has favoured me') and bel ('beautiful' in French and Italian).

However, the name may have been derived from the Old French name Amabel which comes from the Latin for 'lovable'.

Variants: Annabella, Annabelle

Anne

The Biblical name Hannah was thought to be the name of the mother of the Virgin Mary. Anna is the Greek form and Anne, its French equivalent. In Hebrew the name means 'God has favoured me'.

The popularity of this name has led to many variants and independent names. The pet forms Nan and Nanna have led to Nancy and Nanette. Anneka and Anika are Scandinavian versions while, in Russia it becomes Anushka.

Variants: Anita, Ann, Anna, Annalise, Annette, Annias, Nanette, Nansi, Nina, Ninette

Anoushka
This is the Russian form of Anne, which has become an independent name.
Variant: Anushka

Anthea
Although this name has been known since the classical period and has appeared in literature since the 4th century it did not become a popular first name until the 1960s.

Anthea comes from the Greek word for 'flowery'. It was the ancient title of Hera, the Greek queen of the Gods.
Variant: Anthia

Antoinette
Perhaps the most famous bearer of this name is Marie Antoinette, the wife of Louise XVI who was beheaded during the French Revolution in 1793. The young queen was famous for her extravagance, intelligence and wit.

Her name, Antoinette, is the French feminine version of Anthony. Ultimately it comes from the Roman family name Antonius and in Latin means 'without price'. In Greek it means 'flourishing'.
Variants: Anonetta, Antonette, Antonia, Toinette, Toni, Tonneli

Aphrodite
According to Greek mythology Aphrodite was the goddess of love, fertility and beauty. She was also the daughter of Zeus, the supreme god.

Her name is said to mean 'foam born' because she came to life by rising from the sea.

April
The month of April is traditionally associated with spring and for good reason. It comes from the Latin word 'to open' or 'to open to the sun'. Hence its association with growth, renewal and blooming buds.

Girls born during this month are usually given this name or its French equivalent, Avril.
Variants: Aprilette, Averyl, Avril

Arabella
This is a Scottish name of Latin origin, which means 'moved by prayer'. It is also thought to be either another variant of Annabel or to have come from a word that means 'Arab'.
Variants: Ara, Arabel, Arabela, Arabelle, Arable, Arbel, Orabell, Orable

Aria
In opera an aria is sung by one voice. Unsurprisingly the name comes from the Latin for 'melody', 'air' and 'tune'.

Ariana
Ariana has both Greek and Welsh roots. It means 'holy', 'holy one' and 'silver'.

Ashanti
The Ashanti are a West African tribe that once ruled a great empire. The name is traditionally given to African-American girls in celebration of their cultural roots.
Variants: Asante, Shante

Ashley
Originally a surname, Ashley became a popular name for both boys and girls in Australia and North America during the 20th century. The name was originally derived from the Old English for 'ash' and 'wood'.

Ashley is also the name of a pivotal character in Margaret Mitchell's *Gone with the Wind*. Following the success of the novel and the film in the 1930s the name became popular with American parents. That trend continued during the 1980s and 1990s when Ashley was among the top 10 names given to baby girls in North America.
Variants: Ashlea, Ashleigh, Ashlee, Ashlie, Ashly, Ashlynn, Ashton

Atlanta

According to Greek mythology Atlas was a giant who held the sky up on his shoulders. It is from him that the Atlantic Ocean gets its name. Atalanta is the female form of Atlas and Atlanta is its variant.

However, Atlanta is also a city in Georgia, North America and its modern day usage may be attributed to this association and not Greek mythology.

Variant: Atalanta

Audrey

The popularity of the name can be attributed to a 6th century saint called Etheldreda. She was an East Anglian princess who died because of a tumour in her neck, believed by her to be divine retribution for her love of fine necklaces. Etheldreda's name comes from the Old English for 'noble strength', but in Britain she was also known as Audrey. The name was especially popular during the 17th century.

Variants: Atheldreda, Addie, Addy, Aude, Audey, Audra, Audrie, Awdrie, Ethel, Etheldreda

Aura

Of Greek origin, this name means 'gentle breeze'.

Variant: Awal

Aurora

The Romans believed that Aurora was the goddess of dawn, and that the morning dew were the tears that she shed following the death of her son. The name comes from the Latin for 'dawn'.

Variants: Alola, Aurore, Ora, Rora, Rori, Rorie, Rory

Ava

The name Ava resembles Eva and can be taken to be a variant of the name Eve, which means 'living'. Alternatively it could come from the Latin word 'avis' ('bird').

During the early Middle Ages Ava was also considered to be

a pet form of names beginning with those three letters. In fact, in the 9th century an abbess and member of the Frankish royal family bore the name. She was later canonised.
Variants: Eva, Eve

Avalon
According to Arthurian legend Avalon was the island to which King Arthur was taken after his death. The name comes from the Latin for 'island', but also from the Old Welsh for 'apple'.
Variant: Avallon

Avis
The exact meaning of the Germanic name Avis is uncertain. It is believed that it comes from the German name Hedewig, which means 'combat' or 'refuge in war'. But it is also said to have come from the Latin for 'bird'.
   The name was brought to England by the Normans as Havoise.
Variants: Amice, Aveis, Aves, Avice, Havoise

Bailey
Used for both boys and girls, Bailey is the transferred use of a surname. Its exact meaning is unclear. It could come from the Old English for 'berry' and 'wood'. It could equally be an old occupational name given to someone who was a bailiff. Alternatively the surname Bailey may have referred to someone who lived near a city fortification.
Variants: Bailee, Baileigh, Bailie, Baily, Bayleigh, Baylee, Baylie

Barbara
The name Barbara comes from the same root as the word barbarian. Of Greek origin, it means 'foreign' or 'strange'.
   Babs, Barbie and Bobbi are all short forms of this name. Babette is the French interpretation. Meanwhile the singer and actress Barbra Streisand gave the world a variant spelling of the popular 20th century name.
Variants: Bab, Babette, Babs, Barbra, Baubie, Bobbi, Bobbie

Bathsheba

In the Bible Bathsheba was the married woman King David saw taking a bath. He later married her himself after bringing about the death of her husband, Uriah. Bathsheba then went on to become the mother of King Solomon.

This Biblical name has various meanings in Hebrew – 'seventh daughter', 'daughter of an oath' and 'voluptuous'.
Variants: Sheba, Sheva

Bea

An independent name in its own right Bea is also the short form of Beatrice. Beatrice comes from the Latin beatrix which means 'bearer of happiness' and 'blessings'.
Variant: Bee

Beatrice

Occasionally used in England during the Middle Ages the name Beatrice was later used by both Dante and Shakespeare in their works. As mentioned above, it derives its meaning from the Latin for 'blessed' or 'blessings'. But it is also believed that the earliest Latin form of the name was Viatrix, which means 'voyager'.
Variants: Bea, Beah, Beate, Beatrise, Beatrix, Bebe, Bee, Trixie, Trixy

Belle

In French the word belle means 'beautiful'. The Italian word for beautiful is bella. An independent name, Belle is also a short form of Isabelle, just as Bella is a pet form of names such as Arabella and Isabella.
Variants: Bel, Bela, Bell, Bill, Billi, Billie

Belinda

The first part of Belinda, 'bel', comes from the Latin for 'beautiful' while the second part, 'linda', comes from the Old German for 'a snake or serpent'. The serpent is a symbol of wisdom.
Variants: Bel, Bell, Bellalinda, Bindy, Blenda, Linda, Lindi, Line, Lynda, Lynde

Bena
This name comes from the Hebrew for 'wise'.
Variants: Bina, Buna, Bunie

Bernadette
St Bernadette was the French teenager who saw visions of the
Virgin Mary at Lourdes in the 19th century.
Her name is the French feminine form of Bernard – a German
name that means 'strong, brave as a bear'.
Variants: Berna, Bernarda, Bernadina, Bernette, Bernita

Bernice
Bernice is a variant of the Biblical name Berenice which comes
from the Greek for 'bringer of victory'. Well known during both
Greek and Roman times, in the New Testament it was the name
of the sister of King Herod Agrippa II.
*Variants: Berenice, Bernelle, Bernine, Bernita, Bunni, Bunnie,
Pherenice, Vernice*

Bertha
Bertha is the Latinised version of the Germanic name that has
been in England, in some form, since Anglo-Saxon times. The
name comes from the Old High German for 'bright, illustrious'.
In Medieval Europe the name was made famous by the
mother of the Emperor Charlemagne.
Variants: Berta, Berte, Berthe, Bertie, Bertina

Bess
Elizabeth I of England was known as Good Queen Bess and the
name Bess has been long considered a short form of Elizabeth.
However, it is also given as an independent name. Bess shares
the same Hebrew meaning as Elizabeth – 'God is perfection'.
Variants: Bessie, Bessy

Bethany
In the Bible Bethany was the village outside Jerusalem where

Jesus stayed during Holy Week before his crucifixion. It was also used in reference to one of his disciples – Mary of Bethany.

In Hebrew the name means 'house of figs'. In Aramaic the meaning is 'house of poverty'.

Betsy
This name is another pet form of Elizabeth, which has been used independently. It may have been created by blending Betty with Bessie.
Variant: Betsie

Bette
In the 20th century the most famous bearer of this name was the American actress Bette Davis. The Hollywood legend pronounced her name as *'bet-te'*, but it can also be pronounced as *'bet'*.

Like Betsy and Bess, Bette is a short form of Elizabeth, which means 'God is perfection', 'God is satisfaction' or 'dedicated to God' in Hebrew.
Variants: Betsie, Betsy, Bettie, Bettina, Betty

Bettula
Of Persian origin, this name means 'maiden, young girl'.
Variant: Betula

Beulah
This Biblical name was popular among the Puritans in the 17th century. In the Bible the prophet Isaiah referred to Israel as the 'land of Beulah'. The name is of Hebrew origin and means 'she who is to be married, ruled over'.

Beverley
At one time this name was given to both boys and girls in North America. This transferred surname was originally a place name. It comes from the Old English for 'beaver's meadow' or 'beaver's stream'.
Variants: Beverlee, Beverly, Buffy

Bharati
This Hindu name is associated with the goddess of speech and learning. It is said to mean 'India'.

Bianca
In Shakespeare's play *The Taming of the Shrew* Bianca is Katherina's more subdued sister. The name comes from the Italian for 'white' or 'pure'. Shakespeare used the name again for a character in *Othello*.
Variants: Biancha, Blanche

Bibi
Bibi comes from the French beubelot, which means 'toy' or 'bauble'. It is also a short form of Bianca, which means 'white'.

Bijou
Another name derived from the French language. Bijou comes from French for 'jewel'. It also has Old English roots and may stem from a word meaning 'ring'.

Billie
Traditionally a short form of the boy's name William, Billie has also been given to girls. William comes from the Old English for 'resolution' and 'determination'. Legendary blues singer Eleanora Fagan is more famously known by her stage name, Billie Holiday.
Variants: Bill, Billy

Blair
Given to both boys and girls, Blair is more commonly found as a Scottish surname. Fittingly it has Celtic roots and means 'place', 'field' or 'battle'.
Variants: Blaire, Blayre

Blaise
Blaise comes from the Old English for 'torch' or 'shining' and the Middle English for 'proclaim' and 'to blow'.

In the tales of King Arthur Blaise was the name of Merlin's secretary. The name is occasionally given to boys.
Variant: Blaze

Blanche
Like Bianca, Blanche means 'white'. This name comes from the Old French version of this word and was often given to girls who were blonde or fair-haired.

The name was brought to England by the Normans. One famous, early bearer of the name was Blanche of Artois who married Edmund, the Earl of Lancaster in the 13th century.
Variants: Balaniki, Bellanca, Bianca, Blanca, Blanch

Bleu
Of French origin, in English this name simply refers to the colour blue.

Bliss
This girl's name has the same meaning in modern English that it did in Old English – 'happiness' and 'joy'.

Blossom
Blossom comes from the Old English for 'flower'. The name was first given to girls in the 19th century.
Variants: Blom, Bloom, Blum, Bluma

Blythe
In Old English blithe means 'mild', 'gentle' and 'kind'. In old verses it was linked with the name, and affectionate Scottish term, Bonnie. It can also be given to boys.
Variants: Bliss, Blisse

Bo
This name comes from the Chinese for 'precious' and also has the Old Norse meaning 'house-owner'.
Variant: Bonita

Bobbie
Girls called Barbara and Roberta share the pet name Bobbie. However, this name has become an independent name and one that is used in conjunction with others to produce a double-barrelled first name such as Bobby-Anne.
Variants: Bobbi, Bobby

Bonita
Although this is not a common name in Spanish-speaking countries it comes from the Spanish for 'pretty'. It was popular in North America in the 1940s, but can be directly traced back to the Latin for 'good'.
Variants: Boni, Bonie, Bonnie, Bonny, Nita

Bonnie
In Margaret Mitchell's novel *Gone with the Wind* Bonnie was the name of the daughter of Scarlett O'Hara and Rhett Butler. The popularity of this book and film may account for the use of the name in the 20th century.
But the name has long been an affectionate term in Scotland and before that, like Bonita, was associated with the Latin and Middle English for 'good'.
Variants: Bonita, Bonnee, Bonni, Bonny

Brady
This surname is usually found as a boy's name. It is mainly used in North America but it has Irish roots. It is thought to come from a Gaelic word that means 'broad or large chested'

Brandy
The word Brandy comes from the Dutch word brandewijn ('burnt wine'). It arrived in Northern Europe from Southern France and Spain in the 16th century and described wine that had been 'burnt', or boiled, in order to distill it. As a girl's name it is thought to be a feminine form of Brandon. It is popular in North America.
Variants: Brandi, Brandee, Brandie

Breanna

This is a name of recent coinage. One theory suggests it is a blend of the names Bree (a short form of Bridget) and Anna. But it is also believed to be the feminine equivalent of the name Brian, which is of Celtic origin and means 'strong'.
Variants: Breanne, Breeanna, Brenna, Bria, Brianna

Brenda

Logic would suggest that this name is the female version of Brendon – a Celtic name that means 'stinking hair'. But it has also been suggested that Brenda may be of Scandinavian origin, being a short form of the Old Norse word 'brand', meaning 'sword'.

While the name was popular in English-speaking countries during the 1950s and 1960s before the 20th century it was mainly found in Ireland and Scotland.
Variants: Bren, Brenna

Bria

Brianna, the feminine version of Brian, can be shortened into the pet form Bria, which in North America is also used as an independent name. Like Brianna and Brian it means 'strong'.

Bridget

Bridget is the name of the ancient Celtic goddess of fire, light and poetry. It is also the name of two saints – St Brigid of Kildare, the patron saint of Ireland and St Bridget of Sweden, the patron saint of healers.

The Celtic meaning of the name is 'strength' and 'high one', while the Scandinavian interpretation is 'protection'.

Brigitte is the continental form of the name that was popularised by French actress Brigitte Bardot.

Meanwhile, the short form Britt comes from the Swedish forms Birgit and Birgita and is born by the Swedish actress Britt Ekland.
Variants: Biddie, Biddy, Birgit, Bridie, Brigette, Brigid, Brigitte, Britt

Britney
Mainly found in North America, this name means 'from Britain'.
Variants: Britany, Brittany, Brittanie, Brittnee, Brittney, Brittni

Bronwyn
Of Welsh origin, Bronwyn means 'fair bosomed'. In Middle English the name means 'a robust or well-built friend'.

The name is popular in Wales where, according to legend, the name was borne by the daughter of the god of the sea.
Variants: Bron, Bronnie, Bronny, Bronwen

Brook
As a surname Brook was originally the name of someone who lived near a brook or a stream. Hence in Old English it meant 'stream'. But there is another Old English meaning of the word – 'to enjoy, be rewarded by'.

This name has been given to both boys and girls, along with the place name Brooklyn.
Variants: Brooke, Brooklynn, Brooklynne

Bryony
Bryony is often thought to be the feminine equivalent of the boy's name Brian, which means 'strong'. But it is also a variant of the Greek name for a wild climbing plant which, when translated into English, means 'to grow luxuriantly'.

It was first used as a girl's name in the 20th century.
Variants: Briony

Bunty
In the English language bunty has long been a term of endearment and, in the early 20th century, the nickname was used in reference to pets or lambs. It may have been derived from the verb 'to bunt', which means 'to butt gently'.

The pet name for a rabbit, Bunny, can also be given to girls.
Variant: Bunny, Buntie

Girls

Caitlín
Pronounced 'kat-leen', Caitlín is the Irish Gaelic version of Catherine, which was brought to Ireland by the Anglo-Norman conquerors. An Anglicised version of the name, Kathleen, later became popular. So too did Caitlin, without the accent, which is pronounced 'kate-lin'.

The above versions all stem from Catherine, which comes from the Greek for 'pure'.
Variants: Caitlin, Katelyn, Katelynn, Kaitlyn, Kaitlynn

Calista
Calista comes from the Greek meaning 'most beautiful'.
Variants: Calesta, Calisto, Calla, Calli, Callie

Calpurnia
In Shakespeare's play *Julius Caesar*, Calpurnia is Ceasar's wife. The name comes from the Greek for 'beauty' and 'prostitute'.

Camilla
The name Camilla is derived from the Roman family name Camillus, which means 'messenger'. In Roman times a camillus was also an attendant at a religious rite. Boy attendants were known as Camilli and girls were known as Camillae.

According to the Roman poet Virgil the woman who bore the name Camilla was a female warrior known for her speed. Legend has it that she could run so fast that if she ran over the sea her feet would not get wet. Roman mythology also names Camilla as a huntress and attendant to the goddess Diana.

Although the name was used in Europe during the Middle Ages, it was reintroduced during the 18th century. Its popularity was aided by the 1796 novel *Camilla*, which was written by Madame D'Arblay.
Variants: Cam, Camala, Camel, Camila, Camille, Cammie, Milli, Millie, Milly

Caprice
With meanings from Latin, Italian and French, Caprice is thought to mean 'head with hair standing on end' or 'hedgehog-like head'. It could also mean 'fanciful'.

Carlene
A variant of Carla and Karla this name is another feminine form of the name Charles, which comes from the Old German for 'man'. (See also Carol and Karla.)
Variants: Carla, Carleen, Carly, Carlyn, Carol, Karla

Carmel
Carmel is the name of a mountain in Israel that was mentioned in the Bible. It is also the name attached to one title for the Virgin Mary, Our Lady of Carmel.
It comes from the Hebrew for 'garden' or 'orchard'.
Variants: Carmela, Carmelina

Carmen
The famous title of Bizet's opera, *Carmen,* is ultimately the Spanish form of Carmel, which comes from the Hebrew for 'garden'.
The Latin meaning of this name is 'to sing, praise' and 'be lyrical'.
Variants: Carmia, Carmine, Charmione, Charmaine

Carrie
Sometimes thought to be a variant of Carol – the feminine form of Charles – Carrie may also come from the Welsh word for love. As such it would belong to the Carys, Cerys and Ceri family of names. As another form of Carol its roots lie in the Germanic word for 'man'.
Variants: Cari, Carin, Carine, Carol, Carole, Caryn, Carys, Ceri, Cerys

Carol
Though common today the name Carol was not popular as a child's name before the late 19th century. It drew its roots from

the Latin 'carolus' and from the Old German for 'free man' or 'man' as the feminine form of Charles.

However, its cultural roots are varied. It is also linked to the Welsh for 'brave in battle' and the Old French for 'round dance'. Sometimes a short form of the longer name, Caroline, it is also given to girls born at Christmas time.

Variants: Carey, Carrie, Carola, Carolee, Carole, Carroll, Caroline, Carolyn, Cary, Caryl

Catherine

The history books are littered with notable, powerful women who bore this name. The 4th century saint Catherine of Alexandria escaped death on a spiked wheel and in her honour the Catherine-wheel (a firework) was named. It was also the name of Catherine of Aragon, the first wife of Henry VIII of England, whom the king divorced to marry Anne Boleyn.

Whether spelt with a 'k' or a 'c' the meaning is the same. It comes from the Greek word for 'pure'.

Variants: Caitlin, Carina, Cathleen, Cathy, Katerina, Katherine, Katharine, Kate, Kathryn, Katie

Cecilia

This female version of Cecil was first introduced to England by William the Conqueror's daughter who bore the name. During the early Middle Ages Cecily was the preferred version.

The name was also well known because of the fame of St Cecilia – a Christian martyr who is the patron saint of music.

Cecilia comes from the Welsh for 'sixth' and the Latin for 'blind'.

Variants: Cacilia, Cacile, Celia, Cecile, Cecily, Sissy, Cissie, Cissy

Celena

Celena is a variant of the name Selena or Selene who, according to Greek mythology, was the goddess of the moon. The name is also thought to have a French meaning – 'always smiling'.

Variants: Celene, Selena, Selene, Selina

Ceres

According to Roman mythology Ceres was the goddess of corn who was also responsible for the growth of fruits. Because of this association this name is often given to girls born in springtime.
Variants: Cerelia, Corella

Cerys

This name, like Carys, comes from the Welsh word for 'love'. As such it is the equivalent of the English name Amy, which becomes Aimee in French.

Boys are sometimes given the masculine form of the name, Ceri.
Variants: Cari, Caryl, Carys

Chandra

Chandra comes from the Sanskrit for 'illustrious' or 'like the moon'.
Variants: Chan, Chandah, Shan, Shandra

Chanel

As a first name for baby girls this name has been popular among African-Americans since the 1980s. French in origin it means either 'channel' or 'canal'.
Variants: Chanelle, Shanell, Shannel

Chantelle

Another French name, Chantelle either means 'to sing clearly' or 'stone'. The name was associated with the 17th century saint, St Jeanne de Chantal.
Variants; Chantal, Chantel, Shantal, Shantel, Shantell, Shantelle

Charity

Together with faith and hope, charity is one of the three great Christian virtues. In a letter to the Corinthians in the New Testament St Paul declared charity – Christian love – as the greatest of the three.

The word, and the name, comes from the Greek for 'grace', hence Charis the goddess of beauty and grace. Charity also

comes from the Latin for 'kindness' or 'brotherly love'.
Variants: Charito, Karis

Charlotte
Introduced to England in the 12th century by the Earl of Derby's wife, the name Charlotte was especially popular in the UK in the1970s.

It is the French form of the name Charles which comes from the Old German for 'man'.
Variants: Cara, Charlayne, Charleen, Charlie, Lottie

Charmaine
The origin of this name has been disputed as it did not seem to exist before 1920. It is believed that Charmaine was derived from the older name Charmian – used by Shakespeare for the name of a character in his play *Antony and Cleopatra*. If that is the case Charmaine comes from the Greek for 'joy'. Alternatively it may have come from the Latin for 'song'.
Variants: Carman, Charmain, Charmian, Charmayne, Sharmaine, Sharmayne

Chastity
Another Christian virtue, the word chastity comes from the Latin for 'pure, virtuous, decent' and 'undefiled'.

After it was chosen by pop star couple Cher and Sonny Bono for the name of their daughter in 1969, its popularity increased.

Chelsea
In Old English it means 'chalk landing place' but in England the name Chelsea is usually used in reference either to an affluent part of London or a football club. However, since the 1950s Chelsea has been increasingly used as a girl's name.
Variants: Chelsi, Chelsie

Chenoa
This Native American name means 'white dove'.

Chere
Chere comes from the French word for 'dear' or 'beloved'.
Another related name, Cherami, means 'dear friend'.
*Variants: Cher, Cherami, Cherri, Cherie, Cherrie, Cherry, Cheryl,
Cherylie*

Cherie
As above, Cherie comes from the French for 'dear' or 'beloved'.
Variants: Ceri, Cher, Cherami, Chérie, Cherry, Sheree, Sherry

Cheera
Of Greek origin, Cheera is derived for the word for 'face' and
probably implies a cheery, warm expression.

Cherry
A pet form of Charity, Cherry has become an independent
name in its own right. It was used by the 19th century novelist
Charles Dickens as a nickname for his character Charity in
Martin Chuzzlewit.

It also refers to the fruit and, in Middle English, may have
appeared as Cherie.

Cheryl
Another name not found before the 1920s, Cheryl may have
started life as a blend of Cherry and the popular German
name Beryl.

The name may mean 'love' if Cherry is taken to be a short
form of charity. Alternatively, if the name came from the French
Cherie then it also means 'dear, beloved'.
Variants: Chère, Sheryl, Sherrell, Sheralyn

China
Like India and Kenya this is the name of a country that is now being
used as a girl's name. The name originally comes from the word Qin,
which is the name of the dynasty that ruled China from 221 BC.
Variants: Chynna

Chloë
Chloë comes from the Greek word for 'green' or a 'young green shoot'. Hence Chloë was the name of the goddess of young crops.

The name is mentioned in both the Bible and the 19th century anti-slavery novel *Uncle Tom's Cabin*.
Variant: Chloe

Christabel
The English poet Samuel Taylor Coleridge is thought to be the creator of the name Christabel, which was the title of his 1816 poem. The name is a combination of the first syllable of Christine and the feminine suffix 'bel'. Thus it means 'beautiful Christian'.

The suffragette Christabel Pankhurst is one famous bearer of the name.
Variants: Christa, Christabell, Christabella, Christable, Christabelle, Christie, Christobella, Bell, Bel

Christina
The boy's name Christian means exactly what it implies – follower of Christ. Christina is a simplified form of Christiana, the Latin feminine version of this name. Like Christine it has lead to a number of variants from around the world and the independent name Tina.
Variants: Chris, Chrissie, Christiana, Kirstie, Kirsty, Krista, Kristen, Kristine, Krystyna, Tina, Xena

Christine
Christine comes from the Old English word for Christian – in other words a follower of Christ and a member of the Christian faith. The name has been in use, for both boys and girls, in various forms since the 11th century.

Christian is the masculine form. Kirsty and Kirstie are the Scottish variants. Kirsten and Kersten are the Scandinavian forms.
Variants: Chris, Chrissie, Kersten, Kirsten, Kirstie, Kirsty, Krista, Kristen, Kristine

Cicely

A variant of the name Cecilia, Cicely is an independent name in its own right. Like Cecilia it is a feminine form of Cecile and is derived from an ancient Roman family name that means 'blind'.
Variants: Cecily, Cecilia, Celia

Cillian

Of Irish origin this name may have one of two meanings. It either comes from the Gaelic word for 'strife' ('ceallach') or from 'ceall' – another Gaelic word meaning 'monastery' or 'church'. Cillian has been borne by a number of Irish saints. While Cillian is the Irish spelling, Killian is the Anglicised version.
Variants: Keelan, Killian, Killie

Cindy

In the 19th century this name may have been a pet form of the popular name Cynthia. In the classical world Cynthia was an alternative name for Diana, the Greek moon goddess.

Cindy is also the pet form of the names Lucinda and Cinderella. Lucinda comes from the Latin word for 'light', while Cinderella comes from the French for 'ashes'. It is also the name of the fairytale heroine who, once bullied by her stepmother and sisters, went on to marry Prince Charming.

Cindy is now used independently as a girl's name, especially in North America.
Variants: Cindi, Cyndi, Sindy, Syndi

Claire

This name was derived from the Latin word 'clarus', which means 'bright, clear' and 'famous'. It was brought to England by the Normans and has appeared in various forms ever since.

In 1975 it was the most popular name given to girls.
Variants: Clair, Clare, Claribel, Clarrie

Clara

Like Claire the name Clara comes from the Latin word for

'bright, clear' and 'famous'. The name was borne by a 1920s silent film actress, Clara Bow. She was the original 'it' girl and an early Hollywood celebrity.

It is ironic that the name is associated with a woman made famous by the medium of film, for the patron saint of television is St Clare of Assisi who witnessed a mass being celebrated far away. Clara is the Latinised form of Claire.
Variants: Claribelle, Clarinda, Clara-Mae

Claudette

Claudette is the French feminine form of Claudius, which started life as a Roman family name. The Claudii believed their name came from the Latin word 'claudus', which means 'lame'. It may have been a nickname given to one of their ancestors.

Claudii became Claudius, the feminine of which is Claudia. Claudette is a variant of that girl's name.
Variant: Claudia

Cleo

The name Cleopatra was borne by many women in the Ptolemaic royal family who ruled ancient Egypt. The most famous bearer of this name was the final member of this dynasty Cleopatra VII, who was born in either 70 or 69 BC. She had affairs with the Roman leaders Julius Caesar and Mark Antony. Cleo is the pet form of Cleopatra and thus shares its Greek roots and meaning – 'glory of her father'.
Variants: Cleopatra, Clio

Clove

Cloves are dried flower buds that are often used to add flavour to food and drinks. They are also prized for their aromatic and medicinal qualities. The name comes from the Latin for 'nail'.

Clover

Usually clover has three leaves on each stem and flowers. However, according to tradition a four-leaved clover is supposed to bring good luck.

The name is derived from the Old English word for the plant.

Coco

The exact meaning of this name is unclear beyond the fact that it is a French pet name. Its most famous bearer was Coco Chanel, the fashion designer whose given name was Gabrielle.

The variant of Coco, Koko, has both Japanese and Native American roots. The Japanese meaning is 'stork'. The Native American interpretation is 'night'.

Variant: Koko

Colleen

Little used in Ireland but popular in North America and Australia, Colleen comes from the Irish Gaelic word for 'girl'. It may also be a feminine form of the boy's name Colin.

Variants: Coleen, Colena, Colene, Collice, Coline, Collene

Colette

The boy's name Nicholas comes from the Greek for 'victory of the people'. Colette is a French feminine variant of this name. It was popular in the 1920s because of the French novelist Sidonie Gabrielle Colette, the author of *Gigi*.

Variants: Colet, Collette, Cosette, Cosetta, Kalotte

Comfort

To strengthen, give solace to or ease someone's pain is to 'comfort' them. During the 17th century this name was given to both boys and girls by the Puritans. It comes from the Latin word 'confortare'.

Connie

Constance was another name that was popular with the 17th century Puritans primarily because it had an association with Christianity. The Roman emperor Constantine is considered to be the first Christian emperor, and steadfastness, or constancy, is celebrated as a virtue of that faith.

The name was first brought to England by the Normans. One of William the Conqueror's daughters was called Constance. Its popularity declined after the 17th century but was revived by the Victorians. The short form, Connie, is now given as an independent name.

Variants: Conetta, Constance, Constanza

Consuela

Another Puritan favourite, Consuela comes from the Latin meaning 'to free from sadness'.

Variants: Consolata, Consuelo

Cora

The origin of this name is uncertain. It may have been coined by the American writer James Fennimore Cooper, who used it for one of his characters in the 19th-century novel *The Last of the Mohicans*.

The name may have been a derivative of the Greek word 'kore', which means 'maiden'.

Variants: Corabelle, Coretta, Corette, Corinna, Corinne, Kora

Coral

This colourful hard substance that is found at the bottom of the sea is often turned into ornaments and jewellery. Its association with gemstones may have led to its adoption as a girl's name during the 19th century, when names such as Ruby were in vogue. Its meaning is derived from the Greek word for 'pebble'. However, the French name Coralie existed some 100 years before Coral.

Variants: Coralie, Coraline

Cordelia

Cordelia was the name of the youngest of King Lear's three daughters in the 1606 play of the same name. It comes from the Latin for 'from her heart', while its Celtic meaning is 'harmony' or

'daughter of the sea'. The saint of that name was a martyred virgin.
Variants: Delia, Della, Neila, Nellie, Nell, Nelly

Cori
Usually given to boys, especially in North America, Cori began life as a surname. It is derived from an Old English word for 'helmet'. It is especially popular among the African-American community.
Variants: Corey, Corie, Cory, Korey, Kori, Korie, Kory

Corina
Like Cora, the name Corina was derived from the Greek word 'kore', which means 'maiden'. It was also the name of a poetess in ancient Greece.

The Roman poet Ovid called the object of his affection Corina in his work *The Amores*.
Variants: Cora, Corene, Cori, Corinna

Courtney
Once an aristocratic surname Courtney has become popular in North America where it is given to both boys and girls. It was also once the name of a Norman village and refers to a place that still exists in France.

Its French connection implies that the name comes from a phrase which, in French, means 'short nose'. But it is also thought to be an English name that means 'from the court' of 'member of the court'.
Variants: Cortney, Courteney, Kortney, Korteney

Crystal
The name Crystal is derived from the Greek word 'krystallos', which means 'ice'. This probably refers to the clear quality of the gemstone often used to make jewellery and ornaments.

Like Ruby, Emerald and Coral, Crystal was bestowed upon girls as a name from the 19th century onwards.
Variants: Christel, Chrystal, Krystal, Krystle

Cynthia

In Greek mythology to say someone was 'of Cynthus' was to say that they were born on Mount Cynthus on the island of Delos. This applied to Artemis (also known as Diana) the goddess of the moon.

Her epithet became a name in England during the classical revival of the 17th and 18th centuries, but did not enjoy popularity until the 1800s.

Variants: Cynth, Cindi, Sindi, Cindy, Sindy

Cyr

The boy's name Cyril comes from the Greek word for 'lord'. Cyr is its feminine form.

Variants: Ciri, Cirilla, Cyra, Cyrilla

Daffodil

This bright yellow flower is so closely associated with springtime that it is known as the Lent Lily. Its name is taken from the Dutch for asphodel – the Greek name for the lily family of flowers that include daffodils and narcissus.

Variants: Daff, Daffie, Daffy, Dilly

Dahlia

The 18th century Swedish botanist Anders Dahl lent his name to this family of Mexican and Central American plants that produce large, brightly coloured flowers. The root of the name comes from the Old Norse for 'from the valley'.

Variants: Dahla, Dalia, Daliah

Daisy

This name may owe its popularity to the 19th century trend to name baby girls after flowers. The daisy, a European plant, derived its name from the Old English for 'day's eye', which was a reference to the yellow discs of the flower opening their petals to the morning sunlight and closing them at night.

The name is also a pet form of Margaret because of its

association with a saint. The daisy was a symbol of St Margherita of Italy.

Dakota
North and South Dakota are two states in North America. They got there name from the Dakota division of the Sioux tribe of Native Americans, who lived on the plains before the Europeans arrived. Unsurprisingly Dakota is a popular choice for children in the United States where it is given to both boys and girls. It means 'friend'.

Dallas
This Texan city may have been named after George M Dallas, the American vice president from 1845 to 1849. His surname comes from the English and Scottish for place names, meaning 'house or dwelling in the valley'.

In North America this name is given to both boys and girls as a first name.

Damaris
In the Bible Damaris was the name of an Athenian woman who was converted to Christianity by St Paul's preaching. Although the origin of her name is unclear it is believed to come from the Greek for 'calf' or to mean 'gentle'.
Variants: Damara, Damaras, Damaress, Damiris, Mara, Mari, Maris

Dana
Several theories exist to explain the origin of the name Dana. As a female variant of the boy's name Daniel, it has the Hebrew meaning 'God has judged' or 'God is my judge'. But it could also come from the Old English for 'a Dane'.

Again, the name could come from the Irish Gaelic for 'bold' or 'courageous'. In fact, according to Irish mythology, Dana was the goddess of fertility.
Variants: Daina, Danae, Dane, Dania, Danice, Danita, Danna, Danni

Danielle

In the Bible Daniel was an Israelite slave who could interpret dreams. His enemies conspired against him and he was thrown into a den of lions. But it was his faith in God that saved him.

In Hebrew the name Daniel means 'God is my judge'. Danielle is the French, feminine form of this name. Daniella is the Italian equivalent.

Variants: Dani, Danii, Daniella

Daphne

In Greek mythology Daphne was a nymph with whom the god Apollo fell in love. Unfortunately the feeling was not reciprocal and she was turned into a laurel tree to escape his advances. Henceforth, Apollo declared that plant as being sacred to him. The name comes from the Greek for 'laurel, bay tree'.

Used in England from the late 19th century, it was especially popular in the early 1900s.

Variants: Daff, Daffie, Daffy, Dafna, Dafnee, Daphna, Daphnee

Daria

This name is thought to have Persian, Greek and English roots. As the feminine form of the Persian name Darius it means 'protector' or 'royalty'. Its Greek meaning is 'wealthy, rich'. Meanwhile, as a variant of Dara, it comes from the Middle English for 'compassion' and 'to have courage, daring'.

Variant: Dara, Darice, Darya

Darcie

Given to both boys and girls Darcie began life as a Norman baronial name. It was borne by a family who came from Arcy in northern France – hence, d'Arcy ('of, from Arcy').

Darcy also appears as an Irish surname via the Anglicisation of an Irish name that meant 'descendent of the dark one'.

The most famous Darcy in English literature is the hero, Mr Darcy, in Jane Austen's classic novel *Pride and Prejudice*.

Variants: Dar, Darce, Darci, Darcy, D'Arcy, Darsey

Darleen
Common in North America and Australia, the name Darleen comes from the Old English for 'darling', 'beloved', 'highly valued, worthy, favourite'.
Variants: Darlene, Darilyn, Darilynn, Darlin, Darline

Daron
Daron is a feminine form of the boy's name Darren, which is a variant of the Persian name Darius ('protector').

Daryl
The name of the Norman village Airel was derived from the Latin for 'an open space'. A family from Airel would have been given the surname de Airel, which later became Daryl.
   It was in 19th-century North America that this French surname was given to babies of both sexes as a first name. This trend became especially popular towards the end of the 20th century.
Variants: Darrel, Darrell, Darryl

Davina
This Latinate feminine form of the name David originated in Scotland, but ultimately is Hebrew for 'beloved, friend'.
Variants: Davene, Davi, Davida, Davinia, Davita, Devina

Dawn
This name comes from the Old English word for 'daybreak'. It was first used as a given name in the late 19th century. Until then the Latin form Aurora was more commonly used.
   In Greek mythology Aurora was the 'goddess of dawn'.
Variants: Aurora, Dawne, Dawnelle, Orrie, Rora

Dayle
In Old English the word 'dael' meant valley. Thus, the surname Dale originally referred to where a person lived and meant 'dweller in the dale'.
Varients: Dael, Dale, Daile

Deborah

Deborah was the name of more than one Biblical character. In Genesis Deborah was Rebecca's nurse. Later on, in another Old Testament book, it was the name of a prophetess and female judge of the people who helped the Israelites to defeat the Canaanites.

The name, which was favoured by the Puritans in the 17th century, comes from the Hebrew for 'bee'.
Variants: Deb, Debbi, Debra, Debs, Debora, Debbie, Debby

Dee

As a nickname Dee is given to girls whose first names begin with the letter 'D'. However, it is also an independent name in its own right. Welsh in origin, it comes from the word for 'dark' or 'black' and could be given to children – boys and girls – with a dark complexion.
Variants: DeeDee, DD, Dede, Didi

Delwyn

Welsh and of modern origin, this name is a compound of two words. It is derived from the Welsh words 'del' ('pretty, neat') and '(g)wyn', which means 'white, fair' or 'blessed and holy'.
Variant: Del

Delwyth

This is another Welsh name which comes from the word for 'pretty' and 'neat'. The suffix 'yth' gives it the added meaning 'lovely'.
Variant: Del

Deirdre

The tale of Deirdre of the Sorrows is a tragic one. According to Celtic legend this beauty was to be wed to Conchobhar, the king of Ulster, but she rejected him and eloped with his younger brother Naoise instead. Hurt and angry, the king murdered his brother and Deirdre subsequently died of a broken heart. Hence the name Deirdre is taken to mean 'the broken-hearted', but it

could also mean 'the raging one' or 'fear'. This legend was cherished and honoured by Irish authors W B Yeats and J M Synge, who both produced acclaimed works based on this story in the early 1900s.
Variants: Dede, Dee, Deerdre, Diedra, Dierdra

Delia

The originally meaning of the name Delia was 'girl from Delos' – the Greek island that was sacred to Apollo and Artemis in ancient times.

As a first name it has been popular with poets since the 1st century BC. It was the favourite of the Latin poet Tibullus who wrote about Delia in his love poems. In 16th-century England Samuel Daniel produced his own sonnets dedicated to a beloved of the same name.
Variants: Dede, Dee, Dehlia, Delinda, Della, Didi

Delilah

One of the most tragic tales in the Bible is that of Samson and Delilah. Samson was a judge who, famed for his strength and his might, was a great protector of Israel. Delilah was his Philistine mistress who was persuaded to betray him. Discovering that the source of his strength lay in his long hair, she cut it off as he slept. Unable to defend himself Samson was captured by his enemies who blinded him and forced him to work for them.

Despite the negative portrayal of this temptress in the Bible, Delilah was a popular name among 17th-century Puritans. However, perhaps due to its Biblical connotations, its popularity began to wane in the 18th century.

In Hebrew the name means 'full of desire' and also comes from the Arabic for 'guide, leader'.

Delma

This name was derived from the Spanish for 'of the sea'. It also has a German meaning 'noble' and 'defender'.
Variants: Delmar, Delmi, Delmira

Denna

When taken as a feminine form of the name Dean, Denna coincidently shares the Old English and Native American meaning 'valley'.

However, it is also considered to be a variant of the name Diana who in both Greek and Roman mythology was the goddess of the moon.

Variants: Dea, Deana, Deanna, Deanne, Diana

Delta

The term for the Greek letter 'D' also gave its name to the mouth of a river which, like the upper-case letter delta, is triangular in shape.

Dervla

This Anglicised version of the Gaelic name Deirbhile is rarely found outside Ireland. It is a compound of the words 'der' ('daughter') and 'file' ('poet'). Thus the name means 'daughter of the poet'.

Variants: Dearbhla, Derval, Dervilia

Desdemona

In Shakespeare's tragic play *Othello* Desdemona was murdered by her jealous husband Othello, who was led to believe by the cunning Iago (wrongly, as it happened) that she had been unfaithful. Fittingly the name comes from the Greek for 'woman of bad fortune' or 'bad luck'.

Desiree

Desiree, the name of the mistress of Napoleon Bonaparte, is an appropriate one, for it comes from the Latin and French for 'to long for, crave, wish or desire'.

'Desiderata' was the Latin form of the name. Early Christians gave this name to a longed-for child.

Variants: Desarae, Desaree, Desi, Desideria, Desire, Désirée, Deziree

Destiny
This alternative word for 'fate' has found popularity as a given name in North America.
Variants: Destinee, Destiney, Destinie

Deva
Depending on the source Deva can have more than one meaning. According to Hinduism it is the name of the goddess of the moon. Indeed, in Sanskrit Deva means 'god, divine' and the variant 'Devi' is the name of the supreme goddess. However, Celtic mythology suggests Deva was the goddess of the River Dee in Scotland.
Variants: Devaki, Devanee, Devi, Devika, Dewi

Devon
Beyond being the name of an English county it is not certain where Devon comes from. It may derive from the Celtic people who inhabited the south western peninsula of Britain at the time of the Roman invasion, the Dumnoni. Equally it is said to mean 'protector' and 'poet'.
Variants: Davon, Devan, Deven, Devonne

Dextra
This name comes from the Latin for 'right-hand side', the implication being that the bearer is skilful with their hands.

Diamond
This name is more popular in North America than it is in the United Kingdom. Until the 15th century only kings wore diamonds as a symbol of strength, courage and invincibility. The clear, precious stone was given this name that comes from the Greek for 'hardest' or 'unconquerable'.
Variant: Diamanta

Diana
The name was first brought to Britain in the 16th century and has

been a common English first name since the 1700s. Of Latin origin it means 'god-like', 'divine' and 'the bright one'.

Perhaps the most famous bearer of this name in recent times is the late Diana, Princess of Wales who died in 1997. However, the name has been well-known since ancient times.

Diana is another name for Artemis, the Greek goddess of the moon. Meanwhile, according to Roman mythology, Diana was also the goddess of hunting and the protector of wild animals. Beautiful and chaste, disinterested in men, she was also associated with fertility.
Variants: Deanna, Deeanna, Dian, Diandra, Diane, Dianne, Dinah, Dyanna

Diandra
This variant of Diana (see above) has become an independent name in its own right. It is also thought to be a blend of two names – Diana and Andrea ('manly').
Variant: Diandrea

Diantha
Of Greek origin this name means 'heavenly flower'. According to Greek mythology it was the flower of Zeus, the supreme god.
Variant: Dianthe

Dilys
This Welsh name means 'genuine', 'perfect' and 'true'. It is also thought to mean 'steadfast' and 'certain'.
Variant: Dilly

Dinah
Dinah was the Biblical name of Jacob and Leah's beautiful daughter. She was raped but her brothers Simeon and Levi sought revenge for the attack. The Hebrew meaning of Dinah, therefore, is 'vindication', 'judgement' or 'revenged'. It is also believed to be a modern variant of Diana.
Variants: Deanna, Deanne, Deena, Dena, Diana, Dina

Dixie

The Mason-Dixon line (surveyed by Charles Mason and Jeremiah Dixon in 1763 to 1767) is said to divide northern and southern states of North America. The term Dixieland will forever be inextricably linked to the American South and is often used as a wistful reference to that region.

Dixie could have also been been inspired by the French word for 'ten', 'dix'. Thus Dixie was derived from an American-English pronunciation of the word for a ten-dollar bill.

However, it is also thought that Dixie may come from the Old Norse word 'diss', which means 'active sprite'. And the name may originally have been that of a Nordic fairy guardian.
Variants: Dis, Disa, Dix

Dolcila

This name comes from the Latin word 'dolcilis', which means 'gentle' and 'amenable'.
Variants: Docila, Docilla

Dolly

Before this name became used for a child's toy it was the pet form of Dorothy which means 'God's gift'. It is now an independent name.
Variant: Doll

Dolores

Santa Maria de los Dolores is a name given to the Virgin Mary by the Spanish. It means St Mary of the Sorrows or Lady of the Sorrows. Hence the name Dolores comes from the Spanish word for 'sorrows'.

In 1423 the feast day of St Mary of the Sorrows was established on 15 September and henceforth it was common to name girls born on that day Dolores. Often it was a way of naming a child after the Virgin Mary, if the parents felt that the name 'Mary' was too sacred to use.

During the 1930s Dolores was popular in North America.

Variants: Dalores, Dela, Delora, Delores, Deloris, Delorita, Dola, Dolore, Lola, Lolita

Dominique
This French name is the feminine form of Dominic, which comes from the Latin for 'of the Lord'. Traditionally, those born on a Sunday were given this name because they were born on the Sabbath – the day of the Lord.

The name is also thought to mean 'servant of God'.

Donna
Of Italian, and ultimately Latin origin, this name means 'lady, woman worthy of respect' or 'mistress of a household'. It is also thought to be a short form of Madonna and a feminine form of Donald, which comes from the Celtic for 'proud ruler'.

The name has been in use since the beginning of the 20th century.
Variants: Donalie, Donnis, Donny, Dona, Donella, Donelle, Donica, Ladonna

Dora
Charles Dickens used this name for one of his characters in his 1850 novel *David Copperfield*. Although it is now considered to be an independent name, it began life as a diminutive of the names Theodora and Dorothy, both of which mean 'God's gift'.
Variants: Dorah, Doralyn, Doreen, Dorrie, Dorit, Dorita, Dorothy, Theodora

Doreen
The name Doreen is thought to be a combination of Dora – a diminuitive of Dorothy and Theodora meaning 'God's gift' - and the suffix 'een'.

However, Doreen is also associated with the Irish name Dorean, which may come from the Gaelic word 'der' meaning 'daughter' and Finn, the name of a legendary Irish hero which means 'white, fair'.

Whatever its origin Doreen was first introduced to Britain at

the beginning of the 20th century and it has become more widespread since that time. (See also Dora and Dorothy.)
Variants: Dora, Doraleen, Dorean, Dorene, Dorine, Dorletta, Dorothea, Dorothy

Dorit
This is another short form of Dorothy that is associated with Charles Dickens. *Little Dorrit* was the title of one of his novels. Like Dora, Dorothy and Theodora it means 'God's gift'.
Variants: Dora, Dorrit, Dorothy

Doris
In Ancient Greece a person coming from the Doris region was known as a Dorian. However, the name was also associated with a character from Greek mythology who was the daughter of Oceanus, the god of the sea. Doris went on to marry Nereus and bore him 50 daughters who became sea nymphs that were also known as the Nereids.

The name Doris also means 'bountiful sea' and 'sacrificial knife'. It was especially popular during the late 19th century and the early 1900s.
Variants: Dorea, Dori, Doria, Dorice, Dorie, Dorisa, Dorit, Dorrit, Dory

Dorothy
In Greek 'doron' means 'gift' and 'theos' means 'God'. Thus the name Dorothea means 'gift of God'. Dorothy is the English version of this name, which has led to a variety of pet forms including Dolly, Dora and Dorrit.

Dove
This white bird is a symbol of peace and gentleness.
Variant: Dova

Drew
This short form of the name Andrew ('manly') is also a girl's name.

Dulcie
This 19th century girl's name is little used today. It was derived from the Latin word 'dulcis' which means 'sweet'. It is also a variant of the medieval name Dowse.
Variants: Dowsabel, Dulce, Dulcee, Dulcia, Dulcy

Dymphna
The Irish Gaelic meaning of this name is 'eligible', 'one fit to be' or 'little fawn'.
Variants: Damhnait, Dympna

Eartha
The name Eartha means exactly what it implies – 'earth', 'the ground'.
Variants: Ertha, Erthel

Easter
Though the name Easter is associated with the Christian festival the word actually comes from the Middle English for 'ester', which means 'where the sun rises'. It is also thought to be related to the Old High German word 'ostarun' – 'eastern'.

Easter is also thought to be a variant of Esther, which comes from the German for 'radiant dawn' and means 'bride' in Hebrew or 'star' in Persian.
Variant: Esther

Ebony
This name comes from the word for the black, hard wood of a tropical tree.
Variants: Ebbony, Eboney, Eboni, Ebonie

Echo
Greek in origin, the name means 'nymph, repeated voice'. In Greek mythology, Echo was a nymph who had the unfortunate task of talking non-stop to the queen of the gods so she would not notice her husband's infidelity. When her motive was

discovered the queen placed a curse on her and thereafter she could only say what others had just said.

Echo was later the victim of unrequited love. She pined away for Narcissus until nothing was left of her but her voice, which could only repeat the words of others.

Edwina

Edwina, the feminine form of Edwin, was coined in the 19th century but it is derived from far older stock. Edwin is an Old English name that was borne by the 7th century king of Northumbria who was an early convert to Christianity. It means 'fortunate friend', 'happiness' and 'riches'.
Variants: Edina, Edna, Edweena, Edwene, Edwyna

Eileen

Eileen is the Anglicised form of the Irish Gaelic name Aibhilin, which in turn was derived from the Norman French name Aveline. The differences in pronunciation account for the variant spellings of the same name. In Gaelic 'bh' is pronounced as a 'v', but sometimes it is silent – hence, Eileen.

Like Evelyn, Eileen comes from Aveline. So both names are related and mean 'hazelnut'. However, Eileen is also thought to be an Irish variant of the name Helen, which comes from the Greek for 'bright'.
Variants: Aibhilin, Aileen, Eilleen, Elly, Evelyn, Helen, Ileen, Ileene

Elaine

This name is thought to have both French and Welsh roots. While some believe it comes from the Old French form of the name Helen ('bright'), others suggest that it was derived from the Welsh for 'fawn'.

The fact that it was the name of the woman who fell in love with Lancelot in the Arthurian legend gives credence to this theory, as many of the names from those tales are of Welsh origin.

Elaine is also considered to be a short from of Eleanor.
Variants: Elain, Elaina, Elane, Elayne, Eleanor, Ellaine, Helen

Eleanor

As an Old French variant of Helen, Eleanor is thought to mean 'bright'. However, it may also be a derivative of the Old Provencal name, Alienor – which comes from the German for 'foreign'. Brought to England by the French, Eleanor may just be a different spelling of this Gallic name. Another theory suggests it is derived from the Arabic for 'god is my light'.

Variants: Ella, Elenora, Elenor, Elle, Ellie, Elyn, Helen, Nell, Nora, Norah

Electra

Of Greek origin, this name is derived from the word 'elektron', which means 'amber one that shines brightly'. It is from this Grecian element that the word 'electricity' was born.

Variants: Electre, Elektra

Elisha

This name can be viewed in one of two ways. Sometimes it is thought to be a combination of the names Elise (a short form of Elizabeth) and Alicia (a derivative of Alice). When these two names are its source it means 'God's oath' and 'noble'.

However, Elisha is also a derivative of the Biblical name Eli. In the Old Testament Eli was a high priest who raised Samuel from infancy. Eli comes from the Hebrew for 'high, elevated' and Elisha, which is sometimes given to boys, means 'God saves'.

Variants: Alicia, Elise, Elisa

Elizabeth

In the Bible, Elisabeth was the Virgin Mary's cousin and the elderly mother of John the Baptist. In England the name is usually spelt with a 'z', but the meaning is still the same. Elizabeth comes from the Hebrew name Elisheva, which means 'God's oath' or the 'fullness of God'.

The name first appeared in England towards the end of the 15th century and its popularity grew during the reign of the Tudor queen, Elizabeth I, who was also known as Good Queen Bess. The name continued to be fashionable in the 20th century, especially in the United Kingdom where it was borne by both Queen Elizabeth II – whose accession to the throne was in 1952 – and her mother. The name has spawned numerous short forms and independent names including Bet, Libby, Lilibet, Lisbeth, Liesel and Liza.

Variants: Bess, Bessie, Beth, Betsy, Betty, Elise, Elisa, Elsa, Eliza, Lisa

Ella

Of both Old English and Old German origin, Ella means either 'fairy maiden' or 'all'. It was introduced to Britain by the Normans and was particularly popular with the Victorians.

It is also considered to be a pet form of the names Eleanor and Isabella.

Variants: Ala, Eleanor, Ellen, Isabella

Ellie

Now widely considered to be an independent name Ellie is also the short form of a wide variety of names. It is the perfect pet form for any name beginning with El, such as Elizabeth and Eleanor. However, it is also believed to be a short form of Alice, Adelaide and Alicia. Thus this name could have a variety of meanings from 'noble' and 'God's oath' to 'bright' and 'God is my light'.

Variants: Adelaide, Alice, Alicia, Ella, Elle, Eleanor, Elizabeth

Elma

Both Turkish and Greek in origin this name means 'apple' and 'amiable' respectively.

Elsa

As the Scottish short form of the Biblical name Elizabeth, Elsa means 'God's oath'. However, the name may have been derived from another independent source. It is possible that it comes from the Anglo-Saxon word for 'swan' or the Old German for 'noble maiden'. It is even thought to be related to the Greek for 'truthful'.

Variants: Aliza, Elizabeth, Else, Elsie, Elza

Elsie

Now considered an independent name in its own right Elsie is also a variant of Elsa, the Scottish short form of the name Elizabeth. Like Elizabeth and Elsa, Elsie means 'God's oath'. But it has a variety of other meanings.

Elsie also comes from the Greek for 'truthful' and the Germanic for 'noble' or 'nobility'. Like Elsa it also comes from the Anglo-Saxon for 'swan'.

Variants: Elsa, Elisabeth, Elizabeth, Elspeth, Elspie

Emma

The name Emma was originally the short form of names containing the German element 'ermin', which means 'universal' and 'entire'. Thus, like Em or Emmie, it was the short-form of Ermintrude ('universal strength').

Queen Emma brought the name to England from Normandy when she married King Ethelred the Unready in the 11th century. She later went on to marry his successor, Cnut.

In the 19th century the name appeared in a classic piece of literature, Jane Austen's *Emma*.

Variants: Em, Ema, Emily, Emm, Emmie, Emmy, Irma

Emerald

In his novel *The Hunchback of Notre Dame*, Victor Hugo christened the object of Quasimodo's affections Esmeralda. Her name comes from the Spanish word for the precious, green stone which is called emerald in English.

Variants: Emeralda, Emeraldine, Esmeralda

Emily

The name was popular in the 19th century and is derived from the medieval form of the Latin name Aemilia. Aemilia, in turn, came from the name of a Roman family, Æmeli.

Emily is also related to the Germanic name Amelia and, as such, also means 'industrious' and 'hard working'.

Variants: Amelie, Amelia, Em, Emma, Emmie, Emilie

E

Enya
This Irish name means 'small fire'. It is also a variant of the name Eithne, which means 'kernel'.
Variant: Ena, Eithne

Erica
Coined in the 18th century, Erica is the feminine form of the Viking name Eric, which means 'eternal', 'honourable', 'alone' and 'ruler'. In addition to this Old Norse meaning it also comes from the Latin word for 'heather'.
Variants: Ericka, Erika, Rica, Ricki

Erin
This poetic name for Ireland has often appeared in sentimental text about the Emerald Isle. First used as a name in North America, its popularity as a first name has grown since the 1970s. It also means 'peace'.
Variant: Errin

Esmé
Esmé comes from the French for 'esteemed'. However, in the past that word was mistakenly translated as 'aimer' ('to love'), so Esmé is also a variant of the French version of Amy, Aimée.
Variants: Aimee, Aimée, Esme, Esmee, Esma

Essence
Of English origin this name is thought to mean 'beginning'. As a word it means 'the essential characteristic of something'.

Estelle
The name, and its variant Estella, is derived from the Old French for 'star'.
Variants: Essie, Estella, Esther, Stella

Eternity
To say something will survive for eternity is to say that it will be

'everlasting'. The use of this word as a girl's name began in North America.

Etta
This name is the short form of both Henrietta ('home rule') and Rosetta ('rose').

Eugenie
Eugenie is the French feminine form of the name Eugene, which comes from the Greek for 'excellent', 'well-born' and 'fortunate'. It was the name of several saints, one of whom was a fallen woman who became an abbot of a monastery, which she entered disguised as a man.

While the name was well-known during the Middle Ages, in Britain it came back into fashion because of Empress Eugenie – the wife of Napoleon III – who fled to England in 1870 and lived there until her death in 1920.
Variants: Eugenia, Gene, Genie, Ina

Eunice
In the Bible Eunice was the mother of Timothy who introduced him to the Christian faith. Her name comes from the Greek for 'well, good' and 'victory'.
Variants: Niki, Nikki, Unice

Eve
The name of the first woman in the Bible comes from the Hebrew for 'breath of life'. It is also believed to mean 'living', 'lively' and 'mother of all living'.

First found in Britain in the 12th century, it was believed that girls bearing the name would be blessed with longevity. The name has produced many derivatives including Eva, Evie and Evita.

The Greek form of Eve is Zoe. Efa is the Welsh version and Eveleen is the Irish interpretation.
Variants: Eva, Evadne, Eveleen, Evie, Evita, Zoe

Evelyn
Like the Irish name Eileen, Evelyn comes from the Germanic and Old French name Aveline, which means 'hazelnut'. The hazelnut is the Celtic fruit of wisdom.

Evelyn, which is sometimes given to boys, is also believed to come from the Latin for 'bird'.
Variants: Aibhilin, Aileen, Eileen, Eveline, Evelyne

Fabia
This is the Latin feminine form of the old Roman family name Fabianus, which was derived from the word for 'bean'.

Quintus Fabius Maximus, who defeated the renowned general Hannibal Barca and his forces, was a member of the house of the Fabii. The British socialist movement, the Fabian Society, was founded in 1884 and named in his honour.

Faith
One of the three major Christian virtues Faith comes from the Latin word 'fides', which means 'trust', 'devotion' and 'loyalty'. The name was popular with the 17th century Puritans and in the 20th century produced the shortened version Fay.

The Spanish boy's name Fidel has the same meaning.
Variants: Fay, Faye, Fayth, Faythe, Fidelity

Faline
'Feles' means 'cat' in Latin hence the English word 'feline'. Faline, a girl's name, comes from the same root.
Variant: Feline

Fallon
Fallon is an English form of an Irish surname that means 'leader' or 'descendant of the leader'.

Fancy
To fantasise about something is to visualise it or wish that it would come true. Similarly, someone with a 'fancy' has a 'whim'

or a dream that they want realised. So fancy, the word and the name, comes from the Greek for 'to make visible'.
Variant: Fancie

Fanny
This name was especially popular in the 18th and 19th centuries. Originally it was a short form of Frances ('Frenchman') and the Welsh name Myfanwy ('my treasure'). But it is now considered to be an independent name in its own right.

Farrah
Farrah has both Arabic and English roots so consequently this name has numerous meanings.

It comes from the Arabic for 'happiness', 'joy' and 'cheerfulness', but also comes from the Middle English for 'lovely', 'beautiful' and 'pleasant'.
Variants: Fara, Farah, Farra

Fatima
The name Fatima has links to both Islam and Christianity. It is the name of the Portuguese village where, in 1917, the Virgin Mary was said to have appeared to three peasant children.

However, the name is also popular among Muslims because Fatima was the favourite daughter of the Prophet Mohammed.

In Arabic the name means 'chaste', 'motherly' and 'abstainer'.
Variants: Fatimah, Fatma

Faustine
Of Italian and Spanish origin this name means 'fortunate'.

Fawn
In English a 'fawn' is a 'young deer'. It is related to the French word 'feon', which means 'off-spring of an animal' and the Latin word 'fetus' ('offspring').
Variants: Fauna, Fawna, Fawnah, Fawniah

F

Faye
This name started life as a short form of the name Faith, which means 'trust' and 'devotion'. However, Faye was also derived from the Old French word for 'fairy'.

According to legend the name was also borne by King Arthur's half-sister Morgan le Fay. She was also known as the Lady of the Lake.
Variants: Fae, Faith, Fay, Fayette

Fayme
The Latin for 'reputation', 'public esteem' and 'acclaim' is 'fama'. Fayme is the Anglicised feminine form of the word.
Variant: Faym

Felicia
Felicia is a variant of Felicity, which comes from the Roman name Felicitas. Felicitas was the Roman goddess of happiness and good fortune. Hence the name and its derivatives share that meaning.
Variants: Falice, Falicia, Felice, Felicity

Felicity
As mentioned above Felicity comes from the Latin word for 'happiness'. It is also the feminine form of the boy's name Felix. A number of early saints bore the name.
Variants: Falice, Falicia, Felicie, Felicite

Fenella
This name is the Anglicised version of the Gaelic name Fionnghuala which is made up of the words for 'white, fair' and 'shouldered'.

The use of Fenella increased in Britain following its inclusion by Sir Walter Scott in the 19th century work *Peveril of the Peak*.

Fiona is believed to have been derived from the same root.
Variants: Finella, Fionola, Fionnuala, Nuala

Ferelith
A Scottish name Ferelith comes from the Old Irish words for 'true, very' and 'lady or princess'. Thus the meaning of this name is believed to be 'perfect princess'.

In 8th century Ireland Ferelith took the form of Forbflaith, while in 13th century Scotland it was Forreleth.

Fern
Taken from the Old English for 'leaf' the name Fern comes from the word for the flowerless, feathery plant. Its use as a given name began during the late 19th century and its popularity increased during the 1900s.
Variant: Fearne, Ferne

Ffion
In medieval love poetry this Welsh name was used to describe the colour and/or softness of a girl's cheek. But Ffion also comes from the old Welsh word for foxglove.
Variants: Fionn, Ffiona

Fifi
Of Hebrew origin the Biblical name Joseph means 'God shall add another'. In the Old Testament it was borne by Jacob's favourite son whose jealous brothers sold him into slavery. In the New Testament it was the name of Mary's husband and the stepfather of Jesus.

Fifi is associated with this name and its rich history because it is the pet form of the French female equivalent, Josephine.
Variant: Josephine

Filma
This name comes from the Old English for 'misty veil'.

Filomena
Two Greek words are believed to be the source of this name – 'philos' ('beloved') and 'armonia' ('harmony'). Filomena is

believed to be the feminine form of the Latin name Philomenus. It was popular during the 19th century, especially in Ireland, because it was borne by St Philomena – the patron saint of impossible causes.
Variants: Phil, Philly, Philomena

Fiona

According to Irish mythology Fionnuala was a woman who was transformed into a swan and cursed to wander the lakes and rivers until Christianity came to Ireland. The name comes from the Celtic word for 'white, fair' and it is from this that Fenella gets its meaning (see above).

While the name Fiona shares the same Gaelic root, it is also believed to be a creation of the writer William Sharp who penned his romantic works under the pseudonym Fiona Macleod. It is this use that popularised the name from the 19th century onwards.
Variants: Fenella, Finella, Fionola, Fionnuala

Flavia

Flavia is an appropriate name to give a blonde or fair-haired daughter, because it comes from the Latin for 'golden' or 'yellow'. The name Flavius is an old Roman family name, which may have begun life as a nickname for a flaxen-haired person. Flavia is the feminine form of that dynastic name.

Fleur

Like Flower and Flora this name means 'flower' or 'blossom'.
Occasionally used in the Middle Ages, it has Old French roots.
Variants: Ffleur, Fflur, Fleurette, Flora, Flower

Floella

This name is believed to be a compound of two short forms – Flo (a diminutive of Florence) and Ella (an independent name and pet form of Eleanor and Isabella). It is a modern creation.

Flora

Flora Macdonald is the name of the woman who helped Bonnie Prince Charlie to escape the Scottish mainland in 1746 following his defeat at the Battle of Culloden. The name is closely associated with Scotland and was not found in England before the 18th century.

But the history of the name stretches back into Roman times as Flora comes from the Latin for 'flower' or 'blossom'. According to the mythology of that time the goddess of fertility, flowers and spring was called Flora. Florrie is the short form.

Variants: Fflur, Fleur, Fleurette, Flo, Flor, Flores, Florrie, Flossie

Florence

During the Crimean War, in the latter half of the 19th century, the name Florence became associated with the founder of modern nursing, Florence Nightingale. It was the fame of 'the lady with the lamp' that popularised this name throughout the world. She, in turn, had been christened after her birthplace, the town of Florence in Italy.

But the name was popular long before the 19th century. During the Middle Ages it was given to both boys and girls. Florence comes from the Latin for 'blossoming' or 'flourishing'. The name Flo is the pet form.

Variants: Flo, Flora, Florance, Floreen, Florrie, Flossie, Flossy

Flower

This is the English version of the French name Fleur. It is also used as a term of endearment. (See Flora.)

Variants: Fleur, Flora

Fonda

Of Spanish origin this name means 'profound'. It can be used as a first name for both boys and girls and is also a surname.

Variants: Fon, Fondea

France
This short form of the name Frances is sometimes bestowed on boys and girls in honour of the European country.
Variant: Frances

Frances
The Old Middle Latin word 'franciscus' meant 'a free man' and it is from this word that the name Frances is derived. The male version of this name is Francis.
Variants: Fran, France, Francesca, Frankie

Francesca
This is the Italian version of the name Frances (see above) which is now common in the English-speaking world.
Variants: Fran, France, Frances, Frankie

Frankie
The names Frank, Francis, Frances and Francesca are all associated with freedom because of their namesake – the Franks. They were a German tribe who, having won their liberty from the Romans, settled in Gaul, which later became known as France.
Variants: Fran, France, Francis, Francesca

Frayda
Frayda is taken from the Yiddish word for 'joy'.
Variants: Frayde, Fraydyne, Freida

Frederica
Of Old French and German origin, this name is made from the elements 'fred' ('peace') and ric ('power, ruler'). Thus it means 'peaceful ruler'.

The name Frederick was originally brought to England by the Normans. It was reintroduced to Britain during the reign of George I and it experienced another wave of popularity during the Victorian age. Frederica is its feminine form.

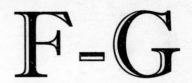
Variants: Federica, Fredda, Freddi, Freddie, Ricki, Rica

Freya
According to Norse mythology Freya was the goddess of fertility, love and beauty. The name means 'noble lady' or 'mistress'. Her male counterpart, Frey, was the god of peace and prosperity.
Variants: Freja, Freyja, Froja

Fulvia
The name comes from the Roman family name Fulvius, which was derived from the Latin word for 'dusky' and 'tawny'.

Gabrielle
The archangel Gabriel makes more than one appearance in the Bible, bringing with him messages from God. It is fitting, therefore, that his name comes from the Hebrew meaning 'messenger of God' or 'my strength is God'.

Gabriel makes his first appearance in the Old Testament where he is seen by David as a vision (see Gabriel in boys' names).

Gabrielle and its variant Gabriella are just two feminine forms of this name.
Variants: Gabbie, Gabi, Gabriella, Gaby, Gigi, Gaye

Gae
Little used as a first name before the 20th century Gae was derived from the English word meaning 'cheerful' and 'merry'.

However, the name fell out of favour from the 1960s onwards when the word 'gay' became synonymous with homosexuality.

In Ireland it is a pet form of Gabriel and Gabrielle. It is also a diminutive of Gaynor. As an independent name it can be given to both boys and girls.
Variants: Gabriella, Gabrielle, Gaenor, Gaye, Gaynor

Gaenor

This name is a diminutive of the Guinevere who according to popular legend was King Arthur's queen and Sir Lancelot's lover. As a short form of this Arthurian name, Gaenor comes from the Welsh for 'beautiful maiden'.
Variants: Gae, Gainer, Gayner, Gay

Gaia

In Greek mythology Gaia was the goddess of the earth and, as Mother Earth, she embodied its richness and fertility. This name is of symbolic importance to environmentalists and feminists.
Variants: Ge, Gaea

Gardenia

The gardenia – sweet-smelling flower – was named after the 18th century American botanist Dr Alexander Garden. The white gardenia also became associated with blues singer Billie Holiday, who would often wear one in her hair when performing in the 1930s.

Gayle

This short form of the Biblical name Abigail is now used independently as a Christian name. It comes from the Hebrew for 'my father rejoices' and 'source of joy'. It is not found before the 20th century.
Variants: Abigail, Abigayle, Gail, Gale

Gazelle

A gazelle is a small, graceful antelope. Thus as a given name it implies 'delicacy' and 'grace'.
Variant: Gazella

Gemma

Popular in 1980s Britain this name implies that the bearer is 'precious' for it is derived from the Latin for 'precious stone' or 'gem'.

The poet Dante, who was born in 1265, was married to a woman called Gemma.

The name was also borne by Gemma Galgani an orphaned Italian girl who had visions of the Virgin Mary. She died in 1903 and was canonised in 1940. Thereafter the name grew in popularity.

Variants: Gem, Germaine, Jemma

Genette
Genette is a variant of Jeanette, Janet and Jean. The afore-mentioned girls' names are all derived from the Biblical name John, which means 'God has favoured', 'God is gracious' and 'God is merciful'.

Variants: Gene, Genie, Genna, Ginette, Ginetta, Jane, Janet, Jean, Jeanne, Jeanette

Geneva
As well as being the name of a city in Switzerland, Geneva is a short form of Geneviève – a French name that comes from the German for 'womankind'.

The name Geneva is also derived from the French, and ultimately the Latin, for 'juniper' which is a bush that does not lose its leaves in winter.

Variants: Gena, Genevia, Genevieve, Geneviève, Genna, Janeva

Geneviève
As mentioned above this French name comes from the German for 'womankind'. Its Gallic connection is further entrenched because St Geneviève is the patron saint of Paris, France's capital city.

This 5th century Gallo-Roman nun devoted her life to prayer and emboldened the city at a crucial hour – when it was threatened by Attila the Hun. Parisians followed her example, stood firm, and the attack failed to materialise. It was believed that her prayers saved the city.

Variants: Geneva, Genevieve, Genny, Genovera, Genoveva, Gina

Georgette

Georgette, like other feminine versions of George, was especially popular in Britain during the reign of the Hanoverian kings which began with the ascendancy of George I in 1714.

It is the French feminine form of George, which means 'farmer'.
Variants: Georgett, Georgia, Georgi, Georgie, Gigi

Georgia

Georgia is also the name of an American southern state that was so-called in honour of King George II. This is not to be confused with the country that was once a part of the former USSR.
Variants: Georgett, Georgette, Georgiana, Georgina, Georgi, Georgie, Gigi

Geraldine

The name Geraldine owes its existence to a poem and the adoration of one man. In 1540 Henry Howard, the Earl of Surrey, professed his love for Lady Elizabeth Fitzgerald in a poem calling her the 'fair Geraldine'. It was a name that he alone invented.

'Fitzgerald' means 'sons of Gerald'. 'Gerald' is derived from a Germanic name that means 'spear' and 'rule'. 'Geraldine' is another, romantic, way of saying 'one of the Fitzgeralds'.
Variants: Deena, Dina, Geralda, Geraldene, Geraldina, Gerrie

Germaine

In the 20th century the feminist writer Germaine Greer was a famous bearer of this name. In the 19th century it was associated with Germaine Cousin, who was canonised in 1867.

The name comes from the Old French for 'German' and from the Latin for 'brother'.
Variants: Gem, Gemma, Germain, Germana, Germane

Gertrude

The name of Hamlet's mother comes from the Old High German for 'spear' and 'strength', 'wizard'.

In Norse mythology Gertrude was a goddess who helped to escort slain heroes to the palace of bliss.

It appeared in England during the late Middle Ages and may have been introduced by migrants from the Low Countries where the name was associated with a mystic saint. Its use increased during the 19th century when Germanic names were in vogue in Britain.

Variants: Gerda, Gert, Gerte, Gertie, Trudie, Trudi, Trudy

Gigi

This French name will forever be connected with the novel and the 1958 Hollywood film *Gigi*. The book was written by Colette who bestowed the name upon her heroine.

In France Gigi is a diminutive of Gilberte and Giselle. Gilberte is a feminine form of the name Gilbert, which is derived from the Old German for 'bright' and 'pledge'. Giselle means 'pledge' and 'hostage'. It too is derived from the Old German language.

Variants: Gilbert, Giselle

Gila

Gila comes from the Hebrew for 'joy'.

Variant: Ghila

Gilda

The origin of the name is uncertain but it is thought to have been derived from the Old English for 'to gild' or 'to gloss over'.

Variants: Gilde, Gildi, Gill, Jill

Gillian

This name is the English form of Juliana, which is the feminine variant of Julian. Julian comes from the Greek for 'soft-haired' or 'fair complexioned'. It was also the name of the first Roman emperor – Gaius Julius Caesar. He belonged to the ancient Roman family, the Julii who traced their descent to Aphrodite, the goddess of love.

Variants: Gill, Gillaine, Gilly, Jill, Jillian, Jilly, Juliana

Gina
Gina began life as a pet form of the names Georgina ('farmer'), Eugena ('well-born, fortunate') and Regina ('queen'), but is now an independent name in its own right. In Japanese Gina means silvery.
Variants: Eugena, Geena, Gena, Georgina, Jeanna, Regina

Ginger
This nickname for someone with red hair is also the pet form of Virginia. The Hollywood actress Ginger Rogers, for example, was born Virginia McMath in 1911.
Variant: Virginia

Giselle
The meaning of this name may have come from a medieval European practice. It was common during those times to leave children to be raised in a foreign court to symbolise an alliance between two states. This was an agreement between two bodies hence the name Giselle comes from the German word for 'pledge'.
The name Gigi is the pet form of Giselle.
Variants: Ghislaine, Gigi, Gisela, Giselda, Gisèle

Gita
As the short form of the Spanish version of Margaret, Margarita, Gita means 'pearl' or 'daisy'. It could also stem from the Sanskrit for 'song'.
Variants: Ghita, Greta, Gretchen, Gretel, Margaret, Margarita, Rita

Gladys
Although it was well known in England since the 1870s, a mystery surrounds the origin of the name Gladys. It may have been derived from the Latin for either 'small sword' or 'lame'.
Its association with the Latin for 'lame' is concurrent with the theory that Gladys comes from the Roman family name

Claduii, which also has the same meaning. This theory is further strengthened by the belief that Gladys comes from the Welsh form of Claudia.

However, Gladys may have been derived from the Welsh for 'ruler' and 'princess'.

Variants: Glad, Gladi, Gladis, Gwladys

Glenda

Glenda is a modern name that was first found in North America and Australia. It is sometimes thought to be a feminine form of the name Glen, which is a Celtic name meaning 'valley'.

Glenda is orginally derived from the Welsh for 'clean, pure, holy' and 'good'.

Variants: Glen, Glennie, Glenny, Glinda

Glenna

Like Glenda and Glen, Glenna is derived from the Scottish Gaelic word 'gleann' which means 'valley'. It is also considered to be a feminine form of the name Glen.

Variants: Glen, Glena, Gleneen, Glenesha, Glenni, Glenice

Glenys

This modern Welsh name is derived from 'glân' which means 'pure' and 'holy'.

Variants: Glen, Glenis, Glennis, Glennys, Glynis

Gloria

Gloria comes from the Latin for 'fame, renown, praise' and 'honour'. It has been a popular name for girls since the late 19th century but appeared in both literature and public life in another form long before that.

During the reign of Elizabeth I in England the poet Edmund Spenser wrote *The Faerie Queen*. In that work the queen of the fairies was known as Gloriana, which itself was a title sometimes given to Elizabeth.

Variants: Glora, Gloriana, Glorianna, Glory

Goldie

Originally a nickname for someone with blonde or fair hair, Goldie is derived from the word for 'gold'. The Hollywood actress Goldie Hawn is perhaps the most famous bearer of this name.

However, Golda stems from the same source. It was the name of former Israeli Prime Minister Golda Meir who led the country from 1969 to 1974.

Variants: Golda, Goldia, Goldina

Gozala

Of Hebrew origin, this name means 'young bird'.

Grace

Favoured by the 17th century Puritans, 'grace' is another quality that has been bestowed upon girls as a first name. It comes from the Latin 'gratus', which means 'pleasing', 'attractive' and 'charming'. To say someone is 'graceful' is to say that they possess beauty, elegance and a certain poise.

In Greek mythology the Three Graces were nature goddesses who brought joy to the world.

In the 20th century the film star Grace Kelly seemed to possess all those qualities associated with her name.

Variants: Gracia, Gracie, Gráinne, Grayce, Grazielle, Grata

Grainne

In English this Irish name is sometimes translated as Grace (see above). For example, Irish heroine Gráinne Ui Mnáille is also known as Grace O'Malley, a female pirate who fought the English during Elizabethan times.

Nevertheless the name Grainne may have been derived from the word for 'love' or the Irish Gaelic for 'grain'. According to legend it was borne by an Irish princess who was betrothed to the warrior Finn, but eloped with his nephew Diarmait (Dermot) instead.

Variants: Grace, Gráine, Gráinne, Granya

Girls

Greer
The late actress Greer Garson was given her mother's maiden name when she was born in London in 1904. This example clearly shows how the Scottish surname Greer went on to become a woman's first name.

It comes from the Greek for 'the watchful mother' and is believed to be a contracted form of Gregor that was coined in the Middle Ages.
Variant: Grier

Greta
The name Greta is a short form of Margarita – a Spanish version of the name Margaret. Margaret is of Greek origin and means 'pearl'. However, the French form Marguerite means 'daisy'.
Variants: Daisy, Ghita, Gita, Gretchen, Gretel, Margaret, Margarita, Marguerite, Maggie, Rita

Gretchen
Like Gita and Greta, Gretchen is a derivative of Margaret, which means 'pearl' or 'daisy'. It comes from Germany.
Variants: Ghita, Gita, Greta, Gretel, Margaret, Margarita, Marguerite, Rita

Guinevere
Like many of the names that featured in the legend that surrounds King Arthur, Guinevere is believed to be of Welsh origin. It is thought to be a compound of two words – 'gwyn' ('fair, white', 'blessed, holy') and 'hwyfar' ('smooth, soft' or 'phantom').

Legend has it that, not only was Guinevere King Arthur's queen, she was also Sir Lancelot's lover. The name Jennifer is a Cornish form of Guinevere.
Variants: Gaenor, Gaynor, Guenevere, Jennifer

Gwendelon
Like Guinevere the name Gwendolina (a variant of Gwendelon)

featured in the story of King Arthur. According to the legend Gwendolina was the wife of Merlin the wizard.

Of Welsh origin, the name Gwendelon was derived from the words 'gwen' ('white, fair') and 'dolen' meaning 'ring or bow'. Hence it means 'white ring'.

According to Welsh legend it was the name of King Locrine's wife. He left her for a German princess and she took her revenge by drowning his daughter Sabrina in the River Severn.
Variants: Gwen, Gwenda, Gwendolina, Gwendolyn

Gwenllian
Another member of the family of Welsh names that begin with 'Gwen', Gwenllian means 'white flood' or 'fair flow'. The name has been in use since the 12th century and probably referred to the pale or fair complexion of the bearer's skin.
Variant: Gwen, Gwenlian

Gwyneth
Popular since the late 19th century Gwyneth may be a variant of the Welsh county name – Gwynedd. Gwynedd comes from the Celtic for 'blessed' or 'happy'. Like Gwendelon and Gwenllian, Gwyneth shares the short form Gwen.
Variants: Gwen, Gwenda, Gwenith, Gwenn, Venetia, Wendi, Winnie

Habiba
Habiba comes from the Arabic for 'lover' and 'beloved'. It is the feminine version of the name Habib.
Variant: Haviva

Haidee
Used by Lord Byron in his 1819 poem *Don Juan*, Haidee is a variant of the Greek name Haido, which means 'to caress'. In the poem the characters Juan and Haidee fall in love.

The name is also a variant of Heidi, which is a Swiss pet form of the German name Adelaide ('noble').
Variant: Heidi

Halina
Halina comes from the Hawaiian for 'likeness' or 'resemblance'.

Halle
Halle is a variant of the name Hayley, meaning 'hay field' in Old English. However, Halle is also thought to come from the Irish Gaelic for 'ingenious' and the Norse for 'hero'.
As well as being a Belgian place name it is borne by the Oscar-winning actress Halle Berry.
Variants: Hayley

Hana
Although it looks as if it could be related to the Hebrew name Hannah, Hana is of Arabic origin. It means 'bliss' or 'happiness'. The same name means 'flower' or 'blossom' in Japanese. It also comes from the Arapaho tribe of Native Americans. In that culture it means 'sky' or 'dark cloud'.
Variants: Hanae, Hanako

Hannah
In the Old Testament Hannah is the mother of the prophet Samuel. The name is also traditionally believed to belong to the mother of the Virgin Mary. It is this latter belief that ensured the popularity of the name Hannah throughout Europe. It was especially beloved by the Puritans in the 16th and 17th centuries.
  The name comes from the Hebrew for 'God has favoured me'. The Greek translation of Hannah is Anna and hence names such as Anne, Annabel, Anoushka and its derivatives all share the same meaning.
Variants: Ann, Anna, Annabel, Anne, Annette, Anoushka, Nanette

Harmony
According to Greek mythology Harmonia was the daughter of Aphrodite, the goddess of sex, love and beauty. Her name – and the variant Harmony – means 'concord' or 'in agreement'.
Variants: Harmonia, Harmonie, Harmonee, Harmoni

Harper

Mainly found in North America, the name Harper is given to both boys and girls. It is a surname that originally described the bearer's occupation as a harpist.

In the 20th century the novelist Harper Lee bore the name. In 1961 she won a Pulitzer Prize for her novel *To Kill a Mockingbird*.

Harriett

The name Henry comes from the Old German for 'home rule'. It was brought to England by the Normans as Henri – the French form. In England that name was later translated as Harry and it is from this that the feminine form Harriett was born.

Hat and Hattie are short forms of this name, which is also related to Henrietta.

Variants: Harrie, Harriet, Hat, Hattie, Henrietta, Hetta

Hayley

The name is also a surname that was probably derived from the description of a place as it comes from the Old English words for 'hay field'.

Like Halle (see page 101) it is also associated with the Norse for 'hero' and the Irish Gaelic for 'ingenious'.

Variants: Hailey, Haley, Hali, Halle, Hallie, Haleigh

Hazel

Derived from the Old English word for 'hazelnut', the word 'hazel' also refers to two separate colours. It could be used to describe something that, like the nut, is reddish-brown. Alternatively it may also describe eyes that are greeny-brown in colour.

As a girl's name Hazel became popular in the late 19th century.

Variants: Hasse, Hazelle

Heather

Heather is another name that grew in popularity as a girl's name towards the end of the 19th century. During that period flower names were especially popular with Victorian parents. The name

Heather was particularly favoured by the Scottish because the brightly coloured plant adorned the moors of Scotland.

In recent times the name has become popular in North America. Heath is the male variant.

Heaven
Heaven is the use of the English word for 'the place where God lives'.

Hebe
In Greek mythology Hebe was the goddess of youth and the daughter of Zeus. Before she married Heracles she was also the cupbearer for the gods and goddesses on Mount Olympus. Fittingly her name comes from the Greek for 'young'.

Hebe is also the name of a flowering shrub.

Hedda
This name was derived from the German for 'combat' or 'war'. It comes from the Germanic names Hedewig and Hedwige.
Variants: Hedy

Heidi
The children's book *Heidi*, written by Johanna Spyri, was about a little orphan girl who lived with her grandfather in the Alps in Switzerland. The heroine's name is a Swiss pet form of the German name Adelaide.

Heidi is also thought to be a German form of the name Hilde, a variant of the English name Hilda ('battle').
Variants: Adelaide, Adeleid, Heide, Heidie, Hilde

Helen
Once described as 'the face that launched a thousand ships', Helen was the great beauty of Greek mythology. The daughter of Zeus, she was married to Menelaus of Sparta but she left him for Paris, the Trojan prince. It was this event, described by Homer in the poem the *Iliad*, which sparked the 10-year Trojan War.

The name Helen comes from the Greek for 'ray', 'bright' and 'light'.
Variants: Elaine, Eleanor, Elena, Ellen, Helena, Helene, Lena, Leonora

Helianthe
This name comes from the Greek for 'bright flower'.

Helga
Brought to Britain by the Normans the name Helga comes from the Old Norse for 'prosperous', 'successful' and 'pious'.

Despite its early introduction Helga was not a popular in Britain and the name was only re-introduced into the English-speaking world in the 20th century.
Variant: Olga

Heloise
Although the name Heloise has been used in England since the 13th century its exact origin is disputed. It may have come from the Old German name Helewise. Alternatively it is thought to be of French origin, meaning 'famous fighter'.
Variants: Eloisa, Eloïse, Eloise

Henrietta
The name Henrietta is the feminine form of the Germanic name Henry, which means 'home rule'. Although the name Henri had been brought to England by the Normans, Henrietta was not used until the marriage of Charles I to the French princess Henrietta Maria de Bourbon in 1625.

As explained above the Anglicised form of Henrietta is Harriett. (See Harriett.)
Variants: Enrica, Harrie, Harriet, Harriett, Hat, Hattie, Henni

Herma
Milestones were often made from a square stone pillar, which in Latin was called 'herma'. Like the stone pillar it is hoped that girls blessed with this name will be strong.

Hermione

With her Harry Potter series of children's novels J K Rowling has thrust the name Hermione back into the limelight. However, centuries ago Shakespeare used the name for one of his characters in *The Winter's Tale*. And, long before that, Hermione featured in Greek mythology. She was the daughter of Helen and Menelaus.

The name, a feminine form of Hermes, means 'stone' or 'support'. According to legend Hermes was the messenger god who protected travellers.

Variants: Erma, Hermia, Hermina, Hermine, Herminia, Mina

Hertha

Hertha is an English name that means 'of the earth'.

Hesper

Of Greek origin, Hesper means 'evening' or 'evening star'. It comes from the word 'hesperos'.

Variants: Hespera

Hester

Used since the Middle Ages, Hester is a variant of the Biblical name Esther. In the Old Testament Esther was the Queen of Persia who saved her people from slaughter.

The name Esther comes from the Hebrew for 'bride'. It is also believed to come from the word for 'myrtle', which is a bush. Alternatively Esther, and Hester, also comes from the Persian for 'star'.

Variants: Esther, Hettie, Hetty

Heulwen

This Welsh girl's name means 'sunshine'

Hilary

During the Middle Ages Hilary was a common boy's name. Its popularity may be associated with the 4th century theologian

St Hilary of Poitiers whose feast day falls in mid-January. It is because of him that the English law courts, and some universities, call their second term in the academic calendar the Hilary Term.

Although the name became less popular from the 1500s onwards it was revived in the 19th century and was given to both boys and girls.

Hilary comes from the Greek word 'hilaros', which means 'jovial', 'lively', 'cheerful' and 'boisterous'.
Variants: Hilarie, Hillary

Hilda

Popular with parents both before and after the Norman Conquest, the currency of this name dipped during Tudor times but rose again in the 19th century. Hilda, believed to be of Germanic origin, also comes from the Old English for 'battle'.

In Anglo-Saxon England the name was borne by St Hilda, a Northumbrian princess who founded the abbey at Whitby.
Variants: Hildie, Hylda

Hina

This Hindu name means 'henna' – the red or black dye that is used to colour hair and decorate the skin and fingernails.

Holly

Like Carol, Noel and Robin, Holly is associated with the Christmas season. It comes from the Old English word 'holen', which means 'holly tree'. This evergreen tree with red berries is traditionally used to decorate homes during Christmas.

First used as a name at the beginning of the 20th century, its popularity grew during the 1960s.
Variants: Holli, Hollie, Hollye

Honor

To honour someone is to give them recognition and respect. Naturally the name Honor has the same meaning.

The Roman emperor Theodosius the Great was given the title 'Honorius' and his niece was given the name Honoria.
Variants: Honora, Honoria, Honour

Honey
Both a sweet substance made by bees from nectar and a term of endearment, Honey is also a name given to girls. The word is of Germanic origin and is related to the Dutch 'honig' and German 'Honig'.

Honesty
Like Charity, Chastity and Honour, Honesty is another quality that has given birth to a girl's name. It comes from the Latin word 'honestãs'.

Hope
Hope is one third of the triumvirate of Christian virtues, which stands alongside charity and faith. It comes from the Old English word 'hopa' and means 'to desire or wish something to happen'. The name was another Puritan favourite.

But a second Old English meaning has been identified, that is unrelated to the Bible. Hope may have also been derived from the word for 'little valley'.
Variants: Hopi, Hopie

Hortense
Widely used in France, the name Hortense comes from the Latin for 'garden' or 'gardener'. Its use in the English-speaking world increased during the 19th century.

The name was borne by Hortense de Beauharnais – the wife of Louis Bonaparte and the mother of Napoleon III.
Variants: Hortensia, Ortense, Ortensia

Hoshi
This Japanese name means 'star'.
Variants: Hoshie, Hoshiko, Hoshiyo

Girls

Hula

Hula comes from the Hebrew for 'to make music'.

Hulda

This Biblical name is also of Old Norse and Germanic origin. In the Old Testament Hulda was a female prophet who predicted the destruction of Jerusalem. According to Teutonic mythology, the name was also borne by a goddess.

The Hebrew meaning of the name is 'weasel'. The Old Norse meaning is 'muffled' or 'covered', while it can also come from the German for 'beloved' or 'gracious'.
Variants: Huldah, Huldi, Huldy

Hyacinth

In Greek mythology a young man called Hyacinthus was accidentally killed by the god Apollo, his lover. A purple flower – the hyacinth – sprang from his blood by way of memory of him.

Although the name was associated with a legendary Greek man it is now commonly given to girls. It was particularly fashionable during the late 19th century.
Variants: Ciancinta, Hyacinthe, Jacinda, Jacinta

Ianthe

This poetic name was used by both Byron and Shelley in their works. It originates in Greek mythology. According to legend Ianthe was a nymph and daughter of Oceanus who was supreme god of the seas. She was also the granddaughter of Uranus and Ge, who ruled the sky and the earth.

The name comes from the Greek for 'violet' and 'dawn cloud'.
Variants: Iantha, Iola, Iolanthe, Iole, Ione

Ida

Mount Ida on the Greek island of Crete was associated with the king of the gods, Zeus. However the name Ida is thought to have more than one source. It is believed to be derived from the Old

Norse words for 'work' and 'woman'. It is also linked to the Old
English for 'protection' and 'possession'.
Variants: Idane, Idina, Ita

Ignatia
Taken from the Latin for 'fiery' and 'ardour', Ignatia is also
derived from the Old Roman family name Egnatius.
 The male form of this name is associated with St Ignatius
who, in the 16th century, founded the Jesuit order. The
youngest of 13 children, Ignatius was a soldier who devoted
his life to Christianity.
Variant: Ignacia

Ilka
Ilka is a Scottish name that comes from the Middle English for
'of that same standing'. It also has a Slavic meaning – 'striving'
and 'flattering'.

Ilona
This is the Hungarian version of the Greek name Helen, which
means 'bright'. In Hungarian it means 'beautiful' and 'sunshine'.
Variants: Eleanor, Helen, Helena, Ili, Ilonka, Lanci

Iman
Of African and Arabic origin, it means 'faith in God'. In the
1970s and 1980s this name became well known because of the
Somali-born model Iman.

Imelda
Imelda comes from the Latin for 'wishful'. It also the Italian form
of the Germanic name Irmhild, which means 'universal battle'.
During the 20th century the name became associated with Imelda
Marcos, the First Lady of the Philippines.

Imogen
This name is of disputed origin. It may be derived from the Latin

word 'imago' ('image, likeness') or it could mean 'innocent'.

However, it is also believed that Imogen could be a misprint of Innogen, a Celtic name that means 'girl' or 'daughter'.
Variants: Emogene, Imagina, Immie, Immy, Imogene, Imogine, Innogen, Inogen

Ina
As a variant of Agnes, Ina comes from the Greek for 'pure' and 'chaste'. It is also used as a short form of names such as Christina and Georgina, which end in 'ina'.
Variants: Agnes, Ena

India
This Sanskrit word for 'river' is also the name of a country. In her 1936 novel about the American Civil War and its aftermath, *Gone with the Wind*, Margaret Mitchell used the name for one of her characters.

Indigo
Indigo is a dark blue colour. But the name comes from the Greek for 'from India'.
Variants: Indie, Indy

Indira
Born in 1917 Indira Gandhi was the daughter of the first Prime Minister of India, Jawaharlal Nehru, who went on to assume the office herself. She was assassinated in 1984.

Her name means 'splendid' in Hindi. It is associated with Lakshmi, the goddess of wealth who was the consort of the god Vishnu.
Variants: Indie, Indy

Inés
Inés is the Spanish form of the name Agnes, which is derived from the Greek for 'pure' and 'chaste'. It is also used without an accent.
Variants: Agnes, Ines, Inez

Inge
In Norse mythology Ing was the god of fertility, who was also associated with peace and plenty. The feminine name Inge comes from the Old Norse for 'meadow', but because it was also known to the Anglo-Saxons the name has an Old English meaning 'to be descended from'.

Inge comes from the same source as the girl's name Ingrid.
Variants: Inga, Ingaberg, Inger, Ingrid

Ingrid
Like Inge the name Ingrid is linked to the Scandinavian god of peace, fertility and plenty, Ing. He was associated with a sacred golden boar and it is from this association that the name Ingrid is thought to stem for it means 'Ing's ride or steed'. Ingrid is also thought to mean 'beautiful under the protection of Ing'.

The Swedish actress Ingrid Bergman, born in 1915 helped to introduce the name to the English-speaking world.
Variants: Inga, Ingaberg, Inge, Inger

Inoke
Hawaiian in origin, Inoke means 'devoted'.

Iola
A variant of the name Ianthe, Iola comes from the Greek for 'violet' and 'dawn cloud'. One version of this name, Iole, appears in Greek mythology. Iole was the daughter of Eurytus who was abducted by Heracles.
Variants: Ianthe, Iole, Yolanda, Yolande

Iona
It was on this Scottish island that St Columba settled and founded his monastery in 563. From that site he spread Christianity throughout Scotland and the north of England.

The name is also believed to come from the Greek for 'violet', 'dawn cloud' or possibly 'purple jewel'.
Variants: Ione, Ionia

Iora
This name comes from the Latin for 'gold'.

Ireland
Like the name Shannon, Ireland is often bestowed upon girls as a tribute to the Emerald Isle.

Iris
In Greek mythology Iris was the goddess who passed messages between the gods and earth using the rainbow as her link. Thus the name Iris comes from the Greek for 'messenger of light' or 'rainbow'.

It is also the name of a flower as well as the term used for the coloured part of the eye.
Variants: Irisa, Irita, Irys, Irisha, Irissa, Risa, Risha, Rissa

Irma
Irmintrude and Irmgard are two examples of German names that begin with the element 'irm(en)', which means 'whole' or 'universal'. Irma is a pet form of names that begin with this element, used independently.

It was first introduced to the English-speaking world in the late 19th century.
Variants: Emma, Erma, Irmina, Irmgrad, Irmintrude

Isabel
The name Isabel is the Spanish equivalent of Elizabeth, which means 'God's oath' in Hebrew. It was first introduced to England in the Middle Ages and henceforth it became a name associated with royalty. The wives of three kings of England bore the name.
Variants: Bel, Bella, Bell, Ezabel, Isabella, Isabelle, Isbel, Isobel, Izzie, Izzy

Isadora
Isadora comes from the Greek for 'gift of Isis'. Isis was the

Egyptian goddess of the moon and fertility who was worshipped during classical times.

In the 20th century the name was borne by Isadora Duncan, an American dancer who was considered to be the mother of modern dance. She died in 1927.

Variants: Dora, Issy, Izzy

Isha

Isha is a variant of the name Aisha which comes from the Arabic for 'prospering'.

Variant: Aisha

Isis

In Ancient Egypt Isis was the goddess of fertility.

Isla

Pronounced 'eye-la', Isla is a Scottish name that means 'swiftly' and 'flowing'. Islay, a Hebridean island, is a variant of Isla.

Variant: Islay

Ismaela

Ismaela comes from the Hebrew for 'God listens'.

Isra

This Turkish name means 'freedom'.

Ita

As a variant of Ida, Ita has a variety of meanings. It could come from the Old English for 'possession' and 'protection' or the Old Norse for 'work' or 'woman'.

But, as an independent name, it is derived from the Italian and Irish for 'thirsty'.

Variant: Ida

Italia

The girl's name Italia means 'Italian' or 'woman from Italy'.

I-J

Ivory
Ivory is a precious bone-like substance that forms the tusks of a certain breed of elephant. White in colour, it is used to make carvings and jewellery.

The girl's name Ivory also comes from the Welsh for 'highborn lady'.

Ivy
Introduced as a girl's name in the 19th century, Ivy was especially popular during the 1920s. It comes from the Old English for ivy – the clinging plant.
Variants: Iva, Ivi, Ivie

Jacqueline
The name Jacqueline was brought to England by the sister-in-law of Henry V, who reigned from 1413 until his death in 1422.

Jacqueline is of French, but ultimately Hebrew, origin. It is the French feminine form of the Biblical name James, which is a variant of Jacob ('follower', 'supplanter').

Jacquetta, another version of the name, has been known in England since the 15th century, while Shakespeare used the name Jacquenetta in *Love's Labour's Lost*. But the popularity of the name Jacqueline increased during the 1960s because it was borne by the glamorous First Lady of America – Jacqueline Kennedy, who went on to marry the shipping magnate Aristotle Onassis.
Variants: Jacki, Jackie, Jacklyn, Jacquelyn, Jacquelynne, Jacquetta, Jacqui

Jade
Jade is a precious green stone that is used to make carvings and jewellery. In Spain it was sometimes referred to as the 'stone of the bowels' because it was believed to protect the body from intestinal disorders. When Mick Jagger, the lead singer of the Rolling Stones, named his second daughter Jade in the early 1970s the popularity of this name grew.
Variant: Jayde

Jaime

In French 'j'aime' means 'I like' or 'I love' and the name Jaime shares this meaning. A unisex name, in Spain it is a form of the boy's name James.

However in North America the name is mostly given to girls where it is also considered to be a variant spelling of Jamie. As a feminine form of James, like Jacqueline, it shares the meaning for James and Jacob – 'supplanter'.

Variants: Jaimi, Jaimie, Jamie, Jaymee

Jamelia

In Arabic this name means 'beautiful'. It is the feminine form of Jamil and is a variant of the North African name Djamila.

Variants: Jameela, Jameelah, Jamilah, Jamillah, Jamillia

Jane

Like Janine, Joan and Jean the name Jane is a feminine form of John, which comes from the Hebrew for 'God has favoured' and 'God is gracious'. It also comes from the Old French name Jehane.

During the Middle Ages Joan was the favoured form of John – a timeless favourite. However, in Tudor England, Jane became the popular choice. It was the name of Henry VIII's favourite wife – Jane Seymour.

Like Anne, Jane has been used in compounds to produce other names such as Sarah Jane and Mary Jane.

Variants: Janelle, Janet, Janette, Janie, Janine, Janice, Janis, Jayne, Jean, Joan

Janelle

In 1989 in North America this variant of Jane was more common than the original. Janelle enjoys more popularity in this region than it does in Europe.

Like Jane, Janet, Jean, Joan and Joanne, Janelle ultimately stems from the Hebrew for 'God is gracious'.

Variants: Jane, Janet, Janette, Janie, Janine, Janice, Janis, Jean, Joan, Jonelle

Janet

Ultimately derived from the Biblical name John ('God has favoured', 'God is gracious') Janet comes from the French variant of Jane – Jeannette. Popular in Scotland, the name Janet was not widely used until the late 19th century.
Variants: Janette, Janie, Janice, Janis, Jeanette, Jeannette, Jennie, Netta, Nettie, Jessie

Janine

Janine is another feminine variant of the name John ('God is gracious'). Of French origin, it is an alternative spelling of Jeannine.
Variants: Jane, Janina, Janice, Janis, Jeanette, Jeannette, Jeanine, Jeannine

Jasmine

This fragrant flower is used to make tea, scented oil and perfume. Of Persian and Arabic origin, the name means 'an olive flower'. Yasmin is the Arabic version of the name.
Variants: Jasmin, Yasmina, Yasmin, Yasmine

Jean

Like Janet, Jean is a Scottish form of the name Jane, which is derived from the French variant Jehane. In the 18th century the name was borne by the mistress of Louise XV, Jeanne Antoinette Poison, who was more commonly known as Madame de Pompadour.

As a feminine variant of John, Jean means 'God is gracious'.
Variants: Gene, Genna, Jane, Janina, Janine, Jeanette, Jeannette, Jeanine, Jeannine, Jeanne

Jemima

In the Old Testament Jemima was the daughter of Job. In Hebrew and Arabic the name means 'dove'.

Favoured by the Puritans, the name was especially popular in the early 19th century. It is also associated with the feminine form of Benjamin, Jemina.
Variants: Jem, Jemimah, Jemma, Jemina, Jona, Jonati, Mima

Jenna
The name Jenna was derived from Jennifer, the Cornish form of Guinevere. Hence, it is ultimately of Welsh origin and means 'fair ghost'.
Variants: Guinevere, Jen, Jenni, Jennie, Jennifer, Jenny

Jennifer
Jennifer is the Cornish version of the Welsh name Guinevere. In Arthurian legend Guinevere was the name of King Arthur's wife and Sir Lancelot's lover. It means 'fair ghost'.

In 1905 the Irish playwright George Bernard Shaw gave the name to one of his characters in *The Doctor's Dilemma*. Jennifer was especially popular in the 1930s. The name has come to the fore again due to the popularity of singer/actress Jennifer Lopez and actress Jennifer Aniston.
Variants: Gaenor, Gaynor, Guinevere, Jen, Jenna, Jenni, Jennie, Jenny

Jessie
The name Jessie may have been derived from a number of roots. In Scotland it is the pet form of the names Janet and Jean, which are feminine variants of John. The Hebrew meaning of John is 'God is gracious', 'God has favoured'.

Jessie is also a short form of the feminine variant of Jesse. In the Bible Jesse was the father of King David. His name was derived from the Hebrew for 'riches, wealthy' or 'a gift'.
Variants: Jane, Janet, Jean, Jess, Jessica

Jessica
In the 1980s Jessica was a popular name for girls born in North America and the United Kingdom. However centuries before Shakespeare had given the name to one of his many characters. In his play *The Merchant of Venice*, Jessica was the daughter of Shylock the moneylender.

Many believe that the name was a Shakespearian creation as a feminine form of the Biblical name Jesse. In the Old Testament Jesse was the father of King David and his name was derived

from the Jewish word 'yisha', which means 'riches', 'a gift'.
Variants: Jess, Jessie

Jewel

During the 19th century it became fashionable to name baby girls after precious stones such as ruby, coral and crystal. In the 1920s this trend was continued when the name Jewel came into use. The name comes from the word jewel and from the Old French for 'plaything'.
Variants: Jewell, Jewelle

Jill

According to the well known nursery rhyme Jack and Jill went up the hill to fetch a pail of water. After Jack fell down, breaking his crown, Jill came tumbling after.

However, the history of the name Jill stems back further than the nursery rhyme. It is derived from the ancient Roman clan of the Julii. Their family name came from the Greek for 'soft-haired' or 'fair complexioned'. Julius Caesar was a descendant of that lineage.
Variants: Gill, Gillian, Julia, Juliana, Julie

Joan

Joan of Arc was the French heroine who led the French army against the English during the 1429 siege of Orleans. As a teenager she said that she heard the voices of St Michael, St Mary and St Margaret telling her to free France from the rule of England and return the Dauphin to the throne. Despite her heroic efforts Joan was captured, sold to the English and burnt at the stake in 1431. She was canonised in 1920.

The popular story of Joan of Arc may have increased the popularity of the name, which comes from the French feminine form of John ('God is gracious').

In Old French the name appears as Jehane, Johanne and sometimes Jeanne.
Variants: Jane, Janet, Jayne, Jean, Jeanne, Jo, Joanna, Joanne, Johanna

Joanne

A derivative of Joan, Joanne is sometimes thought to be a combination of the names Jo and Anne. While that theory is true, the name also stems from the Old French feminine forms of John – Jhone and Johanne. Thus they are related to other feminine variants of that name – Jane, Janet, Jean and Joan. All mean the same thing 'God is gracious' in Hebrew. Siobhan is the Irish version of Joanne.

Variants: Giovanna, Jane, Janis, Jayne, Jean, Jeanne, Joan, Joanna, Joann, Johanna

Jocelin

Brought to England by the Normans, Jocelin has a number of meanings and is thought to have been derived from various sources. It may have come from the Latin for 'sportive' or 'just'. Equally it may have been derived from the Old German for 'descendent of the Goths'. But as a German feminine form of Jacob it shares the same meaning as Jacqueline – 'follower', 'supplanter'.

Jocelin also appears in society as a surname and was once a boy's name before being given to girls in the 19th century.

Variants: Jocelyn, Josceline, Josette, Josie, Joss

Jodi

Jodi began life as a short form of the Biblical name Judith ('Jewish woman'). However, it is also an elaboration of the pet name Jo, which is short for Joan, Joanne or Josephine. As the feminine form of Jude, Jodi means 'praise'. (See Jude.)

Variants: Jo, Joan, Joanne, Jody, Josephine, Jodie, Jody, Judi, Judith

Joleen

Like Josephine, Joleen is a feminine form of the Biblical name Joseph, which in Hebrew means 'God will increase'. It also comes from the French and Middle English word 'joli' ('high spirited').

Variants: Jolene, Jolie, Joline, Josepha, Josephine

J

Jolie
Derived from the French for 'pretty one', Jolie also comes from the Middle English for 'jolly' or 'high spirited'.
Variants: Jolene, Joleen, Joli, Jolly

Jonelle
Jonelle belongs to the family of girls' names that stem from John. Consequently, like Jane, Jean, Joan, Joanne and Janelle it means 'God is gracious'. Mostly found in North America it is a modern elaboration of Jane.
Variants: Jane, Janelle, Jo, Joan, Joanne, Jean

Jonquil
Like Rose, Daisy and Daffodil, Jonquil is a flower name given to baby girls. Introduced in the 20th century, it is less common than other flower names.

Jonquil comes from the Latin for 'reed'.

Jordan
Jordan is the name of a country and a river in the Middle East. Given to both boys and girls, it means 'flowing down'.

In the Bible Jesus was baptised in the River Jordan by his cousin, John the Baptist. Christian pilgrims used to bottle water from the river to use later to baptise their children.

Jordan is also a surname.
Variants: Jourdan, Jordin, Jordyn

Josephine
The Biblical name Joseph comes from the Hebrew 'God will increase'. In the Old Testament it was borne by one of the 12 sons of Jacob, while in the New Testament it belonged to the Virgin Mary's husband.

Josephine is the French feminine form of this name. It was borne by the wife of Napoleon Bonaparte, Empress Josephine, who died in 1814.
Variants: Fifi, Jo, Jojo, Josie, Josey, Josefina, Josephina

Joss

Given to both sexes, Joss is a short form of the name Jocelin that is used independently. Like its source it has a number of meanings. It comes from the Latin for 'sportive' and 'just', as well as the Old German for 'descendent of the Goths'.

Meanwhile the Celtic word 'josse' means 'champion'. As a derivative of the German form of Jacob, Joss also means 'supplanter'.

Variants: Jacqueline, Jocelin, Jocelyn, Josse

Joy

Derived from the Old French word 'joie', Joy means to be 'merry' or 'happy'. It was first found as a name in the 12th century, but its use was revived by the Puritans perhaps because it was connected to the Christian instruction to be 'joyful in the Lord'. It was also favoured by the Victorians in the 19th century.

Variants: Joi, Joyce, Joye

Joyce

Borne by some of William the Conqueror's followers, the Norman name Josce was customarily given to men. However, by the 14th century this practice had died out and it was established as a feminine name.

Modern use of Joyce can be explained by the twin influence of culture and literature. It may have derived its popularity from the transferred use of the Irish surname. Its use in two 19th century works, In the *Golden Days* (1885) and *East Lynne* (1861) could have proved influential to Victorian parents.

The exact meaning of the name is unknown. It may have been derived from the Breton for 'Lord' or, equally, it could be a variant of Joy.

Variants: Joice, Jossi, Jossie, Jossy

Jubilee

Used as a girl's name Jubilee comes from the Latin 'jubilaeus', which means 'a joyful time of celebration'.

Judith
In the Bible Judith was the Old Testament heroine who saved her people by beheading their enemy Holofernes. Judith was also the name of Esau's wife.

The name, which means 'a Jewish woman', was popular in both the 18th and 20th centuries.
Variants: Jodi, Jodie, Jody, Judite, Judithe, Judi, Judy

Julia
Julia is another feminine form of the Old Roman family name Julius, which means 'fair skinned'. A woman bearing that name appears in St Paul's Epistles to the Romans. Juliet and Juliana are both related to this name.
Variants: Gill, Gillian, Gillie, Jill, Jillian, Juliana, Julie, Juliet

Juliana
Popular in England during the 18th century, Juliana is a variant of the Latin name Julianus. Its male equivalent is Julian and like, Jill and Julia it means 'fair skinned'.
Variants: Gill, Gillian, Gillie, Jill, Jillian, Julia, Julie, Juliet

Julie
This French form of the name Julia was first found in English-speaking countries in the 1920s. Like Juliana and Julia it belongs to the family of names derived from the Roman clan of the Julii, who traced their descent to Aphrodite, the goddess of love.
Variants: Gill, Gillian, Gillie, Jill, Jillian, Julia, Julie, Juliet

Juliet
Like Julia, Julie and Juliana, Juliet ultimately stems from the Old Roman name Julius. The form Juliet is an Anglicised version of the French Juliette and the Italian Giuliette. They all share the meaning 'fair-skinned'. The name continues to be well-known to this day because of the influence of the Shakespeare's tragic love story *Romeo and Juliet*.
Variants: Guiletta, Giulletta, Jules, Julia, Juliana, Juliette

June

In the 20th century it became fashionable to name girls born in June after the month of their birth. It was the Roman supreme goddess Juno who gave her name to that month. According to folklore she joined with a magical flower to produce Mars, the god of war.

June also comes from the Latin for 'young' or 'younger'.
Variant: Juno

Juniper

This is another plant used as a girl's name. Berries from the juniper plant are used to flavour gin and foods such as meats and sauces.

Juno

The Roman goddess Juno was also known as 'she who brings children into the light'. In ancient Greece she was worshipped as the goddess Hera.

Not only is the name a variant of June it is also connected to Una, which is Latin for 'one, unity'. Juno is the Irish form of Una.
Variant: June, Una

Justine

Popular in 1960s Britain Justine is a feminine form of Justin, which comes from the Latin for 'just'. The name was derived from the French version Justina. Its popularity may be due to the 1957 Lawrence Durrell novel, *Justine.*
Variants: Justina

Kalila

Kalila comes from the Arabic for 'beloved' and 'sweetheart'.

Kamala

Kamala is derived from the word meaning 'lotus', and is an appellation of Lakshmi, the Hindu god of wealth.

Kamila
This name comes from the Arabic for 'complete', 'perfect' and 'perfect one'.
Variant: Kamilah

Kanani
In Hawaiian the name Kanani means 'beautiful'.
Variants: Ani, Nani

Kara
In Italian the word 'cara' means 'beloved', and like 'dear' in English or 'chéri' in French, is a term of endearment. 'Cara' is also the Irish Gaelic word for 'friend'. It was coined as a name in the 20th century.
Variant: Cara

Karen
Although it is widely held as an independent name in its own right, Karen is actually the Scandinavian form of Catherine, which comes from the Greek for 'pure'. It was brought to North America by Scandinavian settlers, but has been popular in Britain only since the 1950s.
Variants: Caren, Caron, Caryn, Catherine, Karan, Kari, Karina, Karin, Karyn, Katherine

Kari
Used independently, Kari was originally a pet form of the names Karol and Karoline ('free man'). It is also a variant of Karen which stems from Katherine ('pure') and is of Scandinavian and Greek origin.
Variants: Cari, Carol, Caroline, Catherine, Karan, Karin, Karol, Karoline, Karyn, Katherine

Karima
The feminine variant of Karim, Karima comes from 'karam' the Arabic for 'noble' and 'generous'. In the Koran it is also one of

the 99 names of Allah and one of his 99 qualities.
Variants: Kareema, Karimah, Kharim

Karis
Karis is derived from the Greek for 'graceful'.

Karla
As the feminine form of the boy's names Carl and Karl, Karla stems from the Germanic name Charles, which means 'man'. Like Carol and Caroline it can be spelt with either with a 'C' or a 'K'.
Variants: Carrie, Carla, Carol, Caroline, Kari, Karleen, Karlene, Karol, Karoline

Katarina
The Greek name Katherine has spawned a number of derivatives with different countries producing their own variants that are eventually accepted as independent names. Katarina is the Swedish form of Katherine ('pure'). It is sometimes used in the English-speaking world.
Variants: Catherine, Katharina, Katerina, Katherine

Kate
Like the name Katie, Kate is a short form of Katherine which has become a name in its own right. Kate is also a short form of Katerina.
Variants: Catherine, Katarina, Kate, Katerina, Katharine, Katie, Katy

Katherine
The popularity of the name Katherine can probably be measured by the many different forms it has taken throughout the world. In English-speaking countries alone the name can be spelt in at least five ways – Catherine, Catharine, Katharine, Katherine or Kathryn. However it is spelt,Katherine is derived from the Greek word 'katharos', which means 'pure'.

Caterina is the Italian form of the name, while in Sweden Katerina or Katarina are preferred. Kathleen is a well known

Irish variant. (See also Catherine.)
Variants: Catharine, Catherine, Katarina, Katerina, Katharine, Katherine, Katie, Kathlyn, Kathryn, Karen

Kay

At first glance Kay appears to simply be a short form or pet name for names beginning with the letter 'K'. And so it is. But Kay is also an independent name in its own right that is bestowed upon babies of both sexes. Indeed Sir Kay was a knight in Arthurian legend, whose name was believed to be a Celtic form of the Roman name Gaius, the origin of which is unknown.

What is known is that Kay boasts multiple roots. As a short form of Katherine it takes the Greek meaning 'pure' but it could also mean 'rejoice'. There is also a link to the Old Breton word for 'fence' and the Old French for 'quay'. There is a possibility that Kay derives its meaning from the Middle Low German for 'spear' or, equally, from the Old English for 'key'.
Variants: Kai, Kaye, Kayla, Kaylee, Kaylynn

Kayla

More popular in North America than it is in the United Kingdom Kayla is an elaboration of the name Kay (see above). It is also a variant of the Kayleigh – a modern name which is a transferred use of the Irish surname.
Variants: Kay, Kaylah, Kayleigh, Kayley

Kayley

Kayley is a transferred use of the Irish surname Kayleigh, which in Gaelic appears as Ó Caollaidhe ('descendent of Caollaidhe'). Kayley is also derived from the Irish Gaelic word 'caol', which means 'slim'.
Variants: Caileigh, Kailey, Kay, Kaylee, Kayleigh, Kayly

Keeleigh

Keeleigh is another Irish surname that is now being used as a Christian name for baby girls. It stems from the Irish Gaelic for 'beautiful girl' and is also rooted in the word 'cadhla', which means 'graceful'.

It is sometimes used as a variant of Kayley or Kelly.
Variants: Kayleigh, Kayley, Keelie, Keely, Keighley, Kelly

Keira
The Irish word for black, 'ciar' has given birth to a number of Celtic names that mean 'little dark one' or 'dark-haired'. Keira and Kieran, which is a boy's name, are among them.

Like Katherine, Keira can be spelt in a variety of ways but the meaning remains the same.
Variants: Ciara, Ciaragh, Kiara, Kiera

Keisha
Two theories exist about the origin of this name. One theory suggests that Keisha is derived from a Central African language called Bobangi. Taken from the word 'nkisa', Keisha means 'favourite'.

However, another theory suggests that Keisha is a modern blending of the name Aisha with the letter 'K'.
Variants: Aisha, Keesha, Kiesha, LaKeisha

Kelila
This Hebrew name means 'crowned with laurel'. It is also a feminine form of Kyle.
Variants: Kaila, Kaile, Kayle, Kelilah, Kelula, Kyla, Kylene

Kelly
When translated into English the Irish surname Ó Cellaigh means 'descendent of Ceallach' or simply 'Kelly'.

Throughout Western Europe the Celtic warriors were known as warriors or 'keltoi' in Greek. This corresponds with the meaning of Kelly as 'warrior' and its association with the words 'war' and 'strife'. However, the name is also derived from the Gaelic for 'church goer'.
Variants: Kaley, Keeley, Keli, Kellee, Keeleigh, Kelli

Kemba
The name Kemba is derived from the Old English word 'cymaere', which means 'Saxon lord'.
Variants: Kem, Kemp, Kemps

Kendra
The exact origin of Kendra is unknown. It is thought that the name stems from the Old English word for 'knowledge' meaning either the 'know how' or 'ability'. It could also be a blend of the male and female names Ken and Sandra.
Variants: Ken, Kendis

Kenya
Like China, India and Ireland, Kenya is the name of a country bestowed upon girls as a first name. It is sometimes chosen by parents of African descent as a celebration of their cultural heritage.

Keren
According to the Bible the prophet Job had three beautiful daughters – Jemima, Keziah and Kerenhappuch. Keren is a short form of the name Kerenhappuch, which comes from the Hebrew for 'animal horn' or 'horn of eye-shadow'. The name refers to the material from which boxes, which contained kohl to decorate the eyes, were made.

Keren is another Biblical name that was favoured by the Puritans in the 17th century. It is sometimes used as a variant of Karen.
Variants: Kaaren, Kareen, Karen, Karin, Karon, Karyn, Kerryn, Kyran

Kerry
Like Kelly, Kerry has strong links to Ireland and the Irish people around the world. Not only is it the name of an Irish county but it is derived from 'ciar', a Gaelic word meaning 'dark one'.

As a boy's name Kerry's popularity grew in Australia during the 1940s. However, among the Irish in Boston, Massachusetts the name has also been used as a pet form of Katherine. Kerry

is now also common in Britain, while in Wales it assumes the form of Ceri.
Variants: Ceri, Keree, Keri, Kerrey

Keshisha
Keshisha is derived from the Aramaic for 'elder'.

Ketifa
This Arabic name means 'to pluck a flower'.

Keturah
This Biblical name was not very popular during the 20th century but it found favour among the Puritans. For it was the name of the woman Abraham married after Sarah's death. It comes from the Hebrew for 'fragrance, incense'.

Keziah
In the Bible Keziah was the name of Job's second daughter. Her name comes from the Hebrew for 'cassia', a type of fragrant shrub. Thus the meaning of the name ranges from 'cassia tree' to 'bark like cinnamon'.
Keziah is a popular name among African-American parents.
Variants: Kasia, Kerzia, Kesia, Kesiah, Ketzi, Kez, Ketzia, Kizzie

Khadija
Not only was Khadija the first wife of the Prophet Mohammad, she was also the first person that he converted to Islam. So important was she to him and so acutely did he grieve for her, that the year of her death was named 'The Year of Grief'.
The name comes from the Arabic for 'premature baby'.
Variants: Khadeejah, Khadijah, Khadiya

Kiara
Like Kiera and Ciara, Kiara is a feminine form of the Celtic name Kieran, which means 'dark one' or 'dark haired'. However, it is also a variant of Chiara – the Italian form of Clare. Thus it also

means 'bright' and 'clear'.

This is another name that is popular among African-Americans.
Variants: Chiara, Ciara, Clare, Keira, Kiera

Kiki
Like Kay, Kiki is a short form of names beginning with the letter 'K'. It is of Spanish origin.

It is also of African derivation and can mean 'funny girl'.

Kimberly
The name Kimberly became popular with British soldiers during the turn of the last century who were involved in the 1899 to 1902 Boer War – which meant they were stationed in South Africa. It was customary for soldiers to name their offspring after the garrison where they were placed, hence the rise of the name Kimberly in honour of Kimberley, the South African town.

Initially the name was given to boys, but it is now more commonly seen as a girl's name. It is especially popular in North America.
Variants: Kim, Kimberlee, Kimberley, Kimberlie, Kimmi, Kimmie, Kym

Kimi
This Japanese name means 'sovereign', 'best' and 'without equal'.
Variants: Kimie, Kimiko, Kimiyo

Kira
Although Kira looks and sounds like the Celtic name Keira ('little dark one') it is also a Persian name that means 'sun', 'throne' and 'shepherd'.

It is a feminine form of the name Cyrus, which once belonged to a powerful king of Persia who died in 529 BC. Famed for his military prowess and mercy Cyrus was also the founder of the Persian Empire. It was this reputation that earned him the name Cyrus the Great.
Variants: Ciara, Kiara, Keira, Kiera

Girls

Kirsten
As a Scandinavian variant of Christine, Kirsten means 'Christian' or 'follower of Christ'. However, the name is also derived from the Old English for 'church' and the Greek for 'of the Lord'.
It is now also popular in the English-speaking world.
Variants: Christine, Kersten, Kiersten, Kirby, Kirstie, Kirsty

Kirstie
Kirstin is yet another variant of the name Christine ('Christian') but this version hails from Scotland. It produced the short-form Kirstie, which is now considered a name in its own right.
Variants: Christine, Kirsten, Kirstin, Kirsty, Kristen, Kristin

Koko
This Japanese name is supposed to symbolise longevity. It means 'stork'.

Kristen
Bestowed upon boys and girls, Kristen is another Scandinavian form of the name Christine, which means 'Christian'.
Variants: Christine, Kirsten, Krista, Kristeen, Kristina, Krysta, Krystina

Kylie
Kylie is sometimes considered to be a feminine variant of the Gaelic name Kyle ('narrow strait'). However, it actually comes from an Aboriginal word that means 'boomerang' – the wooden toy, which when thrown returns to the thrower. Unsurprisingly it is a popular Australian name which, since the success of actress and singer Kylie Minogue from the late 1980s, has spread throughout the rest of the world.
Variants: Kyley, Kylee, Kyleigh

Kyna
Another Celtic name, Kyna comes from the Irish Gaelic for 'wisdom' and 'intelligence'.

Laila

Although this name is of Arabic origin it was well known in 19th century Britain thanks to the work of two authors. The poet Lord Byron used the variant Leila in two of his works *The Giaour* (1813) and *Don Juan* (1819-24). In *Don Juan* the name was given to a Turkish orphan brought to England by the central character. In *The Giaour* Leila is the name of an Oriental beauty who is the heroine of the romantic poem. Later in the century Lord Lytton used the name again for the heroine of his 1838 novel *Leila*.

However the name is spelt – Laila, Layla or Leila – the meaning of this name is same. It means 'night', 'dark haired' or 'dark complexioned'. In the 20th century the popularity of the name was further emboldened by Eric Clapton's 1972 hit song *Layla*.
Variants: Laili, Laleh, Layla, Leala, Lee, Leigh, Leila, Leyla, Lila, Lilah

Lakshmi

Lakshmi, the Hindu goddess of wealth, beauty, fertility and luck, was married to Vishnu. She is known by more than one name. Kamala is another name for this goddess and Indira is also associated with Lakshmi. (See both Indira and Kamala.) The name comes from the Sanskrit for 'mark' or 'birthmark'.

Lalita

This Indian term of endearment is derived from the Sanskrit for 'charming', 'honest' and 'straightforward'.
Variants: Lal, Lalie, Lita

Lana

Lana is a short form of the name Alana, which is a feminine version of the boy's name Alan. Although the latter name is of unknown origin it is believed to be derived from the Celtic for 'harmony'.

However the name Lana seems to have no shortage of possible sources. It may come from the Latin word 'lanatus', which means 'woolly' or 'downy'. Similarly the Hawaiian word for 'buoyant' is thought to be a source as is the Breton for 'rock'. Another possible Hawaiian meaning is 'offering' or 'light'.

But the name Lana may equally have been derived from the Irish term 'alannah' which itself comes from the Irish Gaelic 'a lenbh', which means 'o child'. The Irish Gaelic for 'good looking', 'cheerful' and 'darling' are all thought to be connected with the name as well.
Variants: Alana, Alanna, Alanah, Alannah, Lanna, Lane, Lanne, Lanette, Lannie, Lanny

Lara
For millions of film enthusiasts around the world the name Lara will forever be associated with the classic 1965 epic *Doctor Zhivago*, which was a dramatisation of Boris Pasternak's 1957 novel. Like the film the name has a Russian backdrop, for Lara is the Russian short form of Larissa (see below).

In Roman mythology Lara was the daughter of the river Almon who could not help revealing secrets. For betraying Jupiter's trust and revealing one of his affairs she had her tongue cut out.

The name is also sometimes found as a variant of Laura. (See also Laura and Larissa.)
Variants: Larissa, Laura

Larissa
Larissa appears in Greek mythology. It was the name of the daughter of Pelasgus. It is also the name of an ancient Thessalian town, a moon and an asteroid.

Although little is known about the origin of the name it is thought that it means 'citadel' in Greek and 'playful' or 'merry' in Latin. Lara is a short form of Larissa, which is also sometimes used as a variant of Laura. (See also Lara and Laura.)
Variants: Lara, Larisa, Laura

Lark
A lark is a small bird notable for its sweet voice, hence the phrase 'to sing like a lark'. But the word 'lark' also means something else in the English language. As well as being associated with 'early rising' it also means to have 'fun' or be 'cheery'.

Laura

In Ancient Greece those who triumphed in the arts, sports or war were crowned with a wreath of laurel. And it is from the Latin for this evergreen shrub that the girl's name Laura is derived. Daphne is of similar origin – it comes from the Greek for 'laurel'.

Although the Romans did not use the name, Laura has appeared throughout history. It was the name of a 9th century nun who died in a cauldron of molten lead and was later canonised. For the Italian poet Petrarch the name was also a source of inspiration. Although he did not meet her, Laura was the name of the woman he loved from afar and many of his sonnets, written in the 14th century, were about her.

Lowri is the Welsh form of the name.

Variants: Lara, Larissa, Lauren, Lauryn, Lola, Loren, Lorraine, Loretta, Lorrie, Lowri

Lauren

A variant of Laura (see above), Lauren is now a name in its own right. Like Laura and Daphne it means 'laurel'. It is also considered to be a feminine equivalent of Laurence.

The film actress Lauren Bacall, who rose to prominence in the 1940s, brought the name to world attention.

Variants: Lara, Larissa, Laura, Lauryn, Loraine, Loren

Lavender

This sweet-smelling plant has clusters of small mauve flowers. Thus the name Lavender is associated with the light purple shade, the herb and the fragrance that is derived from this plant. The name is of Latin origin and means 'to wash'.

Lavern

In Roman mythology Laverna was the goddess of thieves and conmen but her name has a loftier meaning. It comes from the Old French for 'the green one' and the Latin for 'springtime'.

Variants: Laverna, Laverne, La Verne, Luvern

Lavinia

Lavinia is another name that is found in Roman mythology. According to legend she was the daughter of the king of Latinus and the wife of Aeneas, the Trojan and founder of the Roman people. Her son Silvius was said to have named the town Lavinium in her honour.

Although the name was not used by the Romans it was taken up in Europe during the Renaissance. In the 18th century it received attention again when James Thomson wrote the poem *Lavinia and Palemon*.

The name is said to mean 'Latin woman' or 'woman of Rome'.

Variants: Lavena, Lavina, Lavinie, Vin, Vina, Vinia, Vinnie, Vinny

Leah

In the Bible Jacob fell in love with the beautiful Rachel and served her father for seven years in an attempt to win her hand in marriage. However, on the wedding night his beloved was substituted by her less attractive older sister, Leah. Although Rachel was later given to Jacob as a co-wife, Jacob did not like Leah.

Leah, which means 'languid' or 'weary', was a favourite among the 17th century Puritans.

Variants: Lea, Lee, Leigh, Lia, Liah

Leigh

Leigh derives its meaning from other names. As a variant of the English surname Lee it means 'meadow'. As an alternative form of the Biblical Leah it comes from the Hebrew for 'weary' (see above). And as a variant of the Arabic name Laila, Leigh means 'night' or 'dark complexion'. (See also Laila.)

Variants: Laila, Leah, Lee, Leila

Leilani

This Hawaiian name means 'heavenly child' or 'heavenly flower'.

Variants: Lei, Lelani

Leoma
Leoma is derived from the Old English for 'light' and 'brightness'.

Leona
Leona is believed to be the feminine elaboration of the name Leo, which means 'lion' in Latin. However, it is equally regarded as a variant of the name Eleanor via Leonora. As a derivative of this name it means 'bright', 'God is my light' and 'foreign'. (See also Eleanor and Helen.)
Variants: Eleanor, Helen, Leonie, Leonora

Lesley
Lesley belongs to the group of names that are unisex and can be comfortably given to both girls and boys. Leslie is the male form of the name which is Scottish in origin.

Indeed the name Leslie originally belonged to a noble family who rose to prominence in Scotland during the 15th century. Closely associated with the Stewart royal dynasty, the Leslies hailed from Aberdeenshire.

The name Lesley stems from the Scottish Gaelic meaning 'low-lying meadow' and 'garden of hollies'.
Variants: Lea, Lesli, Leslie, Lesly, Lezlie

Letifa
The name Allatif was one of the 99 names and qualities given to Allah in the Koran. Like Letifa it stems from the Arabic word 'latif', which means 'gentle'.
Variants: Latifah, Letipha

Letitia
Letitia comes from the Latin for 'joyful' or 'unrestrained joy'. During the 12th century it was found in England as Lettice, but Letitia and Letisha are the modern variants. It is a favourite among African-American parents.
Variants: Laetitia, Lece, Lecia, Leta, Lettice, Lettie, Letisha, Tisha, Titia

Levanna
In Roman mythology Levanna was the goddess of newborn babies who lifted the babies up from the ground. Hence her name comes from the Latin for 'lifting up' and 'rising sun'.
Variants: Levana, Levona, Livana, Livona

Levina
Levina comes from the Middle English for 'lightning'.

Lianne
The exact origin of the name Lianne is uncertain. It is thought to be the French equivalent of either Juliana or Elaine. As a variant of Juliana, Lianne means 'fair skinned' and ultimately comes from the Roman family name Julius (see Julia and Julie.) But as a variant of Elaine it is connected to the Greek name Helen which means 'bright'.

Lianne may also have been derived from the French for 'to bind' or it could be a compound of Lee ('meadow') and Anne ('God has favoured me'). This blend is English and Hebrew in origin.
Variants: Ann, Anne, Elaine, Helen, Leana, Leann, Leanne, Lee, Lianna

Libby
Like Bess, Betty, Betsy and Liz, the name Libby began as a pet form of Elizabeth. Thus it shares the Biblical meaning 'God is perfection', 'God is satisfaction', 'dedicated to God' and 'God's oath'. It is thought to have been derived from a child's mispronunciation of Elizabeth or one of its short forms.
Variants: Bess, Bessie, Bet, Betty, Elizabeth, Lib, Libbie, Liberty, Lisa, Liz, Lizzie

Liberty
Of Latin origin Liberty is another way of saying 'freedom'. It comes from the word 'libertas'. Libby is also a short form of this name.
Variants: Lib, Libbie, Libby

Lilac
Like lavender, lilac is both a colour and a plant. The lilac shrub boasts sprays of fragrant purple and white flowers. As a colour it is a shade of light purple. The word and name also come from the Persian and Arabic for 'indigo' and 'blue'.

Lillian
As a variant of Elizabeth, Lillian shares the Hebrew meaning 'God is perfection'. However, it is also a derivative of the flower name 'lily'. (See also Elizabeth and Lily.)
Variants: Elizabeth, Liliana, Lilibet, Lily, Lilly

Lilith
According to Assyro-Babylonian tradition Lilith was a female demon who roamed the wilderness on stormy nights and was a threat to newborn babies and little children. She is also said to have been the first wife of Adam who refused to submit to him and was banished from the Garden of Eden as a result. Lilith later became an evil spirit, an ugly demon.

The name is also associated with a serpent, screech-owl and a vampire. Given these dark connotations the name was rarely given to children but it has become symbolic within the feminist movement.
Variants: Lilis, Lilita, Lillith, Lillus, Lily

Lily
In the Sermon on the Mount Jesus asked his followers to 'Consider the lilies of the field, how they grow; they toil not, neither do they spin. And yet I say unto you that even Solomon in all his glory was not arrayed like one of these.'

The lily – the trumpet-shaped genus of flower – is connected with Christianity on another level. It has been portrayed in art as the symbol of purity. Of the 80 types of this flower one is called the Madonna lily, which is associated with the Virgin Mary.

Although this name was first recorded in the late 16th century it was not widely used as a name in England until the

1800s. Lily is also considered to be a short form of Elizabeth ('God is perfection').
Variants: Elizabeth, Lilith, Lilibet, Lillian, Lilly

Lindsey
Like Leslie, Lindsey is an aristocratic Scottish surname which is now given to boys and girls as a first name. It was thought to have been originally borne by Sir Walter de Lindesay who was associated with King David I of Scotland.

In England Lindsey is a name connected with a family from the Lincolnshire district. Indeed Lindsey may stem from the Old English for a place name in Lincoln, meaning 'wetland' or 'waterside linden trees'.
Variant: Lindsay

Linnea
Linnaea is a type of flower named after the 18th century Swedish botanist Carolus Linnaeus. It is the national flower of Sweden.
Variants: Linea, Linna, Linnae, Linnaea, Lynea, Lynnea

Lisa
Widely regarded as a name in its own right, Lisa actually originated as a pet form of the name Elizabeth ('God is perfection'). It is a another form of Liza, which is a variant of Eliza. (See also Elizabeth.)
Variants: Elisa, Elisabeth, Eliza, Elizabeth, Liza

Lois
During the 20th century through comic books, and later television and film, this name became synonymous with Superman. Lois Lane was the love interest of both the superhuman hero and his alter-ego Clark Kent.

But the name has a much longer history. It is actually Biblical and can be found in the New Testament as the name of Timothy's grandmother whose faith was praised by St Paul. This association with Christianity made Lois a favourite among the

Puritans who took the name with them to North America.

Its popularity was reinforced by the French names Heloise and Eloise, as Lois is a contracted form of both. (See also Heloise.) Equally it is a variant of the Germanic name Louise, which means 'famed' and 'warrior'.

Lois, which can be pronounced as either 'Lo-is' or 'Loy' may also be derived from the Greek for 'desirable' and 'good'.

Variants: Eloise, Heloise, Louise

Lola

The 19th century Spanish dancer Lola Montez was neither from Spain nor called Lola. She was Eliza Gilbert who was born in Ireland in 1821. However the plucky performer adopted the stage name Lola and courted fame throughout Europe. French novelist Alexander Dumas was among her lovers before she caught the attention of Ludwig I of Bavaria. But he made the mistake of making his mistress the virtual ruler of his country. His people revolted, Ludwig I abdicated and Lola Montez ended her days in North America where she died in 1861.

Before Lola Montez the name was mostly found in Spanish-speaking countries as a short form of Dolores ('sorrows'). (See also Dolores.)

Variants: Delores, Dolores, Lita, Lo, Lolita

Lolita

Since the publication of Vladimir Nabokov's 1955 controversial novel *Lolita* the name has been associated with underage sex. In the book Dolores Haze is the pre-teen object of the narrator's obsession. Thus the name has become associated with the pejorative term for a pubescent 'sex kitten'.

However, like Lola, Lolita is the short form of Dolores and thus means 'sorrows'. Before the book changed its perception in society Lolita was a popular name.

Variants: Delores, Dolores, Lita, Lo, Lola, Loleta

Lonnie
An independent name in its own right, Lonnie derives its meaning from Leona, which means 'lion' or 'bright'. (See also Leona)
Variants: Eleanor, Elenora, Leona

Lora
Laura comes from the Latin for 'laurel' and Lora is the German form of that name. However, Lora is also derived from the Latin for 'a thin wine made from grape husks'.
Variants: Lara, Laura, Lauren, Lauryn, Lolly, Lori

Lorelei
Lorelei is the name of a cliff near the River Rhine. According to German legend it was from this point that a siren would call luring sailors away from the rocks. As a name Lorelei is believed to mean 'song' or 'melody'.
Variants: Lorelie, Lorilee, Lura, Lurette, Lurleen, Lurlene, Lurline

Lori
Lori is a pet form of the names Lora, Laura and Lorraine. Thus it means 'laurel'.
Variants: Laura, Laurie, Lora, Lorraine

Lorraine
Although it stems from the French place name, Lorraine. It is little used as a first name in France. It has been favoured in England and North America since the 19th century.
Variants: Laraine, Lauraine, Loraine, Lori

Lotus
To be called a 'lotus eater' is to be described as someone who is a work-shy pleasure-seeker. The meaning of this term is connected to Homer's *Odyssey*, written in the 8th century BC. In the poem lotus is the fruit eaten by an imaginary African tribe that makes them drugged and lethargic.

In China and India the fragrant lotus flower has a more

positive connotation. The aquatic bloom that is native to both Asia and Africa is powerful religious symbol of the past, present and future.

Louise
It was the invading Germanic tribe the Franks who brought the name Clodowig with them when they conquered Gaul in the Dark Ages. Clovis, a variant of that name, which means 'famous battle', was the name of the first French king. Clovis eventually became Louis and Louise is its female equivalent. Louise was especially popular in 17th and 18th century Europe.

The variant Louisa was borne by Louisa May Alcott, the American author of the children's classic *Little Women*.
Variants: Aloise, Eloise, Heloise, Louisa, Louisetta

Lourdes
Although the name is of uncertain origin, it is highly regarded within the Roman Catholic Church as the place in southern France where St Bernadette saw a vision of the Virgin Mary in February 1858.

In that same spot a healing spring was uncovered that is believed to cure the illnesses and physical handicaps of the faithful. Lourdes has been a place of pilgrimage ever since. The place name is now also a girl's name.
Variant: Lola

Lowri
An independent name in its own right, Lowri is the Welsh form of Laura which comes from the Latin for 'laurel'.
Variant: Laura

Loveday
This Old English name stems from a quaint tradition. The day of love was the day dedicated to reconciliation and children born on that date were given this name. Although Loveday was originally a unisex name it is now only given to girls.

Lucinda

The Latin word 'lucere' means 'to shine, glitter or be light'. This was at the root of the name Lucia, which predated Lucinda. This longer variant first started making an appearance in the literary works of the 17th century. It was given to a character in *Don Quixote*, the 1605 novel by the Spanish author Miquel de Cervantes. By the 18th century the name was popular in England.
Variants: Cindi, Cindy, Lucia, Lucy, Sindy

Lucretia

The name Lucretia is closely connected to the foundation of the Roman Republic. Lucretia was a Roman noblewoman who was raped by Sextus, the son of Tarquin, the despotic king. Devastated by what happened Lucretia gathered together the men in her family to tell them what Sextus did to her. She then committed suicide. Her husband and father led an uprising, which resulted in the kings being driven out of Rome. In their place a new republic was born.

Although the origin of the name is uncertain it is associated with the twin virtues of purity and chastity.
Variants: Lucrece, Lucrecia, Lucretzia

Lucy

Although Lucy looks like a short form of Lucinda, the latter was actually derived from the former, via Lucia. Like Lucia, Lucy comes from the Latin for 'light' or 'bringer of light'. Lucille is another variant of this popular name.
Variants: Luci, Lucia, Lucille, Lucinda

Lulie

Taken from the Middle English word 'lullen', Lulie means to 'soothe', 'cause sleep' or 'dispel fears'.

Lulu

This pet form of Louise is now widely known as an independent name. Its Germanic interpretation is 'famed warrior' or

'famous battle', but it may also come from a Native American name that means 'rabbit'. As a diminutive of Lucy it borrows the meaning 'light'.
Variants: Lleulu, Louise, Leu, Lucy

Luna
According to Roman mythology Luna was the goddess of the moon. It is fitting, therefore, that her name means 'moon' or 'crescent'. The Latin name 'luna' is the root of many words associated with the moon such as 'lunacy', believed to the acute when the moon is full.
Variant: Lunette

Lynne
The exact origin of Lynne is uncertain. It may have been derived from the Welsh name Eluned, which means 'idol' or 'icon'. Equally it may have come from the short form of various names ending in 'line' such as Caroline.
    Another possible root is the Old English word 'hylynna' which means 'brook'.
Variants: Eiluned, Eluned, Lin, Linn, Lynn

Lys
Lys comes from the medieval French for 'lily'. It is also a variant of Lizi which stems from Elizabeth ('God is perfection').
Variants: Elizabeth, Liz, Lizi, Lizzie

Lysandra
Lysander was a Spartan general who lived during the 5th century BC. His name was derived from the Greek for 'free' and thus Lysander means 'freer of men'. Lysandra is the feminine equivalent.
Variants: Sandie, Sandra, Sandy

Lyzelle
The exact origin of this name is unknown but it is believed to mean 'beautiful'.

Mabel

The name Mabel is thought to stem from another source. It may be a derivation of the Latin word 'amabilis' or 'worthy of love' which developed into the name Amabel and Amabella. Sometime during the 12th century the 'A' was dropped from this name and Mabel was born.

Variants: Amabel, Amabella, Mab, Mabell, Mabella, Mabelle, Mable, May, Maybell, Maybelle

Macy

Although this name is popular in North America it is not derived from the well known department store, Macy's. Instead it is the transferred use of a surname that ultimately came from a French place name. Originally Macy meant 'Maccius' estate'.

Variants: Macey, Maci, Macie

Madeline

In the Bible Mary Magdalene was the reformed sinner who became a devoted follower of Christ. Her second name was not just another way of distinguishing her from the other Biblical Marys, it also told the reader where she came from. Magdala was a village by the Sea of Galilee.

Madeline is the French version of this Biblical place name.

Variants: Madalain, Madaline, Madaliene, Madeleine, Magdalen, Magdalene, Magda

Madison

Throughout the world this name is probably best known as a street name – Madison Avenue, New York City. However, before it became associated with a place in Manhattan, Madison was a surname. Madison means 'Matthew's son', 'Maud's son' or 'Madde's son' – Madde being a pet form of the name Madeline (see above).

As a first name it is given to both boys and girls in North America.

Variants: Maddison, Maddy, Maddie

Madra
Madra comes from the Spanish, and ultimately Latin, for 'mother'.
Variant: Madre

Magdalene
Mary Magdalene was the reformed sinner who bathed Christ's feet with her tears and dried them with her hair at the Last Supper. She was a constant and faithful follower of Jesus. In the Bible Mary can be found at the foot of the cross during Christ's crucifixion and she was one of the few people who discovered his empty tomb on Easter Sunday.

Mary's second name indicated where she was from. Magdala was a village located by the Sea of Galilee.

It is no surprise that the name of this well-known saint has been given to girls throughout history. While Madeleine was the variant used during the Middle Ages, Magdalene has had its place. Sometimes pronounced as 'Maud-e-lin' it has led to variants such as Maudlin and its short form Maude.

Whatever the pronunciation Magdalene is also thought to come from the Hebrew for 'high tower'. (See also Madeline.)
Variants: Madalena, Madelena, Madeline, Madeleine, Magdalen, Magdalena, Maude, Maudlin

Mahalia
Found to have Hebrew and Native American origins, Mahalia sometimes appeared in 17th century Britain. As a variant of the Biblical name Mahala, Mahalia comes from the Hebrew for 'barren' or 'tenderness'. In the Native American culture Mahalia means 'woman'.
Variants: Mahala, Mahelia, Mahila, Mehala, Mehalah, Mehalia

Mahira
Mahira has been found to have a number of meanings. It comes from the Hebrew and Italian for 'energetic' and 'quick' and from the Arabic for 'young' and 'horse'.
Variant: Mehira

Maia

According to Greek mythology Maia was the daughter of Atlas and mistress of Zeus. A fair-haired woman she bore him his blond son Hermes. Her name comes from the Greek for 'nurse' or 'mother'.

In Roman mythology Maia was the goddess of springtime and growth. She was the Earth Mother after whom the month of May is named. Mercury and Jupiter were her children.
Variants: Mae, Mai, May, Maya

Mairin

Mairin is the Irish form of Mary, which means 'dew of the sea'.
Variants: Mary, Maureen

Majesta

Majesty is a word that means 'greatness' and 'grandeur', which is usually used when addressing royalty. Majesta comes from the Latin for majesty.

Makani

Makani is a Hawaiian name that is given to both boys and girls. It means 'wind'.

Malu

The Hawaiian name Malulani means 'beneath peaceful skies'. As a short form of this name Malu simply means 'peace'.
Variant: Malulani

Manuela

This Spanish name is ultimately derived from the Biblical Emmanuel, which means 'God is with us'. The feminine equivalent of Emmanuel is Emmanuella and Manuela is the Spanish version.
Variants: Emanuella, Emmanuela

Marcella

Marcella is the feminine form of Marcel which comes from the

Roman name Marcellus. In Roman mythology Mars was the god of war and it is this meaning that seams to be at the root of Marcellus and the names derived from it.

A 4th century saint who was a Roman noblewoman bore this name, which has been found in Britain since the 1600s.
Variants: Marcela, Marcelle, Marcellina, Marcille, Marcelyn

Mardell
Mardell comes from the Old English for 'meadow near the sea'.

Margaret
The various forms that Margaret has taken across the world throughout the ages demonstrate its enduring popularity. The same name is known as Marguerite in France, Margarita in Spanish-speaking countries and has produced the pet forms such as Maggie and Rita.

All stem from the same source – the Latin for 'pearl'. The French form Marguerite is the exception as here it means 'daisy' because that flower is associated with a saint bearing the name.

In Scotland, where the name was borne by the saint and queen Margaret I, it is especially popular.
Variants: Greta, Maggie, Majorie, Margarita, Margaux, Margherita, Margot, Marguerite, Meg, Rita

Margot
The name Margot is of French origin. Usually pronounced without sounding the 't' Margot is a pet form of Marguerite – the French form of Margaret. Hence it means 'daisy' and 'pearl' (see above).
Variants: Margaux, Margaret, Margo, Marguerite

Marigold
The marigold is a yellow and orange flower that was named after its gold hue. Originally it was simply called 'a gold', however, in the 14th century it became associated with the Virgin Mary. Thus the name stems from the Old English for 'Mary's gold'. At the turn of the last century this flower name

was especially popular with parents.
Variants: Goldie, Goldy, Mari, Marie, Mary, Marygold

Maria
A variant of the Biblical name Mary, Maria is also related to the earlier name Miriam. It comes from the Hebrew for 'longed for child' and 'rebellion'.
Variants: Mariah, Mariam, Mary, Maryam, Miriam

Mariah
Mariah is a variant of the name Maria (see above) which has now become a first name in its own right. Although it shares the Hebrew meaning for Mary and Maria ('longed for child', 'rebellion'), Mariah is also said to come from the Latin for 'bitter' and 'God is my teacher'.
Variants: Maria, Mariam, Mary, Maryam, Miriam

Marilyn
Marilyn is yet another elaboration of Mary and is indeed a combination of two names – Mary ('longed for child') and Lyn ('brook' or 'idol'). (See also Mary and Lynne.)

In the second half of the 20th century the name Marilyn became inextricably linked to the screen goddess Marilyn Monroe.
Variants: Lyn, Lynne, Mari, Marilynn, Mary, Marylyn, Marylynn

Marina
A marina is a harbour specially designed to accommodate yachts and small boats. Unsurprisingly the word comes from the Latin 'marinus', meaning 'belong to the sea' or 'produced by the sea'. It is from this word that the girl's name Marina is derived.

In 20th century Britain the popularity of the name soared thanks to the marriage between Princess Marina of Greece and Prince George, the Duke of Kent. The couple married in 1934 and such was her popularity that a shade of blue-green was named marina blue in her honour.
Variants: Mare, Maren, Marena, Maris, Marissa, Marna, Marne, Rina

Marini
Of African origin, this name comes from the Swahili for 'healthy', 'fresh' and 'pretty'.

Marissa
Like Mariah and Marilyn, Marissa is an elaboration of the Biblical name Mary. Consequently it comes from the Hebrew for 'longed for child' and 'rebellion'. Marissa, which is sometimes spelt with one 's', also comes from the Latin for 'of the sea'.
Variants: Mareesa, Mari, Maria, Mariah, Marie, Marina, Marisa, Mary, Risa, Rissa

Marquita
A marquee is a large tent that is used as a venue for social occasions. The name Marquita comes from the French for this word.
Variant: Marquite

Martha
For centuries the name Martha has been associated with hard work and the roots of this link can be found in the Bible. In the New Testament Martha was the sister of Lazarus, the young man who Jesus raised from the dead. She was also the sister of Mary. But while Mary sat and listened to Christ's stories during his visit to their house, Martha diligently attended to the housework, complaining to Jesus about her sister as she did so.

The name comes from the Aramaic for 'lady'. It was borne by Martha Washington, the wife of the first American president, George Washington.
Variants: Mardi, Marta, Marthe, Martie, Mat, Mattie, Matty, Pattie, Patty

Marva
Marva is taken from the Hebrew word for the fragrant herb, 'sage'.

Mary
One of the most popular Biblical names of all time belongs to the

mother of Jesus, the Virgin Mary. According to the Christmas story Mary was betrothed to the carpenter Joseph when the Archangel Gabriel appeared to her. He told the teenager that she would give birth to the Son of God and the conception would be brought about by the Holy Spirit, not through intercourse with a man.

Though the mother of Jesus is the most well known Mary in the Bible the name is borne by others in the New Testament including Mary of Magdalene and Mary the sister of Martha and Lazarus. In the Old Testament the name appears as Miriam and comes from the Hebrew for 'sea of bitterness' or 'child of our wishes'.

The popularity of the name Mary has led to a plethora of variants and short forms, some of which have gone on to be independent names in their own right. They include Maria, Mariah, Marissa, Moira and Maureen. Mary has also been used in numerous compounds including Marilyn, Marianne and Marylou.

The name was especially popular in North America where it was consistently the first choice for baby girls in the 19th, and well into the 20th, century. In England and Wales Mary was also the favourite of parents during the 18th and 19th centuries.
Variants: Maria, Mariah, Marianne, Marie, Marilyn, Marissa, Marylou, Maureen, Moira, Molly

Marylou
The names Mary ('bitterness' and 'longed for child') and Louise ('famed battle') were joined together to form this name.
Variant: Lou, Louise, Marie, Marilou, Mary, Miriam

Matilda
The Normans brought the name Matilda to English shores. This distinctly Germanic name was borne by the wife of William the Conqueror. It is made up of two elements – 'maht', or in English 'might', and 'hild', which means 'battle'. The name Hilda shares the same Germanic root.

The French translated Mahthilda into Maheud, which the English transformed into Maude – now an independent name.

The granddaughter of William the Conqueror, Empress Maud, was also called Matilda. The name is also associated with the popular Australian song *Waltzing Matilda*.
Variants: Matelda, Mathilda, Matildis, Matti, Maud, Maude, Maudie, Mawde, Tilda, Tillie

May
The name May is commonly associated with the springtime month, which was named after the Roman goddess Maia. However, the popularity of May was strengthened by its use as a pet form to other well known names. As a short form of Mary it assumes the Hebrew meaning of 'longed for child' and as a diminutive of Margaret it becomes 'pearl'.

During the month of May the Romans celebrated the festival of spring, fertility and birth. That tradition continues in some form today as many calendars around the world recognise May Day, 1 May, as a public holiday. However the link between the festival and springtime has not always been maintained.

In Wales May took the form of Mai and in America it is often spelt with an 'e' instead of a 'y'. (See also Maia.)
Variants: Mai, Maia, Mae, Margaret, Mary, Maya, Maybelle, Mei

Mavis
Little used as a given name before the 19th century, Mavis is derived from the Old French 'mauvis', which means 'song thrush'.
Variants: Mave, Maeve,

Meave
Taken from the Irish word 'meadhbh', Meave means 'joy'. However, as a variant of Maeve it also means 'intoxicating'.
Variants: Maeve, Meaveen

Meera
This Indian name means 'saintly woman'. But it also has the meaning 'radiant' and 'light' in Hebrew.

Megan
In Scotland and Wales Meg is a pet form of Margaret, which means 'pearl'. Megan is the Welsh elaboration of Meg.
Variants: Maegan, Maygen, Meag(h)an

Melanie
In Greek mythology Melanion won the hand of Atalanta by beating her in a race. Legend has it that the speedy Atalanta successfully competed against all but one of her suitors. To win her hand Melanion knew he had to win the race so he asked the goddess Aphrodite for a solution. She gave him three golden apples which he threw down as he ran. He won the competition because Atalanta, distracted by the apples, slowed down long enough to pick them up. Melanion's name was derived from the Greek for 'black' or 'dark complexion'.

In the 5th century two saints bore the female version of that name, Melania. Although it was re-introduced to England in the early 1900s it was first imported from France during the Middle Ages.
Variants: Melany, Melony

Mercy
This Christian quality was used by Charles Dickens as a name for one of his characters in his 1843 novel *Martin Chuzzlewit*. To have 'mercy' on someone is to be 'compassionate' and to 'pity' them. The phrase 'God's mercy' also demonstrates his forgiveness of sinners, hence the popularity of the name among the 17th century Puritans.

Mercedes is the Spanish equivalent of this name. Another version, Mercia, was an Anglo-Saxon kingdom.
Variants: Mercedes, Merica, Mercille, Merry

Merit
Of Latin origin, Merit comes from the word 'meritus', which means 'earned' and 'deserved'.
Variant: Merritt

Merle

Though often thought of as a girl's name, in North America Merle is also given to boys. Country music veteran Merle Haggard, who was born in 1937, is a perfect example of its use as a man's name. However in Britain Merle, or the variant Merlene, is traditionally given to baby girls.

The name comes from the Latin for 'blackbird'. As a variant of Muriel, Merle comes from the Irish Gaelic for 'sea' and 'bright'.

In the 1930s the popularity of the name increased thanks to the fame of the actress Merle Oberon.

Variants: Merla, Merlene, Merlina, Muriel, Myrl, Myrle

Merrie

In Charles Dickens' novel *Martin Chuzzlewit* Merry was used as a pet name. The sisters Charity and Mercy were also known as Cherry and Merry.

The word 'merry' comes from the Old English for 'pleasant', 'festive' and 'jolly' and from the Hebrew for 'rebellious'. But as the pet form of other names Merry has taken on more than one meaning. When it is used as a variant of Mercy (as Dickens did) it means 'compassion', 'pity' or 'clemency'. As a short form of the Welsh name Meredith it means 'magnificent chief'.

Variants: Mercy, Meredith, Merry

Mia

The Italian name Mia can be pronounced in one of two ways, either as 'Me-ah' or as 'My-ah'. Its meaning is derived from the Latin for 'mine'.

Michaela

This feminine form of Michael comes from the Hebrew for 'who is like God'.

Variants: Miia, Mica, Michael, Michaelle, Michelle, Mikelina

Michelle

Like Michaela, Michelle is a feminine form of the Biblical name

Michael, which means 'who is like God' It is of French origin. During the 1960s interest in this name soared thanks to the popularity of The Beatles' hit song *Michelle*.
Variants: Chelle, Michael, Michaela, Michaelle, Shell

Milly
Although it is widely considered to be an independent name in its own right Milly began life as a short form of a number of names. They include Amelia ('toil'), Camilla ('one who helps at sacrifices'), Mildred ('gentle stength') and Millicent ('strong worker', 'determined'). As a short form of all these names Milly has adopted these meanings. However, it also comes from the Israeli for 'who is for me?'.
Variants: Amelia, Camilla, Mildred, Millicent, Millie

Mina
Mina has a number of meanings from the Old German word for 'love', the Japanese for 'south' and the Persian for 'daisy'. It is also a short form of the German name Wilhelmina, which means 'will' and 'protection'.
Variants: Minella, Minna, Minnie, Wilhelmina, Willa, Wilma

Mirabel
Although Mirabel was used by the Victorians it was actually common in Europe during the Middle Ages. The name is derived from the Latin word 'mirabilis', which means 'marvellous', 'admirable' and 'lovely'. It is also related to the Spanish for 'beautiful'. Mirabella is the Italian version.
Virants: Bella, Belle, Mira, Mirabella, Mirabelle, Mirella

Miranda
Like Mirabel, Miranda is derived from the Latin for 'wonderful' and 'admirable'. But it also comes from the Latin word 'mirandus', which means 'to be wondered at'.

The name has also been used by playwrights and authors: Shakespeare in his play *The Tempest* whilst D H Lawrence

featured a character called Miranda in his novel *Sons and Lovers*.
Variants: Maranda, Marenda, Meranda, Mina, Mira, Mirabel,
Mirinda, Myranda, Randi, Randy

Miriam
In the Bible Miriam was the sister of Moses and Aaron who led
the rejoicing after the Israelites crossed the Red Sea. In Hebrew
it means 'longed for child' and 'rebellion' and it is from this
source that Mary is derived. An earlier form of the name is
Maryam.
Variants: Maria, Marian, Marianne, Mary, Maryam, Meryem, Mimi,
Minnie, Mitzi

Misty
Misty comes from the Old English for 'clouded' and 'obscure'.
As a girl's name it is popular in North America.
Variants: Misti, Mistie, Mystee, Mysti, Mystie, Mystique

Moira
In Ireland the Biblical name Mary was transformed into the Gaelic
name Maire which, when Anglicised, became Moira. Hence, Moira
comes from the Hebrew for 'longed for child' and 'rebellion'.

Aside from the Biblical origin of his name, in Greek mythology
the Moirae were the Three Fates who were the embodiment of
destiny. Clotho spun the thread of life, Lachesis was the drawer
of lots or the goddess of luck and Atropos represented the
inevitable or inescapable fate, cutting the thread.
Variants: Maire, Mary, Maura, Maureen, Miriam, Moirae, Moreen,
Moyra

Molly
Molly is another short form of Mary. Thus it shares the
Hebrew meaning 'longed for child' and 'rebellion'. Originally
the pet form of Mary was Mally, which eventually became
Molly.
Variant: Mary

Mona

In 1503 the Italian painter Leonardo da Vinci started painting the portrait that would henceforth become known as the Mona Lisa. The exact origin of this name is unknown, but there has been no shortage of theories about its meaning. One possibility is that Mona stems from the Greek for 'alone' or 'just'. In Ireland Mona is thought to have been derived from three different Gaelic words 'noble', 'nun' and 'angel', but in Arabic there is only one meaning 'wish'. The Old English interpretation is 'month'. Another equally legitimate possibility is that Mona came from the Latin name for the Welsh island, Anglesea.

Mona also appears as a short form of Monica, which means 'to advise'.

Variants: Madonna, Monica, Monique, Monna, Moyna, Muna

Monica

St Monica is recognised by the Roman Catholic Church as the mother of St Augustine. She was born in Algeria in 322 and was frequently mentioned in the writings of her famous son.

Monica's name comes from the Latin 'monire', which means 'to warn'. It is also derived from the Latin for 'to counsel' and 'to advise'.

Variants: Mona, Monique

Morag

This Irish Gaelic name was popular in Scotland during the 20th century. It means 'great', 'sun' and 'young one'. But, as the Scottish version of Sarah, it also shares the Hebrew meaning 'princess'.

Variants: Marion, Moirin, Moreen, Sarah

Morgan

According to Arhurian legend Morgan Le Fay was the half-sister of King Arthur. Her name comes from the Welsh for 'sea' and 'bright' or 'great' and 'born'. In North America Morgan is given to both boys and girls. In Britain it is frequently found as a surname.

Variant: Morgana

Morwenna

Borne by a little known 5th century saint, the Welsh name Morwenna was especially popular during the Middle Ages. It is derived from the word 'morwyn', which means 'a maiden'.

In the 20th century Morwenna was favoured by Welsh parents as a symbol of their nationalism. It is also thought to be related to Maureen, an Irish version of Mary ('longed for child').

Variants: Maureen, Morwen, Morwyn, Wenna, Wennie, Wenny

Muriel

Muriel was brought to the British Isles by William the Conqueror's Celts from Brittany. Thus the name comes from the Irish words 'muir' ('sea') and 'geal' ('bright').

Variants: Marial, Meriel, Merril, Merrill, Meryl, Muriell, Murielle

Myfanwy

First found in medieval times this Welsh name means 'rare one' or 'my treasure'. It was revived during the 19th century and spawned the short form Fanny.

Variants: Fanni, Fannie, Fanny, Myf, Myfi, Myfina

Myrna

According to the Christmas story the Three Wise Men brought the baby Jesus gifts of gold, frankincense and myrrh. It is from this reddish brown material that the Arabic name Myrna is derived. Considered to be valuable in ancient times, myrrh was frequently used in perfumes and incense.

Myrna also has roots in Ireland and is thought to be a variant of the Irish name Muirne, which means 'blood'.

Variants: Merna, Mirna, Morna, Muirna, Muirne

Naama

Naama comes from the Hebrew for 'beautiful' and 'pleasant' and the Arabic for 'good fortune'.

Variants: Naamah, Naava

Nadia

Nadia is the pet form of the Russian name Nadezhda, which means 'hope'. The French variant of this name is Nadine. Nadia is also believed to come from the Spanish for 'nothing' and from the Arabic word 'nazir' or 'opposite to zenith'.

In the English-speaking world Nadia grew in popularity during the 20th century.

Variants: Nada, Nadeen, Nadie, Nadina, Nadine, Nadja, Nadka

Naia

In Greek mythology the Naiads were water nymphs who dwelled in rivers, brooks, streams, fountains, ponds and lakes. Blessed with the gift of prophecy, they had the ability to heal the sick and were associated with fertility. Though they lived for thousands of years they were destined always to look young. Fittingly the name Naia comes from the Greek for 'to flow'.

Variants: Naiad, Naida, Naiia, Nalda

Nancy

The name Nancy has a long history that stretches back to the Biblical name Hannah. Hannah comes from the Hebrew for 'God has favoured me'. It is from Hannah that the name Anne was derived and Nancy was a pet form of Anne as far back as the 18th century.

Nancy may also be related to the name Agnes which comes from the Greek 'hagnos' meaning 'pure' or 'holy'. (See also Agnes, Anne and Hannah.)

Variants: Agnes, Ann, Anna, Anne, Hannah, Nance, Nancie, Nanette

Nanette

Nanette is the French version of the name Nancy, which is a pet form of Anne, itself a derivative of Hannah ('God has favoured me').

It is now considered independently of Nancy, Anne or Hannah.

Variants: Ann, Anna, Anne, Hannah, Nance, Nancie, Nancy, Nannie, Nanny

Naomi
Naomi is another Biblical name that proved popular with the
Puritans of the 17th century. It comes from the Hebrew for
'delightful', 'pleasant' and 'charming' and for good reason. In
the Old Testament Naomi and her family were Israelites living in
the land of Maob. When her husband and sons died Naomi
decided to return to her homeland, but her daughter-in-law
Ruth, a Maobite refused to leave her side. She loved her mother-
in-law so much that she determined to leave her birthplace and
go to Israel with her.
Variants: Nae, Naome, Noemi, Nomi

Natalie
The Latin word 'natalis' means 'anniversary', 'birthday' or
'festival' and traditionally it is associated with the birth of
Christ. Thus like Noel, which is the French for Christmas, the
name Natalie is linked to the festive season.
　　Natalia, Natalya and Talia are the Russian forms of the name.
Nathalie is the French spelling.
Variants: Natalia, Natalya, Natasha, Natassia, Nathalie, Talia

Natasha
Natasha is sometimes given to girls as the feminine version of
Nathan, which comes from the Hebrew for 'gift'. However, it is
more commonly seen as the Russian pet form of the name
Natalie.
　　As mentioned above, Natalie is derived from the Latin for
'birthday' or 'anniversary'. But the Russian pet form Natasha
was given prominence in Leo Tolstoy's classic novel *War and
Peace*, published from 1865 to 1868. In the English-speaking
world the name proved popular from the 1960s onwards.
*Variants: Natacha, Natalia, Natalie, Natalya, Nathalie, Natasja,
Natassia, Tasha*

Nayer
Nayer is taken from the Persian for 'sunshine'.

Girls

Nebula
This name comes from the Latin for 'mist', 'smoke' and 'darkness'.

Nell
Eleanor Gwyn, the English actress who died in 1687, was the most famous mistress of King Charles II. The name she was given at birth betrays the origin of her pet name, the one that she is more commonly known by – Nell.

Now an independent name, Nell is also a pet form of Ellen and Helen. Ellen and Eleanor share the Greek meaning of Helen – 'bright'.
Variants: Eleanor, Ellen, Helen, Nellie, Nelly

Neoma
Neoma comes from the Greek word 'neomenia', which means 'new moon'.

Nerissa
The exact origin of Nerissa is unknown but the name was used by Shakespeare in his play *The Merchant of Venice*. Nerissa was maid to the wealthy heiress Portia.

In Greek mythology the Nereids were the daughters of Nereus, the god of the sea. Thus the name Nerissa is believed to mean 'sea nymphs'.
Variants: Nerida, Nerina

Nerys
Nerys derives its meaning from the Welsh word 'ner', which stands for 'lord'. Although it has long been in the Welsh vocabulary it has only come into use as a girl's name within recent times.

Ngaire
This Antipodean name comes from the Maori word, 'ngaio' which means 'clever'.
Variant: Ngaio

Niamh
Irish mythology holds that Niamh was a goddess who fell in love with Oisin, and took him back with her to Tir na n'Og – the land of youth where there was no sadness, dying or ageing.

Pronounced as 'Neev' Niamh means 'bright'. In Wales the name is shortened to Nia, which as a first name comes from the Swahili word for 'purpose'.
Variants: Nia, Niar

Nicole
The boy's name Nicholas comes from the Greek for 'people's victory'. Nicola is the Italian feminine form of the name and Nicole and Nicolette are popular in France. Nicole has enjoyed great popularity in North America.
Variants: Nichole, Nicola, Nicolette, Nicci

Nikita
Although Nikita is currently perceived as a girl's name, it was originally a boy's name in Russia that came from the Greek for 'unconquered'. But it is also an Indian name that means 'the earth'. Like Nicole, Nikita is popular among North American parents.

Nissa
Nissa has meanings in both Hebrew and African. Its Hebrew meaning is 'sign', 'emblem' or 'to test'. But it also comes from the Hausa for 'never forgotten loved one'.
Variants: Nissie, Nissy

Nokomis
This Native American name means 'daughter of the moon'.

Nola
As the feminine version of the Irish name Nolan, Nola means 'son of the noble one'. However, it is also derived from the Celtic name Fionnuala, which means 'fair-shouldered'.
Variants: Fiona, Fionnuala, Nolana, Noleen, Nolene, Nuala

Nona

In Victorian England, when big families were common, Nona was bestowed upon the ninth child if she were a baby girl for the name comes from the Latin for 'ninth'. Nona could also be given to babies born in September, the ninth month in the calendar, or to those born on the ninth day of any month.

The name is also associated with the Roman goddess of foetal development.

Variants: Noni, Nonie

Norah

Eleanor, Leonora and Honoria are all shortened to form the name Norah. As a variant of Eleanor and Leonora this short form assumes the Greek meaning for Helen 'bright' or 'light'. Honoria provides Norah with the meaning 'honour'.

In Ireland, where it is especially popular, Norah is sometimes adopted as a derivative of Nuala and ultimately Fionnuala ('fair-shouldered').

Variants: Eleanor, Fionnuala, Helen, Honoria, Honor, Nora

Nova

In astronomy a nova is a star that burns brightly for a time but eventually returns to its normal state in a few weeks, months or years. Both the word and the name come from the Latin 'novus', which means 'new', 'newcomer'.

Variant: Novia

Nuala

Nuala is another popular Irish name that is derived from the Celtic name Fionnuala ('fair-shouldered'). It is pronounced 'New-la'.

Variants: Fenella, Fionnghuala, Fionnuala, Nola, Nora

Octavia

Octavia comes from the Latin for 'eighth', thus traditionally the name was given to the eighth child in a family.

Octavia may have also been derived from the Ancient Roman

family name, Octavius. The first Roman emperor, Augustus Gaius Julius Octavius, was born in 63 BC. His sister, Octavia, married Mark Antony.
Variants: Octavio, Octtavia, Tave, Tavia, Tavy

Odessa
Written by the Greek poet Homer, *The Odyssey* recounts the story of Odysseus, the king of Ithaca, who spent 10 years trying to return home after the fall of Troy. His name, and the female equivalent Odessa, means 'extended wandering' or 'epic voyage'.

Olga
The first Russian state was established by Scandinavian settlers in the 9th century and with them they brought the name Olga. Olga comes from an Old Norse adjective that means 'prosperous' and 'successful'.

Although it was not introduced into the English-speaking world until the late 19th century it was born by a saint, Olga of Kiev, who died in 969. This Russian saint, who was baptised in Constantinople (Istanbul), helped the spread of Christianity.
Variants: Helga, Ola, Olenka, Olia, Olina, Olli, Ollie

Olive
Olives are the fruit of the evergreen tree that is grown in the Mediterranean. They can be eaten alone, used in food or pressed into oil, but traditionally the branches of that tree have been offered as symbol of peace. Consequently the name Olive is taken from the Latin word 'oliva'. and is associated with peace. In Greece brides traditionally carry an olive garland and the wreath is seen as a mark of success.
Variant: Olivia

Olivia
Like Olive the name Olivia is associated with the olive tree and the symbol of peace. It is also considered to be the female equivalent of Oliver, which shares the same Latin root 'oliva'.

However, Oliver may have also been derived from the Old Norse for 'ancestor, remains'.

Olivia has been in currency in Britain since the Middle Ages and Shakespeare used the name for the heroine of his 1599 play *Twelfth Night*. Although Livia is a pet form of Olivia it also comes from the Roman family name Livius and was borne by the wife of the Emperor Augustus.
Variants: Livia, Livvy, Oliva, Olive

Olwyn

In Celtic mythology Olwyn was the daughter of the giant Ysbadden, who would die if he were separated from his offspring. Prince Culhwch wanted to win Olwyn's hand in marriage and to do so he had to perform a series of difficult tasks.

According to Welsh legend Olwyn was so-called because her footprints were covered in white clover. Her name is made from the word 'ôl', 'footprint' and '(g)wen', which means 'white' or 'fair'.
Variants: Olwen, Olwin

Olympia

It is the tallest mountain in Greece but, according to the mythology of that country, Mount Olympus was also the heavenly abode of the gods and goddesses. It is from this place that the Olympic Games derived their name, for they were held every four years in honour of the great Olympian, the supreme god Zeus.

The girl's name Olympias was later borne by the mother of Alexander the Great, the king of Macedon who conquered Persia and Egypt. She died in 316 BC, but the 4th century St Olympia helped the name to become popular throughout Europe.
Variants: Olimpia, Olimpie, Olympias

Omega

In the Greek language omega stands for 'O', the last letter of the Greek alphabet. Traditionally it was given to the last child in the family.
Variant: Mega

Opal
The Sanskrit word 'upalas' means 'precious stone' and like Diamond, Emerald, Ruby and Crystal, Opal is a gemstone that is now used as a girl's name. Opals are pale in colour and are said to bring luck.

Ophelia
Ophelia is thought to be a name created by Shakespeare and derived from the Greek word 'ophelos', which means 'help'. In his play *Hamlet* Ophelia is the tragic girlfriend of the lead character and the daughter of Polonius, an advisor to King Claudius. When Hamlet kills her father accidentally Ophelia goes mad and drowns herself.

Although the name featured in a Shakespearian play it did not become popular until the 19th century.
Variants: Ofelia, Ofilia, Ophelie

Orchid
Like Daisy, Orchid is a girl's name derived from a flower. The flower is considered to be exotic, rare and is generally associated with luxury.

Orla
The name Orla comes from the Irish for 'golden lady' or 'golden princess'.
Variants: Orfhlaith, Orlagh

Paige
In medieval times a 'page' was a young boy who attended a knight as the first step in becoming a knight himself. The occupational title became a surname and in modern times has become a girl's first name. It was especially popular in 1980s North America.

The name comes from the Greek for 'child' and the Italian for 'page boy'.
Variant: Page

Girls

Palma

Christian crusaders who went to the Holy Land were known as Palmers because they returned from their journey with crosses made from palm leaves. But the name Palma is probably derived from the Latin word 'palmus' which means 'the palm of the hand'.

Traditionally a large palm is associated with victory, success and happiness.

Variants: Palmeda, Palmer, Palmyra, Pelmira

Pamela

The name Pamela was the creation of the English poet Sir Philip Sidney who used it in his 1580 work *Arcadia*. The Greek words 'pau' ('all) and 'meli', ('honey') were believed to be the source of his inspiration.

However, the name only became popular once it was used by another English writer, Samuel Richardson in *Pamela, or Virtue Rewarded* (1740).

Variants: Pam, Pamelia, Pamelina, Pamella, Pammi, Pammy

Pandora

Pandora was the first woman, created by Zeus for the confusion of men. She was given a box that she was forbidden to open, but her curiousity got the better of her and out spilled all the evils of the world. The only positive present to be released from the box was hope.

Pandora's name comes from the Greek for 'all gifts' or 'gift in everything'. The phrase 'Pandora's box' stems from this story.

Variant: Panda

Paris

The capital city of France is associated with elegance, sophistication and romance. But as a given name Paris was originally bestowed upon boys. Indeed Paris was the name of the Trojan prince who instigated the 10-year Trojan War by stealing Helen, the wife of Menelaus and queen of Sparta.

Paris is now a common first name for girls.

Patience

Early Christians associated the virtue of patience with those who suffered persecution because of their faith without complaint or loss of devotion. The word comes from the Latin word 'pati', which means 'to suffer'.

As a given name Patience was popular with the Puritans of the 17th century.

Variants: Pat, Pattie, Patty

Patricia

The feminine form of Patrick. The origins stem from the Latin for 'noble one'.

Variants: Patrice, Patrizia, Patsy, Patty, Pattie, Pat, Tricia, Trish, Tish, Rickie, Ricky

Paula

Paula is the feminine form of the boy's name Paul. St Paul was originally known as Saul, a man who persecuted Christians during Biblical times. However, after seeing Christ in a vision on the road to Damascus he changed his belief and subsequently his name. Paul comes from the Latin for 'small'.

The girl's name Paula was carried across Europe by a saint of the same name. Born in 347, she was the founder of a number of convents in Bethlehem. Paulette is the French version of the name and Paola is the Italian equivalent. (See also Paul.)

Variants: Paola, Pauletta, Paulette, Paulina, Pauline, Paulita

Peace

The name is taken from the Latin 'pax', which means 'peace'.

Variants: Paz

Pearl

Pearl is sometimes used as a pet form of the name Margaret, and for good reason. The Greek word for 'pearl' is 'margaretes'. As a name in its own right Pearl became popular among parents during the late 19th century when it was extremely fashionable to bestow gemstone names on girls.

However the name Pearl boasts a much longer history. The variant Perle is an Anglicised version of the Yiddish name Penninah, which means 'coral'. The name was borne by the co-wife of Elkanah, the father of Samuel.

Variants: Margaret, Pearlie, Pearline, Peninnah, Pennina, Perla, Perle

Penelope

In Homer's *The Odyssey* Penelope is the faithful wife of Odysseus who, for 20 years, faithfully waits for his return. During that time she is approached by a string of suitors, all who want to marry her so that they can control the kingdom. She promises to remarry, but only after she has woven a shroud for her father-in-law. Cunningly Penelope weaves all day and unpicks her work at night, thus she never completes her task and her devotion to her husband remains unbroken. Thus Penelope means 'weaver'.

Variants: Penelopa, Pennie, Penny, Popi

Peta

This Scandinavian feminine version of the name Peter was little used before the 1930s. In the Bible Saint Peter was one of Christ's apostles and his name comes from the Latin and Greek for 'stone' or 'rock'. (See also Peter.)

Variant: Pet, Petra

Petra

In Latin and Greek the word 'petra' means 'stone'. Thus, Petra, like Peta, is a female equivalent of Peter. (See also Peta and Peter.)

Variants: Pet, Peta, Petie

Petula

The exact origin of Petula is uncertain but it is thought to come from the Latin for 'forward', 'saucy' and 'impudent'. Another possibility is that it came from the Latin word 'petulare' meaning 'to ask'.

There is a theory that Petula is connected to the plant name 'petunia' or that it is an elaboration of 'pet' – an English term of endearment.

Phoebe
Phoebe is also a Biblical name and was mentioned by Paul who associated it with a Corinthian woman in the New Testament. The name comes from the Greek and the Latin for 'bright' and 'shining'. The name Phoebe was borne by more than one person in Greek mythology. It was the alternative name for Artemis, the goddess of the moon and sister of Apollo who was known as Diana to the Romans. It was also the name of her grandmother, one of the original Titans.
Variant: Phebe

Phoenix
In Ancient Egypt the phoenix was regarded as a sacred bird that was said to live for 500 years. At the end of its life it would set itself and its nest alight and from the ashes a new bird would arise.

The Greeks also had a myth surrounding the phoenix. To them it was a bird that dwelled in Arabia and bathed in the water of a well each morning. Apollo, the sun god, always stopped to listen.

Phoenix comes from the Greek word 'phyllidis', which means 'leafy branch'. The name Phillis shares the same root.
Variants: Phillis, Phyllida, Phylis, Phyllis

Philippa
The Biblical name Philip is a combination of the Greek words 'philos', 'loving' and 'hippos', 'horse'. Thus Philip and its feminine equivalent Philippa mean 'someone who loves horses'.
Variants: Felipa, Filipa, Phillipa, Philly, Pippa

Pippa
This pet form of Philippa is now independently given as a name. In England the name became more popular following the

publication of Robert Browning's 1841 poem, *Pippa Pauses.*
Variants: Felipa, Filipa, Philippa, Phillipa, Philly, Pip

Poppy
In the United Kingdom red poppies are worn during the month
of November to commemorate the soldiers who died in the two
World Wars and subsequent conflicts. This emblem was chosen
because red poppies littered the battlefields of Flanders during
the Great War of 1914 to 1918.

The word was derived from the Old English 'popaeg'. As a
girl's name it has been in use since the turn of the last century
and it was especially popular during the 1920s.
Variants: Poppi, Poppie

Portia
William Shakespeare used the name Portia for characters in
two of his plays. In the historically-based *Julius Caesar* Portia
was the wife of Brutus, the man who played a pivotal role in
the plot to assassinate the Roman emperor. In *The Merchant of
Venice* Portia was the cross-dressing heroine who disguised
herself as a man.

As a girl's name Portia is derived from the old Roman
family name Porcius, which comes from the Latin for 'pig'.
Variants: Porsha, Porsche, Porchia, Porshia

Precious
To say something or someone is 'precious' is to suggest they are
'invaluable', 'priceless' and 'treasured'. Often used as a term of
endearment, it is now also given to baby girls.

Primrose
Like Daisy and Rose, Primrose is a flower name that became
popular with parents during the turn of the last century. The
plant, with its pale yellow flowers, derives its name from the
Latin 'prima rosa' meaning 'first rose'.
Variant: Rose

Priscilla
The Biblical Priscilla was a follower and supporter of St Paul. Her name was derived from the Latin word 'priscus', which meant 'ancient', 'old-fashioned' and 'antique'. The Roman family name Priscus came from the same root.
Variants: Cilla, Precilla, Prescilla, Pricilla, Pris, Prissy, Silla

Quintana
This name derives its meaning from the Latin word for 'fifth', traditionally given to the fifth child, or to a baby born in May, or on the fifth day of a month.
Variants: Quinn, Quinta, Quintilla, Quintina

Quinn
Like Quintana, Quinn is associated with the Latin word for 'fifth'. However it is also a variant of the name Queenie, which comes from the Old English and Old Norse for 'wife', 'companion' and 'woman'. Queenie also means 'ruler' or 'queen'.
During the Middle Ages the name was associated with the Queen of Heaven, the Virgin Mary, but during the 19th century it was often used in reference to Queen Victoria.
Variants: Queenie, Quintana, Quinta, Quintilla, Quintina

Rachel
The name Rachel comes from the Hebrew for 'ewe', a female sheep. In the Bible it was borne by the beautiful second wife of Jacob. She was the mother of his last two sons – Joseph and Benjamin.
Upon meeting Rachel, Jacob laboured seven years to win her hand, but on the wedding night he realised that his father-in-law had tricked him into marrying her older sister Leah. Although Jacob later took Rachel as a second wife, she died in childbirth. (See also Leah.)
Variants: Rachael, Rachele, Racheli, Raquel, Ray, Raye, Rochell, Shell, Shelley

Girls

Raquel
Although this name is considered to be an independent name in its own right, it is actually the Spanish form of Rachel. As mentioned above Rachel is derived from the Hebrew for 'ewe'. In the 1960s the name was popularised by the actress Raquel Welch who was born Raquel Tejada in 1940.
Variants: Rachael, Rachel, Rachelle, Raquelle

Rashida
In Sanskrit and Arabic Rashida means 'follower of the correct path'. It is the feminine equivalent of Rashid.
Variants: Rasheeda, Rashi

Reba
This modern name is believed to be a short form of Rebecca. In the Bible Rebecca is the wife of Isaac and her name comes from the Hebrew and Aramaic for 'knotted cord'.
Variants: Bec, Becca, Becky, Rebecca, Rebekah

Rebecca
In the Bible, Rebecca was the wife of Isaac and the mother of Esau and Jacob. She conspired with Jacob to trick her blind and elderly husband into bestowing the older son's blessing and inheritance on to him. Rebecca dressed the younger twin in Esau's clothes and adorned him in goatskin so that he would smell and feel like his hairy, hunter brother. The deception worked.

The Old Testament spelling of Rebecca (Rebekah) closely resembles the Hebrew and Aramaic word that the name was taken from. 'Ribkah' means 'knotted cord' and implies a faithful wife.

Rebecca was one of the many Biblical names favoured by the Puritans in the 1600s. In 1938 the name was the title of Daphne Du Maurier's classic novel, which went on to become an Oscar-winning film directed by Alfred Hitchcock.
Variants: Bec, Becca, Beck, Beckie, Becky, Bekky, Bex, Reba, Rebe, Rebekah

Reese

This Welsh name was once borne by a 12th century warrior, Rhys. His name meant 'ardour' or 'rashness'. He earned his place in history by fighting against the English invaders of Wales. Reese is the feminine equivalent of his name.

Variants: Reece, Rees

Rhea

In Greek mythology Rhea was the mother of Zeus, the supreme god, but the exact origin and meaning of her name is unknown. It may come from the Greek for 'flowing' or 'protector'.

According to Roman legend Rhea was a Vestal Virgin raped by the god Mars, who gave birth to twin boys, Romulus and Remus, the founders of Rome.

Variants: Rea, Reanna, Ria

Ria

Ria comes from the Spanish for 'small river' or 'river mouth'. It is also a variant of Rhea, which is thought to mean 'flowing' or 'protector' (see above). But it can also be used as a pet form of names ending in 'ria', such as Maria ('longed for child') and Victoria ('victory').

Variants: Maria, Rhea, Victoria

Rita

Margarita is the Spanish version of the name Margaret, which comes from the Latin and Greek for 'pearl'. Rita is the short form of this Spanish variant.

However, as an independent name it also boasts Hindu roots. Rita is an Indian name that means 'brave', 'strong' or 'proper'.

Famous Ritas include the actress Rita Hayworth and St Rita of Cascia, the patron saint of desperate causes and unhappy marriages.

Variants: Daisy, Margaret, Margarita, Margherita, Marguerita, Marguerite, Reda, Reeta, Reida

Robyn

The boy's name Robin is sometimes used as a pet form of Robert, a name of Germanic origin that means 'fame' and 'bright'. But children are also named Robin after the red-breasted bird associated with Christmas. Thus, like Carol, Noel, Nicholas and Nicola, Robin is often given to children born during this time. Robyn is the feminine equivalent.

Rose

Throughout history roses have been associated with love and beauty. In the ancient world this flower was sacred to several goddesses and later it became a symbol of the Virgin Mary. The red rose is the national flower of England and is also represents love and romance.

While the girl's name Rose may be derived from the flower it may also stem from the German word for 'horse'. It could equally have been derived from the Germanic word 'hrad', which means 'fame'.

Variants: Rosa, Rosanna, Rosabella, Rosalie, Rosalind, Rosemary, Rosetta, Rosie, Rosina, Rosita

Rosanna

This popular North American name was derived by combining the names Rose and Anna. As mentioned above the name Rose may either be associated with the flower or may be derived from the German words for 'horse' and 'fame'. Anna ultimately comes from the Biblical name Hannah, which means 'God has favoured me'.

Variants: Anna, Hannah, Rosa, Rosanne, Rose, Roseanna, Roseanne

Roxanne

Roxana was the name of a beautiful Asian princess who married Alexander the Great in 327 BC. The name was later used by Daniel Defoe in his 1724 novel *Roxana, The Fortunate Mistress*.

However, the variant Roxanne is best known as the heroine in Edmond Rostand's 1897 play *Cyrano de Bergerac*, which is

based on the life of a writer of the same name.

The exact meaning of Roxanne is unclear but it is thought to come from the Persian for 'dawn'.

Variants: Roxana, Roxane, Roxy

Ruby

Ruby was a popular gemstone name for baby girls born during the late 19th century and early 1900s. It comes from the Latin word 'rubeus', which means red.

Variants: Rubetta, Rubette, Rubi, Rubia, Rubina

Ruth

In the Old Testament Ruth was the devoted daughter-in-law of Naomi. Following the death of her husband and father-in-law, Ruth left her homeland to return to Israel, the birth place of Naomi.

Although the exact meaning of the name is unknown it is associated with companionship and friendship and is also of Hebrew origin.

Variant: Ruthie

Sabrina

In England, in ancient times, the River Severn was known as Sabrina. According to Celtic legend its name was derived from the illegitimate daughter of a Welsh king whose stepmother ordered that she be drowned in its waters. In his writings the Roman historian Tacitus refers to the river by its ancient name.

Variant: Zabrina

Saffron

As a girl's name Saffron was little used (if at all) before the 1960s. It comes from the crocus that produces yellow dye and spice that adds flavour to food.

The name is derived from the Arabic word 'zafaron', which means 'crocus'.

Variants: Saffie, Safflower, Saffrey, Saffy

Sage
The herbal plant sage is used to flavour food and is as also used as a tea. In English the word means an old, wise man. Today it is given to both boys and girls as a first name.

Sahara
Situated in North Africa, and covering 9,065,000 sq km, the Sahara Desert is the largest desert in the world. It sprawls between the Atlantic Ocean on the west and the Red Sea of Egypt in the east. To its north lay the Atlas Mountains and the Mediterranean. Its southern boundary is the valley of the Niger River.

Fittingly the name comes from the Arabic word 'sahra', which means 'desert'.
Variant: Zahara

Salena
The name Salena comes from the Latin word 'sal', meaning 'salt' and 'salt water'. To say someone is the 'salt of the earth' is to say they are genuine, selfless and blessed with common sense.

The similar-sounding name Selena, comes from the Greek for 'moon'.
Variant: Salina

Sally
Today Sally is considered to be an independent name, but originally it was a pet form of Sarah, a Hebrew name meaning 'princess'. It is sometimes combined with Ann to produce the separate name Sally-Ann.
Variants: Sal, Sallie, Sally-Ann, Sarah

Salome
Although this name comes from the Hebrew word for 'peace' ('shalom') in the Bible it was not borne by a peaceful woman. In the New Testament Salome was the stepdaughter of King Herod who was asked to dance for him at a banquet. In return he promised to give her anything her heart desired. Prompted by

her mother she asked for the head of John the Baptist, the preacher and cousin of Jesus.

In 1893 the Irish playwright Oscar Wilde wrote a play about Salome, which Richard Strauss later developed into an opera.
Variants: Sal, Salama, Saolma, Salomi, Shulamit

Samantha
The exact origin of Samantha is unknown. It could be the feminine equivalent of the Biblical name Samuel, which comes from the Hebrew for 'heard by God'. Alternatively it may have been derived from the Aramaic for 'one who listens'.

Whatever its origin, the name first came into use in the 18th century when it was especially popular with parents in the southern states of North America.
Variants: Sam, Sammie, Sammy

Samira
This name derives its meaning from the Arabic for 'entertainer' and 'companion in night talk'.
Variants: Mira, Sam, Sami, Sammie, Sammy

Sarah
Sarah was the wife of Abraham – who, to Christians, Jews and Muslims is the patriach of their faiths. Sarah, at 90 bore him a son, Isaac, who went on to father Esau and Jacob.

In the Old Testament God changed Abraham's name from Abram ('exalted father') to Abraham ('father of many'). Although he changed his wife's name from Sarai to Sarah, the meaning in Hebrew remained the same – 'princess'.

The popularity of this name increased throughout the English-speaking world after the Reformation. The Scottish Gaelic version of Sarah is Morag.
Variants: Morag, Sara, Sarai, Saran, Sarann

Saskia
The 17th century Dutch artist Rembrandt first brought this name

to England. He was married to a woman called Saskia von Uylenburg who modelled for many of his paintings.

The exact origin of the name is unknown but it is thought to stem from the Germanic word 'sachs', which means 'Saxon'.

Selma

Selma is of both Celtic and Scandinavian origin. Its Celtic meaning is 'fair' but it is also derived from the Old Norse for 'divinely protected'.

Scandinavian immigrants brought the name with them to the shores of North America, ensuring its spread throughout the English-speaking world.

Previously the name Selma had grown in stature in Sweden thanks to the works of the poet Frans Mikael Franzen who used it in his work. He died in 1849. Later the Swedish novelist Selma Lagerlöf brought the name further public attention. In 1909 she became the first female writer to win the Nobel Prize for Literature.

Variants: Aselma, Zelma

Shannon

Located in Ireland and stretching over 200 miles the River Shannon is the longest river in both Ireland and Britain. As a surname Shannon means 'descendent of Sean' in Gaelic.

Despite its connections Shannon is little used as a first name for babies born in Ireland. It is generally given to girls whose parents are of Irish descent but live abroad. Shannon is sometimes used as a boy's name as well.

Variants: Shanna, Shannagh

Siân

Siân is the Celtic version of the name Jane, which is the feminine equivalent of John ('God is gracious'). Like the boy's name Sean it is pronounced 'Shaw-an'.

Variants: Jane, Janet, Jayne, Jeanette, Sian, Siani, Shani

Sierra
The name Sierra is derived from the Spanish for 'mountain range'. It is especially popular in North America.

Sinéad
The Irish name Sinéad is the Gaelic version of Jane and Janet, both of which are feminine versions of the Biblical name John. John comes from the Hebrew for 'God has favoured', 'God is gracious' and 'God is merciful'. Sinéad is pronounced as 'shin-aid' or 'sin-aid'.
Variants: Jane, Janet, Jayne, Jeanette, Sinead

Skye
During the hippy flower-power age of the 1960s it became popular to choose children names from the world of nature. The Phoenix family – an American acting clan – are a perfect example of this trend. The family boasted the names Rain, River and Summer. The popularity of the name Skye is indicative of this movement. However this name is sometimes given to children in honour of the Scottish island of Skye.
Variant: Sky

Sophie
The Greek word 'sophia' means 'wisdom' and throughout history it has been used in connection with the holy wisdom of God. In 6th century Constantinople (Istanbul, Turkey) a large cathedral was built as part of the Christian Orthodox Church. It was called Hagia Sophia, meaning 'Sacred Wisdom'. Although it was torn down in 532 it was rebuilt over the next few years and still stands in the city today.
Variants: Sofi, Sofia, Sofya, Sonia, Sondya, Sonja, Sonni, Sophia

Stella
In Latin 'stella' means 'star' and the Virgin Mary is sometimes known as 'Stella Maris' or 'star of the sea'.
   The Elizabethan poet Sir Philip Sidney was said to be the first

person to use this Latin word as a girl's name in his sonnets and songs called *Astrophel and Stella*. But the French name Estelle, which was popular in the 19th century, was derived from the same root. (See also Estelle.)

Susan

Popular in the 20th century, Susan is a short form of the name Susannah. The 1616 painting by Ludovico Carracci depicts the Biblical story of Susannah and the Elders, the beautiful woman who was seen bathing in her garden. Lusting after her, the men tried to blackmail Susannah into sleeping with them by threatening to say they had seen her having sex. Susannah refused, the elders carried out their threat, and the young woman faced the punishment of stoning. However she was exonerated when the judge Daniel interviewed the two men separately. Their stories did not match and Susannah was saved.

Her name comes from the Hebrew word 'shoshana' meaning 'lily'. Although it was not common until the 1700s, Shakespeare gave the name to one of his daughters.

Variants: Chana, Shoshan, Siusan, Suki, Susana, Susannah, Susanne

Tabitha

According to the Bible Tabitha is the name of a follower of Jesus who was raised from the dead by St Peter. Her name comes from the Aramaic for 'gazelle'.

Although Tabitha was favoured by the 17th century Puritans it was not popular with the Victorians.

Variants: Tab, Tabatha, Tabbi, Tabbie, Tabbitha, Tabby

Tamara

Tamar was the name of a 12th century queen of Georgia, a region that was once part of Russia. Her name comes from the Arabic and Hebrew for 'date palm tree'.

There were two Tamars in the Bible. One was the daughter-in-law of Judah. The other was the daughter of King David who

was raped by her half-brother Amnon. Tamar's other brother Absalom, another son of David, took revenge by killing their mutual sibling. Tamara is an elaboration of Tamar.
Variants: Mara, Tam, Tamah, Tamar, Tamarah, Tammi, Tammy, Timi

Tammy

The name Tammy was first used as a pet form of Tamara and Tamsin. As a short form of Tamara it assumes the meaning 'date palm tree'. As a variant of Tamsin, which is the feminine equivalent of Thomas, it means 'twin'.

Today Tammy is given to girls as an independent name, especially in North America where it was borne by the Country music singer, Tammy Wynette. She was given the name Virginia Wynette Pugh when she was born in 1942 but adopted Tammy when she became a singer.
Variants: Tami, Tammi, Tammie

Tamsin

There are a number of feminine versions of the Biblical name Thomas. They include Thomasina and Tomasina, but Tamsin is the Cornish form. Like Thomas it comes from the Arabic for 'twin'.
Variants: Tamasin, Tamasine, Tami, Tammie, Tammy, Tamzin, Thomasina, Thomasine

Tania

In Russia the name Tatiana is associated with royalty. Not only was it associated with a fairy queen it also belonged to a daughter of Nicholas II, the country's last Tsar. Tatiana was also borne by an early Christian martyr who died in 228.

Tania is the pet form of Tatiana, which is now used as an independent name.
Variants: Tatiana, Tanya, Titania, Tita.

Tara

In Margaret Mitchell's novel *Gone with the Wind*, Tara was the name of the fictional home of the O'Hara family. In Ireland Tara was the name of the hill in County Meath, which was the seat of the country's ancient kings.

Now used as a girl's name, Tara also comes from the Aramaic 'to throw' or 'carry'. It was little used in Britain before the 1960s.
Variants: Tarrah, Taryn, Tatiana

Tatum
The exact origin of this modern-day girl's name is unknown. It may be a feminine version of Tate, which comes from the Middle English for 'cheerful' and 'spirited'. Tate is also believed to stem from the Old English for a variety of other words and phrases. They include 'dear', 'dice', 'hilltop', 'tress of hair' and 'treat'.

Tatum is also believed to come from the Native American for 'windy' or 'garrulous'.
Variants: Tata, Tait, Tayte

Taylor
The word 'tailor' is derived from the Anglo-Norman word 'taillier', meaning 'to cut'. Thus the surname Taylor was originally a tag for someone who was a tailor by profession. However, in modern times Taylor has been given to babies of both sexes as a first name. It is especially popular in North America.

Tempest
Used by William Shakespeare as the title of one his plays, Tempest is also bestowed on girls as a first name. It comes from the Old French for 'storm'.
Variant: Tempestt

Terri
As the feminine variant of the boy's name Terence, Terri ultimately comes from the Old Roman name Terentius. It is also used as a pet form of Theresa, which may come from the Greek for 'to reap'. (See also Theresa.)

In North America it is used as an independent given name.
Variants: Teresa, Teri, Theresa

T

Thalia

Thalia comes from the Greek word 'thallein' which means 'to flourish', 'to prosper' or 'to bloom'. According to Greek mythology she was one of the Three Graces (also known as the Charites) – the daughters of Zeus who were associated with charm, beauty, creativity, fertility and nature. Thalia was also the name of one of the nine Muses who were goddesses of the Greek arts and sciences. Thalia presided over comedy.
Variants: Talia, Talya

Theresa

The exact origin of the name Theresa is unknown, but it is thought to come from the Greek for 'harvest' or 'to reap'.

The name was first brought to England via Roman Catholicism but it fell out of favour once the country became Protestant. In the 20th century Mother Theresa was perhaps the most famous bearer of the name. Born in 1910 she died in September 1997 after a life devoted to caring for the poor and sick in Calcutta, India. A Roman Catholic nun and the founder of her own order, the Missionaries of Charity, she was awarded the Nobel Peace Prize in 1979.
Variants: Teresa, Thérèse, Theresia, Terri, Tess, Tessa, Tracy, Tracey

Tia

This short name derives its meaning from others. As a pet form of Christina it means 'Christian', but as a variant of Tatiana it means 'fairy queen'.
Variants: Christina, Christine, Tatiana, Tania, Tanya, Tina

Tina

Although Tina is now used as an independent name in its own right it was first used as a pet form of Christina, which means 'Christian'. It is also used as a short form for other names ending in 'tina', such as Valentina.
Variants: Christina, Christine, Tatiana, Tiana, Tia, Tyna

Toni

The boy's name Anthony was derived from the Old Roman family name Antonius, which may have come from the Greek for 'flourishing' or 'flower'. Antonia is the feminine equivalent of that name and Toni is its short form.

Toni is now given to girls as an independent name.

Variants: Antonia, Tonie, Tonya

Tonya

Like Toni, Tonya is an independent name that derives its meaning from Antonia, the feminine form of Anthony. Thus it assumes the Greek meaning 'flourishing'.

Variants: Antonia, Toni, Tonie, Tonia

Tracy

While the exact meaning of Tracy is unclear the source of its popularity is not. The name became more widespread following the 1940 film *The Philadelphia Story* and the 1956 musical *High Society*. Katharine Hepburn played the central character, Tracy Lord, in the first film and Grace Kelly assumed the role in the second.

The name is sometimes used as a pet form of Theresa, which comes from the Greek for 'to reap'. However, it may also derive its meaning from the Latin word 'tractare', which means 'to manage, handle or lead'.

Another possibility is that Tracy was taken from the Gallo-Roman personal name meaning 'inhabitant of Thrace'.

Variants: Teresa, Terese, Theresa, Thérèse, Trace, Tracie, Tracey

Troy

Troy derives its meaning from two surnames and one place name. According to Greek legend Troy was an ancient city located in the Asia Minor and the scene of the 10-year Trojan War.

As a surname Troy was given to those who lived in the French town of Troyes. But as an Irish last name it comes from the Gaelic for 'a foot soldier'.

T-U

Tuesday
According to Teutonic mythology Tiw was the god of war and the brother of Thor. The second day of the week, Tuesday or 'Tiwesdaeg', was named after him. The fourth day 'Thor's day' or Thursday, was named after his brother.

Tyler
In North America this surname is popular as a first name for both boys and girls. It comes from the Old English for 'tile' and was used as an occupational name for someone who was a tiler. Its popularity in North America may be due to the 10th president of the United States, John Tyler.

Uma
Uma is the name of the Hindu goddess of beauty and sunlight. Her name is derived from the Sanskrit word for 'flax' and 'turmeric'.

R L Stevenson used the name in his 1893 novella *The Beach of Falesa*.

Unity
The girl's name Unity is derived from the Latin 'unitas', which comes from 'unus' meaning 'one' or 'together'.

The name Unity is also a variant of Una, which is taken from the Irish word for 'lamb'. In Latin 'una' also means 'together'. In 1930s and 1940s Britain the name was borne by Unity Mitford, one of the glamorous Mitford sisters.
Variants: Una, Unique

Ursula
Ursula is derived from the Latin for 'little bear' or 'female bear'. In the 5th century it was borne by a saint who, according to legend, was martyred in Cologne with 11,000 martyrs as they returned from a pilgrimage to Rome. Ursula was a popular saint during the Middle Ages.

It is also the feminine equivalent of the name Orson ('bear').
Variants: Orsa, Orsola, Ursala, Urse, Ursel, Ursie, Ursola

Valentina

Valentina is the feminine version of Valentine, the name of the saint whose feast day is celebrated on 14 February. Valentine was a 3rd century Roman martyr and his name is derived from the Latin word 'valens' which means 'healthy', 'strong', 'vigorous' and 'powerful'.

Both Valentine and the feminine equivalent Valentina are traditionally bestowed upon children born on St Valentine's Day – a day associated with love and romance.
Variants: Valeria, Valerie

Valerie

Like Valentina and Valentine, Valerie is derived from the Latin for 'healthy' and 'vigorous'. It is the feminine form of the Old Roman family name.

The variant Valeria was borne by Valeria Messalina, the granddaughter of Mark Antony. Valeria became the third wife of the Roman emperor Claudius and bore him two children. But she conspired with her lover to kill him and suffered the fate of execution.
Variants: Val, Valaree, Valari, Valeria, Valery, Valentina

Vanessa

The name Vanessa is thought to be the invention of the Anglo-Irish 18th century writer Jonathan Swift who used it as a nickname for his friend Esther Vanhomrigh. He appears to have combined the first part of her surname, 'Van', with the suffix 'essa'. Swift used the nickname in the title of his poem *Cadenus and Vanessa.*

The name may also be associated with the Greek word for 'butterflies'.
Variants: Nessa, Nessie, Van, Vania, Vannie, Vanny

Vashti

Vashti was the name of a Biblical woman who was married to the King of Persia. However, she was later replaced by Esther, when she refused to place herself at her husband's feet.

Vashti comes from the Persian for 'beautiful'.

Venus
Venus was an Italian goddess who became associated with Aphrodite, the Greek goddess of love. It is also the name given to the second planet from the sun.
Variants: Venita, Vinita, Vin, Vinnie

Verdi
The name Verdi is usually associated with the Italian composer Giuseppe Verdi. However, it can also be given to girls as a first name.
Verdi comes from the Latin word 'vivere', which means 'to be green'. It is associated with lush vegetation and springtime.
Variants: Vera, Veradis, Vere, Verene, Verina, Verine, Verita

Verity
Verity is another name favoured by the Puritans of the 17th century because of its value as a Christian virtue. It is derived from the Old French and Latin words for 'truth'.
Variants: Vera, Verena

Veronica
St Veronica was the woman from Jerusalem who was said to have taken pity on Christ as he carried his cross on the road to Calgary. She offered him a cloth to wipe the sweat from his face and, when it was returned to her, it bore the imprint of his image.
Thus the name Veronica is derived from the Latin for 'true image' and, fittingly, Veronica is the patron saint of photographers.
The French variant Veronique, was carried to Scotland in the 17th century, but the name was not popular in England until the 1800s.
Variants: Berenice, Bernice, Nika, Ron, Roni, Verenice, Verona, Veronika, Veronique, Vonni

Victoria
Queen Victoria, the Empress of India, died in January 1901 after reigning over Britain and its Empire for over 63 years. But when

she was born in 1819, the name that would lend itself to an era was little used in the nation she went on to rule.

Queen Victoria was named after her German mother Mary Louise Victoria of Saxe-Coburg. Their shared name came from the Latin for 'victorious' and during Victoria's reign it was bestowed upon both a Canadian city and an Australian state in her honour.

More than a century after Victoria's death the name continues to be used as a girl's name. However, it was especially popular in 1970s Britain.

Variants: Tora, Tori, Tory, Vic, Vicci, Vicki, Vicky, Victoire, Victoriana, Victorina

Violet
Violet is both a colour – bluish-purple – and a flower. Although it was a popular girl's name during the 19th century a variant of the name was used by Shakespeare in *Twelfth Night*. Viola is the name of his heroine who disguises herself as a man when she is shipwrecked in a hostile country.

Variants: Viola, Violetta

Virginia
The American state of Virginia was christened by the explorer Sir Walter Raleigh who named it in honour of Elizabeth I, the Virgin Queen. The name was derived from the Latin for 'virgin' or 'maiden', but it was also the feminine version of the Old Roman family name, Virginius. Virginia is also associated with the Latin for 'manly race'.

In Ancient Rome the name was borne by a young girl who received the unwelcome sexual attention of a corrupt ruler. She was killed by her father to save her virtue.

Although the name Virginia enjoyed great popularity in 18th century France, it was not as widespread in Britain until the late 1900s.

(See also Ginger.)

Variants: Gina, Ginger, Ginia, Ginni, Ginny, Virgie, Virginie

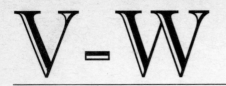

V - W

Vivian

Although this name was originally given to baby boys it is now more frequently associated with girls. Vivian comes from the Old French, and ultimately Latin, word for 'alive'. To say someone is vivacious is to say they are bubbly and full of life.

The name existed in England as far back as the Middle Ages. In the 20th century it was associated with the British actress Vivien Leigh who won an Academy Award for her portrayal of Scarlett O'Hara in the film adaptation of *Gone with the Wind*.

Variants: Vivi, Vivien, Vivienne, Vyvian, Vyvyan

Wallis

The origin of the name Wallis is disputed. One theory suggests that it is derived from the Old French for members of the Celtic race, 'waleis'. Another possible theory points to the Old Norse word 'val', meaning 'choice' or 'selection'. It could also come from the Old English for 'defence' or 'fortification'.

Wallis Simpson was the twice-married American divorcee who created a constitiutional crisis in Britain in 1936. It was for the love of Mrs Simpson that Edward VIII abdicated the British throne in favour of his younger brother Prince Albert, the Duke of York. Albert became King George VI and was succeeded by his daughter, Elizabeth II.

In Scotland the surname Wallace is associated with the patriotic hero William Wallace who led an army against the English. Wallis may be a transferred use of this surname or it could equally be derived from the Latin for 'Welshman'.

Variants: Wallace, Wallie, Wally

Wednesday

Wednesday is the name given to babies of either sex who are born on that day of the week. The practice is more common in North America than in the United Kingdom.

In England the name comes from the Old English for 'Woden's Day'. Woden was a one-eyed Anglo-Saxon god.

Wendy

Wendy is another name that was a literary invention. The Scottish writer J M Barrie created the name for a character in his play *Peter Pan*. The inspiration for the name was a child called Margaret Henley who called Barrie 'my friendy', 'friendy-wendy' or 'fwendy-wendy'.

The popularity of the children's story about Peter Pan, the boy who refused to grow up, helped to spread the use of Wendy.
Variants: Wanda, Wenda, Wendi, Wendie

Whitney

Situated in California, Mount Whitney is the highest point in North America outside of Alaska. It was named after Josiah Whitney who was a professor of geology at Harvard University during the 19th century.

Although Whitney was associated with a surname in North America it came from the Middle English for 'by the white island'. Thus it was originally a place name.
Variants: Whitnee, Whitni, Whitnie, Whitny, Witney

Willow

The willow is pliant and graceful and it is from this tree that the girl's name is derived.

Wilma

Wilma is the short form of the German name Wilhelmina, which is the feminine form of William. William comes from the Old German for 'resolute protection'.
Variants: Wilhelmina, Mina, Minnie

Winona

Winona comes from the Old High German and Old English for 'blissfully happy' and 'joy'. It also has a Native American meaning – 'firstborn daughter'.

In North America Winona is also known as a place name. For example, in the Midwestern state of Minnesota there is a county

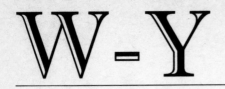

bearing the name. It is a popular first name in North America.
Variants: Wenona, Wenonah, Winnie, Wynona

Winter
The name of the season is sometimes used as a girl's name.

Yasmin
Yasmin is a variant of the name Jasmine, which is also used as an independent name. The two names share the same meaning. They are both derived from the jasmine flower, the sweet-smelling plant from which oil is made. Yasmin is the Arabic form of this name.
Variants: Jasmine, Yasmina, Yasmine

Yoko
Yoko comes from the Japanese for 'positive' and 'female'. In the Western world the most famous bearer of this name is Yoko Ono, the widow of former Beatles' member John Lennon. Yoko's name is rooted in Japanese philosophy, which says that 'Yo' and 'In' lay still in an egg until they are split to form heaven and earth.

Yolanda
This name stems from the Greek word 'ion', which means 'violet'. Thus it is closely related to the name Iolanthe, which means 'violet flower'. In France Iolanthe became Yolande and Yolanda is its variant. The Latin meaning of Yolanda is 'modest'.
Variants: Iolanthe, Violet, Yolande

Yoshiko
Yoshiko is a Japanese name that is given to boys and girls. It means 'good' and 'respectful'.
Variant: Yoshi

Yvette
Yvette is of both French, German and Hebrew origin. Its Germanic meaning is 'yew' and 'small archer'. But in France it is held as the feminine version of Yves, the French form of the

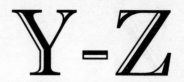
Biblical name John. John comes from the Hebrew for 'God has favoured', 'God is gracious' and 'God is merciful'.
Variants: Ivetta, Yevette, Yve, Yvonne

Yvonne
Like Yvette, Yvonne borrows its meaning from the French and ultimately Germanic word for 'yew'. It is also associated with 'small archer' because the yew tree was used to make long bows. As the feminine form of Yves, the French for John, Yvonne also means 'God has favoured', 'God is gracious' and 'God is merciful'. It has produced a plethora of variants and is not confined to the French-speaking world.
Variants: Evona, Evonne, Ivetta, Yevette, Yve, Yvette

Zara
A granddaughter of Queen Elizabeth II, Zara Phillips, bears this name. It is taken from the Arabic word 'zahr', which means 'flower'. It is also thought to come from the Arabic for 'brightness' and 'splendour of the dawn'. Sometimes it also appears as a variant of Sarah, which comes from the Hebrew for 'princess'.
Variants: Sara, Sarah, Zahra, Zarah

Zita
Zita comes from the Italian for 'child'. It was borne by a 13th century Tuscan saint who was canonised in 1696. St Zita is the patron saint of domestic servants because that was once her profession. A bunch of keys are her emblem. St Zita also represents bakers, home-makers and those who have misplaced their keys. The last empress of Austria also bore this name.
   As a short form of the Spanish name Rosita, Zita means 'little rose'.
Variants: Citha, Rosita, Sitha, Zeta

Zoe
The name Zoe was popular with early Christians because of its association with eternal life. The name is the Greek translation of

the Hebrew word 'hawwah', which means 'life'.

Zoe was borne by martyrs in the 2nd and 3rd centuries and was popular among British parents during the 1800s. It is also a variant of the name Eve, which shares the same meaning.

Variants: Eva, Eve, Evita, Vita, Zoë, Zoey, Zowie

Zola

Zola may be a combination of the name Zoe ('life') with the ending 'la'. However, it is more likely that it is the transferred use of a surname made famous by the French novelist Emile Zola who died in 1902.

Whether used as first name or surname Zola comes from the German word 'zoll', which means 'toll', 'tax' and 'price'.

Variant: Zoe

Unisex names

The concept of unisex names is steeped in history. Back in medieval times, names were translated between languages, and most children were named after religious figures. But while most Romance languages distinguished between masculine and feminine in the way names ended – Alexander and Alexandra, for example, the English didn't. Hence, Alexander would be Alexandra in French, but when translated into English, it remained as Alexander. Medieval names used for girls and boys include Alexander, and also names like Patrick, Basil, Nicholas and Simon.

When French and Latin influences started to creep into English during the following centuries, the feminine endings for these names were adopted, and girls stopped being called Philip, as the daughters of the educated classes served as beacons of their parents' educated status by being given the original Latin/French versions of names, hence Patricia, Juliana, Philippa, etc.

By the 19th century, many new girls ' names were created by adding 'a' or 'ina' suffixes to boys' names, creating the likes of Roberta and Edwina. But in the late 19th and early 20th centuries, a fashion started in the US for shortening girls' names, and making them sound masculine in the process – Jimmie, Jamie, Eddie, etc. By the 1960s, and the arrival of feminism, names like Ashley, Cameron and Alexis were given to girls. Pop culture has further spread this habit, and below are some of the more popular names considered to be gender–free. ∎

Unisex names

Addison	Dusty	Judd	Riley
Aden		Kasey	Robbie
Ainsley	Eddie	Kelly	Ronnie
Alex	Elisha	Kendall	Rowan
Alexis	Emmanuel	Kennedy	Ryan
Andy	Evelyn	Kingsley	
Angel			Sacha
Asa	Fletcher	Lacey	Sage
Asher	Flynn	Lane	Sam
Ashley	Frankie	Lee	Sandy
	Freddie	Leslie	Sawyer
Bailey	Francis	Lindsay	Sean
Beau		Lorne	Shae
Berkeley	Gabriel	Lynn	Sheridan
Beverly	Gale		
Billie	Gerry	Mackenzie	Tara
Blair	Grady	Misha	Tate
Bobby	Greer	Murphy	Tatum
Brady			Tegan
Brooke	Haley	Nat	Terry
	Harley	Nevada	Toby
Cade	Hillary	Nicky	Tracy
Cameron	Hunter	Nikita	Tristan
Carol	Hyatt		Tyler
Casey		Ocean	
Charlie	Indiana		Val
Christy	Ireland	Palmer	Valentine
Cody		Paris	
Connor	Jackie	Pat	Wallis
Corey	Jan		Warner
	Jean	Quinn	Wynne
Darcey	Jermain		
Dale	Jocelyn	Rae	Xerxes
Dallas	Jody	Randy	
Dana	Jordan	Ray	Yancy
Drew	Jordy	Regan	Young

Surnames as first names

Using surnames as first names dates back to 17th century Scotland, when Protestants, newly freed from having to call their offspring after various saints, started to give sons their mother's maiden name as a first name. The idea soon caught on, spreading throughout families, and by the 19th century, parents were looking outside the family circle, using the last names of various notaries and heroes as their children's first names. Military heroes and, for those with more pious inclinations, religious figures, all had children named after them.

In keeping with those male-dominated times, most children named in this fashion were boys, but by the 20th century, the practice had spread to girls. However, even now the vast majority of surnames-used-as-first names are boys: Barry, Clifford, Milton and Zane, for example, are all most definitely boys' names. There are some which can now be considered unisex: Ashley, Casey, Lindsay and Mackenzie.

Others that might formerly have been thought of as boys' names are now being used for girls as well, with the likes of Hunter and Dylan popping up on the birth certificates of female children. There are also a few which are specifically female, including Audrey, Kimberly, Shelby and Tiffany. The following are a list of common last names found as first names. ∎

Surnames as first names

Addison	Cambell	Darryl	Hadley
Ainsley	Cameron	Dawson	Hailey
Allen	Carlton	Dean	Haley
Alison	Carson	Delaney	Hayley
Anderson	Carter	Denzil	Harley
Avery	Casey	Desmond	Harrison
Alton	Cassidy	Dewitt	Hartley
Ashley	Chance	Dexter	Hogan
Aubrey	Chandler	Dillon	Howard
Audrey	Chase	Dylan	Hudson
Austin	Chauncey	Douglas	Hunter
	Chester	Drake	
Bailey	Clark	Dudley	Irving
Baron	Clayton		
Barrie	Clifford	Earl	Jamison
Barrington	Clifton	Elmer	Jameson
Barry	Clinton	Emerson	Jackson
Bentley	Clive	Everard	Jefferson
Beverly	Cody	Everett	Jensen
Beverley	Colby		Jenson
Blake	Cole	Forrest	Johnson
Bradley	Colton	Franklin	Jordan
Brady	Cooper		
Brandon	Corey	Garnet	Kayley
Brent	Cory	Garrett	Keith
Brewster	Courtney	Garrison	Kelly
Bria	Craig	Gary	Kelsey
Bryan	Curtis	Gerard	Kendall
Bronson		Glanville	Kennedy
Brooke	Dale	Glenn	Kent
Bruce	Dallas	Gordon	Kenton
Bryson	Dalton	Graham	Kerry
Byron	Dana	Grant	Kimberly
	Darby	Grayson	Kirk
Cade	Darcy	Greyson	Kyle
Calvin	Darrell	Grover	

Porter
Preston

Quentin

Ramsay
Randall
Riley
Rodney
Roosevelt
Ross
Roy
Royston
Russell
Rutherford
Ryan

Sawyer
Scott
Shane
Shawn
Shelby
Sheldon
Sheridan
Sherman
Shirley
Shannon
Skylar
Spencer
Stacey
Stanley
Stuart
Sullivan

Tanner
Tate

Taylor
Todd
Tiffany
Tracey
Travis
Trevor
Troy
Truman
Tucker
Turner
Tyler
Tyson

Van
Vance
Vaughan
Vernon

Wade
Walker
Wallace
Warren
Wayne
Wendell
Wesley
Whitney
Wilbur
Willard
Willis
Wilson
Winston
Woodrow
Wyatt
Wynne

Zane

Lacey
Lance
Lane
Laurence/
Lawrence
Lawson
Lee
Leigh
Leland
Leslie
Lesley
Lester
Lindsay
Linsey
Logan
Lucas
Luther
Lyle

Mackenzie
McKenzie
Macy
Madison
Marshall

Mason
Maxwell
McKinley
Meredith
Michael
Millard
Milton
Mitchell
Morgan
Morris
Mortimer
Morton
Nelson
Neville

Odell
Otis

Page/
Paige
Parker
Percival
Perry
Peyton

Place names as first names

Place names can make excellent first names, especially if the name chosen will have some meaning to the child, i.e. being the place their parents met, where they were born, or, in extreme cases, where they were conceived. It may be a country, county, town, river, desert or mountain range.

Not all place names work, however, as a child named Scunthorpe or Bognor is less likely to take to the name than one named Atlanta or Paris.

The following are a list of names inspired by places, most are unisex, although some may suit boys better than girls, or vice versa.

Adelaide	China	Iona	Nile
Africa	Clyde	Ireland	
Alabama		Israel	Odessa
Albi	Dakota		Olympia
Arabia	Dallas	Jamaica	Ohio
Arizona	Derry	Jordan	
Asia	Denver		Paris
Aspen	Devon	Kelly	Persia
Atlanta		Kent	Phoenix
Austin	Eden	Kenya	
Avalon		Kerry	Sahara
	Florence	Kingston	Savannah
Brazil	Florida	Korea	Shannon
Brittany			Sienna
Brooklyn	Geneva	Lincoln	Sierra
	Georgia	London	Sydney
Cairo		Loiusiana	
Caledonia	Hamilton	Lourdes	Texas
Camden	Houston		
Carolina	Hudson	Manchester	Valencia
Catalina		Memphis	Venetia
Chelsea	Idaho	Milan	Verona
Chester	India		Vienna
Cheyenne	Indiana	Nevada	Virginia

Boys

Aaron

Although the exact meaning of the name is unknown it is believed to come from the Hebrew for 'mountain of strength' or 'brightness'. Its Arabic meaning is 'messenger'.

In the Old Testament Aaron was the older brother of Moses who became the founder the Jewish priesthood. As well as being the first high priest of the Israelites, Aaron was also his brother's spokesman.

Variants: Aharon, Ahron, Ari, Arnie, Aron, Arron, Haroun, Ron, Ronnie

Abdul

Although Abdul is considered to be an independent name in its own right, it is actually a short form of Abdullah, which means 'servant of Allah' in Arabic.

Variants: Ab, Abdal, Abdel, Abdullah

Abel

Abel is another well-known Biblical name that is of uncertain origin. Two Hebrew meanings have been suggested as possible interpretations – 'son' or 'source of God'. It is also thought to mean 'herdsman'.

In the Bible Abel is the second son of Adam and Eve who is murdered by his older brother Cain. Abel is also significant to the Muslim faith because in the Koran it is his non-violent attitude – his refusal to defend himself – which is emphasized.

Variants: Abelard, Abeles, Abell, Able

Abir

In Hebrew this short name has a significant meaning – 'strong' and 'heroic'.

Variants: Abira, Amoz, Amzi, Azaz, Aziz, Aziza

Abner

In the Old Testament Abner was King Saul's cousin and the commander of his army. In Hebrew his name means 'father of

light' or 'my father is light'. In Britain the name was popular after the Reformation.
Variants: Ab, Abbey, Abby

Abraham
In the Christian, Jewish and Islamic faiths Abraham is the spiritual father who connects the three religions. In the Old Testament Abraham was originally known by the name Abram, which in Hebrew meant 'exalted father'. He and his elderly wife longed for a child. Unable to give her husband what he desired most, Sara suggested that he conceive a child with her Egyptian attendant, Hagar. The result was Ishmael, who went on to become the forefather of the Arab race.

To signify that Abram would indeed have a child with his wife Sara, God changed Abram's name to Abraham, 'father of many' or 'father of a multitude'. Sara became Sarah. Both names mean 'prince'. The couple went on to have a son, Isaac, who fathered the twins Esau and Jacob. The latter's children later gave birth to the 12 tribes of Israel.

This popular Jewish name was also favoured by Christians in 17th century England. In North America the name is associated with the twice-elected President Abraham Lincoln, who fought to preserve the Union during the Civil War. The Islamic version of Abraham is Ibrahim.
Variants: Ab, Abe, Abi, Abie, Abrahan, Bram, Ham, Ibrahim

Absalom
Absalom was a popular name in the Middle Ages. Taken from the Old Testament, it was the name of one of King David's sons who fell out of favour with his father after he brought about the murder of his brother Amnon. Absalom took revenge on Amnon for raping their sister Tamar.

The name was later used by the 17th century British poet and playwright John Dryden in his poem *Absalom and Achitophel* (1681). The name means 'father of peace' in Hebrew.
Variants: Absolun, Axel

Ackley
This name is taken from the Middle English words for 'acorn' and 'meadow'. Thus Ackley means 'acorn meadow' or 'meadow of oak trees'.
Variant: Ackerley

Adam
The name Adam has long been a favourite with Christians and Jews alike. According to the Book of Genesis in the Bible, it was the name of the first man created by God. It is appropriate that the Hebrew meaning of Adam is 'earth', for this holy text says that God created him from a handful of dirt. The name also comes from the Hebrew for 'mankind' and 'red earth'.

Adam has been used as a name by early Christians from the 7th century. Widespread in Celtic areas such as Wales and Ireland, the name has been popular throughout the English-speaking world since the 1960s.
Variants: Ad, Adamo, Adamson, Addie, Adom, Edom

Adolph
The Old Germanic name Aethelwulf was used in England from the 11th century onwards. It was formed from the elements 'athal', meaning 'noble', and 'wolfa', which means 'wolf'. The implication was that the bearer would be like a 'noble wolf' guarding the home and family.

It was the House of Hanover – whose period of British rule began with the reign of King George I in 1714 – that brought the Latin form of Aethelwulf, Adolph, with them.

The popularity of the name in Britain plummeted during the 1930s with the rise of the Austrian-born German dictator Adolf Hitler. The name has been associated with the Nazi leader ever since.
Variants: Ad, Adolf, Adolfo, Adolphe, Adolpho, Aethelwulf, Dolf, Dolph, Dolphus

Adrian

The Adriatic Sea and the neighbouring northern Italian town of Adria are believed to be the sources of the name Adrian. Both place names derive their meaning from the Latin word 'ater' or 'black' in English – a direct reference to the black sand of the beaches in that area. In the days of the Roman Empire a man from Adria or Hadria was known as Adrianus or Hadrianus.

The name Hadrian was born by the Roman Emperor Publius Aelius Hadrianus who ruled from 117 to 138. During that time the defensive border Hadrian's Wall was built in the north of England to separate that province from Scotland. Hadrian was also the adopted name of the only Englishman to head the Roman Catholic Church. Born Nicholas Breakspear in the 12th century, Hadrian IV – also known as Adrian IV – was Pope from 1154 until 1159. (See also Adrienne.)
Variants: Ade, Adriano, Adrien, Hadrian

Adriel

In Hebrew this name means 'God's majesty' or 'one of God's congregation'.
Variants: Adri, Adrial

Aelwyn

More than one theory exists to explain the origin of this name. It may have been derived from two Old English first names – Athelwine, 'noble friend', and Alfwine 'elf friend'. After the Norman Conquest both names became Alwin, which can also be spelt with a 'y' replacing the 'i'. In Wales Alwen and Alwyn also mean 'great', 'child' or 'brow' and 'white, fair'. An alternative Old English interpretation is 'friend of all'.
Variants: Alvan, Alvy, Alvyn, Alwen, Alwin, Alwyn

Ahmed

This Arabic name means 'greatly adored' or 'praised the most'. The character Prince Ahmed appears in the classic tale *Arabian Nights*.
Variants: Ahmad

Aidan

In the 7th century, St Aidan was a missionary from Ireland who helped to convert the north of England. His name comes from the Irish Gaelic for 'little fiery one', but it also has Latin roots, which give it the meaning 'to help'.

The use of Aidan as a given name was revived during the 20th century. It was primarily bestowed upon boys but has also been given to girls.

Variants: Aiden, Aden, Aodán, Aodham, Edan, Eden

Ainsley

Today Ainsley is considered to be a boy's name, but during the 12th century it was given to children of both sexes. It is a Scottish name that was once a surname associated with a powerful family. They derived it from a place name – possibly Annesley in Nottinghamshire or Ansley in Warwickshire. Ainsley, therefore, comes from the Old English word 'ān' – 'one', 'only' or 'own' – and 'lēah', which means 'wood', 'clearing' or 'field'. Thus the name means 'my meadow or land'.

Variants: Ainie, Ainslee, Ainslie

Alan

The exact meaning of this name is unclear. It is a known Old Celtic name that appeared in early Welsh records and means 'harmony'. It may also come from the Irish Gaelic for 'good looking' and 'cheerful'.

The use of the name in Britain died out only to be reintroduced by the Normans shortly after their conquest of England. Indeed, two members of William the Conqueror's court bore the name – the Count of Brittany and the Earl of Richmond. The Breton meaning of Alan is 'rock'.

Variants: Al, Allan, Allen, Alleyn, Alyn

Alban

Although this name was borne by the first British martyr its use as a given name was not widespread until the 19th century. Alban was the name of a 3rd century Roman soldier who was born a pagan, but offered shelter to a priest during a time of Christian persecution. Under the priest's instructions he converted to Christianity and when his fellow Roman soldiers came to seize his house guest, he swapped clothes with the priest and allowed them to take him instead. Alban was executed in the priest's place. The town where he lived, Verulamium, is now known as St Albans in his honour.

Alban's name means 'white', 'man from the town of Alba' or 'from Alba Longa' in Latin. Alba Longa was a Roman city.
Variants: Al, Alba, Albany, Alben, Albin, Albion

Albert
When Prince Albert of Saxe-Coburg-Gotha married his cousin Queen Victoria in 1840, he not only had a major influence on her rule but on the popularity of the name Albert in Britain. Its use became more widespread once it was associated with the Queen's consort.

Albert comes from the Old High German name Adelbrecht, which consists of the elements 'adal' and 'beraht' meaning 'noble' and 'bright' or 'noble' and 'illustrious'.
Variants: Adalbert, Adel, Adelbert, Al, Albe, Alberto, Bert, Berty, Burt

Aldous
This rare name comes from the Old German for 'old' and may have been a short form of various Norman names including Aldebrand, Aldemund and Alderan. All were formed using the German element 'ald' – 'old'. It was borne by the British novelist Aldous Huxley, who wrote *Brave New World* in 1932.
Variants: Aldan, Alden, Aldin, Aldis, Aldo, Aldos, Aldus

Aled
Aled is the name of a river in Wales. It means 'offspring' or 'noble brow' in Welsh.
Variants: Al

Alexander

According to Greek mythology the first bearer of this name was the Trojan prince Paris – the man who caused the 10-year Trojan War by abducting Helen, the Queen of Sparta. He was given the nickname Alexander because he helped to defend the flock of some shepherds. They called him Alexandros, which means 'defender of men'. The name has been popular ever since.

It appeared in the Bible, was borne by a number of early saints and belonged to Alexander the Great, the King of Macedon who lived from 356 to 323 BC. He is credited with spreading the name throughout the world because he conquered Persia, Egypt and his realm touched the borders of India.

The name is especially popular in Scotland where it is associated with Scottish royalty. Three kings of Scotland bore the name Alexander. It was also bestowed upon more than one Tsar of Russia. In that region, Sacha is a pet form of Alexander.
Variants: Al, Alec, Aleksander, Alex, Alexei, Alexis, Ali, Alistair, Sacha, Sandy

Alfred

The name Alfred was frequently used in Britain before the arrival of the Normans in 1066. Until that time its most famous bearer was Alfred the Great the celebrated king of Wessex – a kingdom that stretched from Sussex to Devon. It was this 9th century king who was credited with building Britain's first navy and forcing the Danes out of southern England.

Although the name Alfred was adopted by the Normans, who used it in the form of Avery, it fell out of favour during the 16th century. It was the Victorians – fascinated by Anglo-Saxon and medieval culture, history and folklore – who revived the name.

Alfred comes from the Old English for 'good counsel' or 'elf counsel'.
Variants: Alf, Alfie, Fred, Freddie

Algernon

It was William de Percy, a companion of William the Conqueror,

who brought the name Algernon to British shores at the time of the Norman Conquest. Most of the Normans were clean-shaven, but Percy had a moustache. Algernon was his nickname, which came from the Old French for 'with whiskers' or 'with a moustache'.
Variants: Alger, Algie, Algy

Alistair
The name Alistair has enjoyed popularity in Scotland for many centuries. It is an alternative spelling of the Gaelic name Alasdair, which is a version of the Greek name Alexandros – more commonly known as Alexander. Like Alexander, Alistair means 'defender of men' or 'warrior'.
Variants: Alasdair, Alastair, Alexander, Alister

Alphonse
Alphonse comes from the Old High German for 'noble' and 'ready' or 'apt'. In Spain the name is associated with royalty as it was borne by more than one king of Castile – a former Spanish kingdom.
Variants: Al, Alfonso, Alphonso, Alphonsine, Fons, Fonsie, Fonz

Ambrose
In Greek the name Ambrose means 'divine' or 'immortal'. It comes from the same root as the word 'ambrosia', the food of the gods and goddesses according to Greek mythology.
Variants: Ambie, Ambros, Ambrosio, Ambrosius, Brose

Amir
This Arabic name means 'prince'.
Variant: Emir

Amos
Amos was the Old Testament prophet who predicted that Judah and Israel would be destroyed if the people did not change their ways. The Hebrew meaning of his name is 'to carry', 'bearer of a burden' or 'troubled'.

Andrew

Andrew is a name that has been borne by more than one saint, including the patron saint of Scotland and Russia. In the Bible the Galilean fisherman Andrew was the first of Christ's Apostles to be called to join him. He was accompanied by his brother, Simon Peter. The name is of Greek origin and means 'manly'.
Variants: Anders, Anderson, André, Andreas, Andrei, Andres, Andy

Angus

Angus is another name that has a special place in the hearts of the Scots for it belonged to one of the Irish founders of their nation. Angus is a form of the Gaelic name Aonghus, which means 'one choice'.
Variants: Aengus, Ennis, Gus

Anthony

Anthony comes from the Old Roman family name Antonius. The most famous bearer of the surname was Marcus Antonius, better known as Mark Antony. A soldier and statesmen, he was a follower of Julius Caesar who went on to co-rule the Republic following Caesar's assassination.

The exact origin of the name is unclear but is thought to have been derived from the Greek for 'flourishing'. The Romans believed that it meant 'inestimable' or 'priceless'.

The name has since been borne by a number of saints and early Christians, including St Antony, the patron saint of lost property. The 'h' was added to the name in the 16th century.
Variants: Antoine, Anton, Antonio, Antony, Toni, Tonio, Tony

Anton

Anton is the French form of the name Anthony, which, during Roman times, was known as Antonius. Like its source the exact meaning of Anton is unknown. It may come from the Greek for 'flourishing' or has the Roman meaning of 'priceless'.

Anton is now commonly used in the English-speaking world.
Variants: Anthony, Antoine, Antonio, Antony, Toni, Tonio, Tony

Archibald
This name comes from the Germanic for 'noble' and 'bold'. In England a similar name, Ercanbald ('very bold'), was used. It was James VI of Scotland who brought the Scottish variant to England when he ascended the English throne in 1603. He brought with him his jester Archie Armstrong.
Variants: Archie, Archy, Baldie

Ardal
Ardal is an Irish name that stems from the words for 'high valour'. It may also mean 'bear'.
Variants: Ardgal, Ardghal

Arden
The name Arden comes from the Latin for 'to be on fire', 'ablaze', 'sparkle', 'glitter' and 'dazzle'. It was used by Shakespeare as a place name – the Forest of Arden – in his comedy *As You Like It* (1599).
Variants: Ard, Arda, Ardie, Ardin, Ardy

Argus
According to Greek mythology Argus was a giant who had 100 eyes and was the servant of Hera, wife of Zeus. Jealous of his affair with the nymph Io, she sent Argus to watch over Io, but her plan was foiled when Zeus instructed Hermes to kill the giant. After his death Hera decorated the tail of a peacock with his eyes.

Unsurprisingly, the Greek meaning of Argus is 'highly observant' or 'bright-eyed'.

Arnold
Arnold is a Germanic name that was adopted by the Normans and brought to England as Arnaud. This name, which means 'eagle' and 'rule', was a popular surname in Britain during the Middle Ages before it died out, only to re-emerge as the first name Arnold in the 19th century.
Variants: Armand, Armant, Arn, Arnald, Arnaud, Arnie, Arny

Arthur

More than one theory exists to explain the origin of the name Arthur. It is thought to stem from the Greek for 'bear-keeper' or the Celtic for 'bear'. Equally it could mean 'stone' or 'rock' in Irish Gaelic, 'noble' in Welsh or 'follower of Thor' in Norse. A link between Arthur and the Roman family name Artorius has also been suggested.

During the reign of Queen Victoria, Arthur became the name of choice for many parents. Another reason for its popularity is that it was the first name of the first Duke of Wellington, Arthur Wellesley, who defeated Napoleon in 1815 at the Battle of Waterloo. The Duke's name was later bestowed upon his godson, Prince Arthur, whose mother was Queen Victoria herself.

However, another Arthur had also captured the imagination of Victorian parents – King Arthur, the mythical 6th century British figure who, according to legend had a court at Camelot, and presided over the Knights of the Round Table.

Variants: Art, Arth, Artie, Arty

Asher

In the Bible Asher was one of Jacob's 12 sons and one of the children that he had with his first wife Leah. His mother gave him the name Asher, which means 'happy' in Hebrew. It is also thought to mean 'martial', while the Swahili interpretation is 'born during Asher (a Muslim month)'.

Ashley

This unisex name has enjoyed popularity in North America and Australia. Its growing use from the 1940s onwards may be explained by the success of Margaret Mitchell's 1936 novel, *Gone with the Wind*, and the Hollywood epic made of the book in 1939. Ashley Wilkes was the object of Scarlett O'Hara's affection, if not obsession. His name comes from the Old English for 'ash' and 'wood'. Hence originally it may have been given to someone who lived either in or near an ash wood.

Variants: Ashlie, Ashly

Ashton

Like Ashley, Ashton is a name with Old English roots that can be given to children of either sex. It is derived from the words 'æsc', meaning 'ash-tree', and 'tūn' ('enclosure' or 'settlement'). Hence the name means 'settlement where ash trees grow' or 'dweller on the ash tree farm'.

Auberon

This Old French name is believed to be of Germanic (Frankish) origin. It means 'noble' and 'like a bear'. It is also a pet form of Aubrey, which is related to Alberic – the name of the Scandinavian king of the elves.
Variants: Alberic, Aubery, Oberon

Aubrey

The Norman-French name Aubrey comes from the Germanic name Alberic, which means 'elf-ruler'. The name enjoyed some popularity during the Middle Ages but its use subsequently declined only to be revived during the 19th century.
Variants: Alberic, Alberich, Aubary, Auberon, Aubri, Aubry

Augustus

Augustus was the name of the first emperor of Rome – Gaius Julius Caesar Octavianus. Emperor Augustus, who was the grandnephew and adopted son of Julius Caesar, acquired the name in 27 BC. His successors also bore the title and Augustus eventually came to mean 'majesty'. It also means 'great' and 'magnificent'.

Augustine, a variant of Augustus, was borne by the great Saint Augustine of Hippo and also by another early saint St Augustine who converted King Ethelbert of Kent to Christianity and became the first Archbishop of Canterbury.
Variants: August, Augustine, Austen, Austyn, Gus, Gussie

Aurelius

The Roman family name Aurelius comes from the Latin for

'golden'. It was adopted by the Roman Emperor and philosopher Marcus Aurelius who ruled the empire from 161 to 180 AD. The name was also borne by several early saints.
Variants: Aurea, Aurek, Aurel, Aurelio, Aurelo, Aury

Avi
This name comes from the Hebrew for 'my father'. It is traditionally used in reference to 'God'. Thus the name Avidan means 'God of wisdom and justice', Avidor stands for 'father of a generation' and Aviel is interpreted as 'God is my father'.
Variants: Abi, Av, Avodal

Axel
The name Axel has two meanings. In German it stands for 'oak' or 'small oak tree'. But it may also come from the Scandinavian for 'divine reward'. It is also a variant of the Biblical name Absalom.
Variants: Absalom, Aksel

Azaria
The name Azaria was another favourite of the 17th century Puritans probably because it was the name of a Biblical prophet. In Hebrew the name means 'God is my help'.
Variants: Azariah, Azriel

Bailey
See Bailey in the Girls' section.

Baldwin
This Old German name was adopted by the Normans who brought it to England. It is the combination of two words 'balda', meaning 'bold', and 'wini', 'friend'. Thus, Baldwin means 'courageous friend'.
Variants: Baldawin, Baudoin, Bawden, Boden, Bodkin, Bowden

Balthazar
Balthazar is said to be the name of one of the three wise men

who came to visit baby Jesus bringing him gifts of gold, frankincense and myrrh.

In Hebrew Balthazar means 'may Bel (God) protect the king'. It was popular in Britain during the Middle Ages.
Variants: Balthasar, Belshazzer

Bancroft
The Middle English meaning of this name is 'bean' and 'small field' or 'small holding'. Thus, Bancroft means 'bean field'.

Barclay
Barclay comes from Berkeley, a place in Gloucestershire. In Old English it means 'birch-tree' and 'wood' or 'clearing'. It is also the name of a powerful Scottish family.

Barnabas
This Biblical name has been used in Britain since the 13th century. In the New Testament Barnabas was an early Christian who assisted St Paul in spreading the tenets of the faith through Asia Minor. The two men also took Christianity to Cyprus.

The Aramaic meaning of this name is 'son of consolation' or 'son of exhortation'. Barnaby is a popular short form.
Variants: Barn, Barnabe, Barnaby, Barnie

Barry
In the 20th century this name became well-known and was widely used, especially in Australia. However, until the 1800s use of the name Barry was largely confined to Ireland. It is from Ireland – and Wales – that the name derives its meaning.

There are four theories of the origin of Barry. One suggests that it comes from the Gaelic name Bearrach, which means 'spear' or 'good marksman'. Another theory is that Barry comes from the Welsh for 'son of Harry'. Alternatively it could be a short form of the Irish name Finbar, which means 'fair head'. Finally, Barry may have been taken from a Welsh place name – Barry Island – 'bar' meaning 'dune' or 'mound'.

B

Variants: Bari, Barnard, Barnett, Barra, Barrie, Barrington, Barrymore, Baz, Bazza, Finbar

Bartholomew
In Hebrew Bartholomew simply means 'son of Talmai'. Talmai is the surname of Nathanial, one of Christ's Apostles, and it means 'abounding in furrows'.
Variants: Bart, Bartel, Bartholomieu, Bartlett, Bartley, Bate, Tolly, Tolomieu, Tolomey

Basil
Widely associated with the green herb, 'basil' it also comes from the Greek for 'royal' or 'kingly'. It also has an Irish Gaelic meaning – 'war'.

An early Christian bore the name in the 4th century. The bishop and theologian St Basil the Great was not the only member of his family to be canonised. Six of his relatives also received sainthood – his grandmother, his parents, elder sister and two younger brothers.
Variants: Bas, Basie, Basile, Baz, Bazza, Brasil, Vas, Vasil

Baxter
Originally used as a surname, Baxter comes from the Old English for 'baker'. A feminine equivalent of this name existed during the Middle Ages, but today Baxter is usually given to boys.

Beasley
This name comes from the Old English for 'field of peas'.
Variants: Peasley

Beau
The French meaning of the name Beau is 'handsome', making it the male equivalent of the girl's name Belle, which means 'beautiful'. A young woman's suitor is also traditionally known as her 'beau'.

However in Hanoverian Britain the name Beau became associated with a one-time friend of the Prince Regent. George Bryan Brummell was a fashionable man, well known for his outrageous style of dress. Beau was his nickname and eventually it was used in reference to any 'dandyish' young man obsessed with beautiful clothes. In 1816, after his friendship with the Prince of Wales ended and he had run up a number of gambling debts, Brummell fled England. He died penniless on the Continent in 1840.

Beau is also the short form of the name Beauregard, which means 'handsome look'. This name was borne by the Confederate general Pierre Gustave Toutant Beauregard who successfully defended the southern city of Charleston during the American Civil War. In the south Beauregard was bestowed upon children in his honour.

Variants: Beauregard

Bede

In 1899 the Venerable Bede was canonized and named a doctor of the Catholic Church by Pope Leo XIII. It is a title that underscores the importance of the work of this gentle Benedictine monk and priest.

St Bede, who lived from 673 until 735, was an author, historian, theologian and one of the most influential writers of his time. In particular *The Ecclesiastical History of the English People*, is one of the most valuable historical works.

His name comes from the Middle English for 'prayer'.

Variant: Bedivere

Benedict

The Latin meaning of Benedict is 'blessed'. The name comes from the word 'benedicere', which means 'to bless', 'speak well of' or 'praise'.

Fifteen popes and a number of saints bore this name, which could explain its widespread use throughout the ages. One such bearer was an Italian monk and hermit who founded the first

Benedictine monastery in Monte Cassino, Italy in 529.
Variants: Ben, Benedicto, Benes, Beniton, Bennett, Benny, Dick, Dixie

Bentley
Today this name is widely associated with the expensive type of car. However it was originally a surname that was derived from a number of place names throughout England. Bentley comes from the Old English words 'beonet', 'bent grass', and 'leah', which means 'wood' or 'clearing'. Thus the name means 'place where there is bent grass'. Another Old English meaning of the name has been suggested – 'to exist' or 'to become'.

Charles Dickens used the name for a character in his novel *Great Expectations* (1860-61).
Variants: Ben, Benny, Bently

Bernard
Bernard is an Old French name that is of Germanic origin. It is derived from two words meaning 'bear' and 'hardy, brave or strong'. Hence Bernard means 'to be as bold or brave as a bear'. An Old English form of the name existed in Britain before the Normans arrived bringing their variant that became Bernard.

The popularity of the name may have been influenced by two holy men who lived in medieval Europe. St Bernard of Clairvaux was a French abbot, theologian and monastic reformer who criticised the luxurious lifestyle of his contemporaries. Another St Bernard, of Montjoux, founded hospices on each of the Alpine passes that bear his name. He died in 1008 and later become the patron saint of mountaineers and skiers. The breed of Alpine rescue dogs is named after him.
Variants: Barnard, Barnet, Barney, Bernardo, Bernhard, Bernhardt, Bernie, Björn

Björn
Björn is the Scandinavian version of Bernard, which has the Germanic meaning of 'bear' and 'strength'.
Variants: Bernard, Bjorn

Blain

Blain comes from the Gaelic word for 'yellow', thus the name Blain may have originated as a nickname for someone with blond hair. Another Irish Gaelic meaning of the name is 'narrow' or 'servant of St Blane' – an early Celtic saint who lived during the 6th century. The name is given to children of both sexes.

Variants: Blaine, Blane, Blayne

Blair

This Scottish surname was originally a place name. It comes from the Gaelic for 'plain', 'field' or 'battle' and is taken to mean 'marshy plain'.

Although Blair can be given to children of either sex, in North America it is frequently given to girls.

Variants: Blaire, Blayre

Blake

Blake comes from the Old English for two words that are directly opposed to each other – 'black' and 'white'. In that language the word 'blæc' means 'black' and 'blāc' means 'pale' or 'white'. Thus Blake was originally a nickname for someone with fair hair and pale skin and also for someone who had a dark complexion.

Variants: Blanchard, Blanco

Benjamin

In the Bible Benjamin was the youngest and favourite son of Jacob. His mother, Jacob's second wife Rachel, died giving birth to him. Like his brothers he went on to head one of the 12 tribes of Israel.

This popular Jewish name means 'son of my right hand' and 'son of the south' in Hebrew. During the 16th century – a time when giving children Old Testament names was in vogue – Benjamin became a favourite among Christian parents.

Variants: Ben, Benjy, Bennie, Benny

Bodi
This Hungarian name means 'may God protect the king'.

Bonamy
Bonamy comes from the French for 'good friend'.
Variants: Bonaro, Boni, Bunn

Boris
The name comes from the Slavonic for 'battle' or 'stranger'. It also has the Tartar meaning of 'small'.

The patron saint of Moscow is called Boris, which is also the short form of the Russian name Borislav meaning 'battle' and 'glory'.
Variants: Borislav

Boyd
Boyd is the name of a clan in Scotland. It comes from the Gaelic for 'yellow hair'.
Variants: Bow, Bowen, Bowie

Brad
Brad shares the Irish meaning of Bradley – 'descendant of Brádach'. The Old English interpretation of the name is 'wide meadow'.

Brad is also the pet form of Braden, which comes from the Old English for 'to broaden', 'make spacious' or 'plain spoken'. It also means 'to be broad minded'. (See also Brady.)
Variants: Bradd, Bradford, Bradleigh, Braden, Bradley, Brady

Brady
Like Bradley, the name Brady comes from the Gaelic for 'descendant of Brádach'. The exact meaning of Brádach is unknown although it is thought to come from the word for 'large-chested'. Brady also comes from the Old English for 'to broaden'.
Variants: Brad, Bradd, Bradleigh, Bradley

Boys

Brandon

As a variant of the Irish name Brendan, Brandon has a rather inauspicious meaning – 'stinking hair'. Nevertheless the name was borne by two 6th-century Irish saints, one of whom was said to have sailed to America long before Christopher Columbus.

The name Brandon has more than one meaning. It comes from the Old English for 'broom' and 'hill'. However the Middle English meaning is 'torch', 'fire' or 'sword'.

Variants: Branden, Brandt, Brant, Brendan, Brent

Brian

This Celtic name was borne by a High King of Ireland who reigned during the 11th century. Known as Brian Boru, he successfully drove the Viking invaders out of his homeland. His name comes from the Old Celtic for 'high' or 'noble' and the Irish Gaelic for 'strong', 'hill' and 'elevated'.

The name Brian was brought to England during the Middle Ages by the Celtic-speaking Bretons, but it is also linked to the classical world. It comes from the Greek for 'strong' and, according to legend, the name Briareos was borne by one of the offspring of Uranus and the earth goddess Gaea.

Variants: Briant, Briar, Bryan, Bryant

Brent

During the 1970s and 1980s the name Brent enjoyed popularity among parents in Britain and North America. Both a surname and a first name, it was originally a place name in England.

Its Celtic meaning is 'high place' or 'hill' but the Old English interpretation is 'burned'.

Variants: Brendt, Brenten, Brenton

Brett

This name comes from the Old French for 'a Breton or Briton' and was originally used in England following the Norman Conquest as a way of identifying the newly-arrived Bretons.

Variants: Bret, Brit, Briton, Britton, Bretton

Brice

The name Brice has more than one meaning. It comes from the German for 'rich' and 'wealthy', but it also means 'powerful ruler'. The Welsh interpretation of the name is 'dappled'.

A 5th century bearer of the name was St Brice who became the bishop of Tours. His fame may have helped to encourage the use of the name, which today enjoys popularity in North America where it is given to children of either sex.

Variants: Bryce, Bryson, Bryston

Brock

The Old English meaning of the name Brock is 'badger'. In children's stories the character of a badger is traditionally called Brock.

Variants: Badger, Braxton, Brook

Bruce

Although popular in modern-day Australia its roots stretch back to the time of the Normans. Its exact meaning is uncertain, but Bruce may come from the French for 'wood' or 'copse'. It was the name of a Norman feudal lord, a relative of whom came to Britain with William the Conqueror.

Robert the Bruce was a descendant of this Norman feudal lord but his fame is connected with Scotland, not France. In 1306 Robert the Bruce, also known as Robert I, secured Scotland's independence from England.

Variants: Brucey, Brucie, Bruis, Brus

Bruno

Like Brock the name Bruno is traditionally used in children's stories as a Christian name for a particular animal – a bear. This is fitting because the German meaning of the name is 'bear' or 'brown like a bear'. Bruno became popular throughout the English-speaking world when German immigrants took the name to North America with them.

Variants: Bronson, Bruin, Bruna, Bruns

Brynn

A unisex name, Brynn comes from the Welsh for 'hill'. It is also a short form of the name Brynmor – a place name in Gwynedd, Wales which means 'big hill'.
Variants: Brin, Brinn, Bryne, Brynmor, Bryn, Brynne

Bryson

Bryson is a variant of the name Brice which means 'rich, wealthy' and 'powerful ruler' in German. It also shares the Welsh meaning of the name, 'dappled'. (See also Brice.)

However, Bryson derives its meaning from another root, the Irish Gaelic language. It is the Anglicised version of the surname Ó Briosáin, which itself was another form of Ó Muirgheasán – 'descendant of Muirgheasán'. The personal name Muirgheasán means 'sea' and 'vigour'.
Variants: Brice, Bryce

Buck

In English the word 'buck' has taken on numerous meanings. It still has the Old English meaning of 'stag', 'male deer' and 'he-goat'. It is also used in North America as a slang term for 'dollar'. Furthermore, to say that a man has the qualities of a young 'buck' is to say that he possesses the robust spiritedness of an animal. This word is also now used as a boy's name.

Bud

The name Bud comes from 'buddy', the English for 'friend' or 'brother'. Like Buck, this vocabulary word is given to boys as a nickname and is sometimes bestowed upon them as a first name.

The American comedian and actor Bud Abbott was one half of the popular screen pairing Abbott and Costello. He was born William Alexander Abbott in 1895. His countryman, the musician Buddy Holly, born Charles Hardin Holly in 1936, also took this name.
Variants: Budd, Buddy

Burgess

This name comes from the Late Latin for 'fortified place'. In Old French it was used to describe a free man in a borough or town. It was also once the name for a member of parliament who represented his local area.
Variants: Burgiss

Burr

The Middle English meaning of this name is 'rough edge', but the Scandinavian interpretation is 'youth'.
Variants: Burbank, Burrell, Burris, Burton

Burt

Burt is a variant of Bert, which is the short form of a variety of names ranging from Albert and Bertram to Gilbert and Robert. It comes from the Old English for 'bright'.
Variants: Albert, Bert, Bertram, Cuthbert, Egbert, Gilbert, Herbert, Lambert, Osbert, Robert

Burton

Burton comes from the Old English words 'burh' and 'tūn' and means 'fortress' and 'enclosure' or 'fortified place' and 'settlement'. It is both a surname and the name of various places in England.

Buster

In the early days of Hollywood Buster was the screen name of silent movie actor Joseph Francis Keaton. In North America the nickname means 'smasher' or 'breaker'. It comes from the verb 'to bust'.

Byron

In Old English the word 'byre' means 'stall', 'hut' or 'cottage'. Thus Byron comes from the Old English for 'cow shed' or 'cattle herder'.

In Britain the first Lord Byron was the 17th-century supporter of

Charles I who received the title in recognition of his loyalty during the Civil War. His descendent, George Gordon Byron, inherited the baronetcy at the age of 10 although he was best known for his poetry and was one of the standard-bearers of the British Romantic Movement. Nineteenth century boys may have been given the name Byron in his honour.
Variants: Biron, Byram, Byrom

Caesar
Caesar is a Roman family name that became associated with leadership and eventually became a title by which Roman emperors were addressed.

The most famous bearer of this name was the Roman political and military leader Gaius (or Caius) Julius Caesar who was born in 100 BC. It was this Caesar who romanced Cleopatra and made her Queen of Egypt. He invaded Britain in 55 BC.

Several theories exist to explain the meaning of his name. It is thought to come from the Latin for 'to cut', 'blue-grey', 'dark hair', 'long hair' and 'head of hair'.
Variants: Casar, Cesar, César, Cesare, Cesareo, Cezar, Czar, Tsar

Cahil
This Turkish name means 'young' and 'naïve'.

Caleb
In the Bible this name belonged to the man who led the Israelites into the Promised Land alongside Joshua following the death of Moses. Its Hebrew meaning is 'bold' or 'without fear'. The Arabic interpretation is similar – 'brave in victory'.

Caleb also has another Hebrew meaning, 'dog', which apparently symbolises devotion to the Almighty.
Variants: Cal, Cale, Kalb, Kale, Kaleb, Kalev

Callum
Although the two names may not look the same, Callum comes from Columba, a Late Latin personal name that means 'dove'. It

is through Columba that Callum derives its association with Scotland, for it was the Irish saint of that name that used the Scottish isle of Iona as a base for the conversion of that nation. From Columba we also get the name Malcolm, which means 'follower of St Columba'.
Variants: Calum, Colm, Colum, Kallum, Kalum, Malcolm

Calvin
John Calvin was the French-Swiss Protestant theologian whose doctrines were the foundation of Presbyterianism. His beliefs centred upon learning, the belief that God was all powerful and the adherence to a strict moral code. It was from this man that the Calvinist movement derived its name. Religious Nonconformists also bestowed his surname upon their children in his honour.

Its meaning is derived from the French for 'bald' or 'little bald one'.
Variants: Cal, Vin, Vinny

Cameron
This Scottish surname was borne by one of the great Highland clans. Its meaning comes from the Gaelic for 'crooked nose', which may suggest that it was once a nickname given to an ancestor. Today it is bestowed upon children of both sexes.
Variants: Cam, Camaron, Camron, Kam, Kamaron, Kameron, Kamron

Carl
This Old German name is a German and Scandinavian form of Charles, which means 'man'. It can also be spelt with a 'K' as demonstrated in Karl Marx.
Variants: Carlo, Carlos, Karl

Carlton
Carlton is an Old English surname and place name that refers to numerous locations in England. It is derived from two words 'carl', meaning 'free man or peasant', and 'tūn', 'town'

or 'settlement'. Thus Carlton means 'settlement of free men or peasants'.
Variants: Carl, Carleton, Carlson, Charles, Charlton

Carson
Carson is another Scottish surname that has gained currency as a first name, especially in North America. Its exact meaning is unknown but it may be of English derivation, meaning 'son of Carr', or it could have referred to someone who lived in a marsh.

Carter
Carter comes from the Old Norse for 'cart for transporting goods' and 'driver of a cart'. It is a first name derived from a surname, which once indicated an occupational name.

Cary
In the 20th century the name Cary became associated with the British-born American actor Cary Grant who was born Archibald Leach. Grant's stage name is thought to have more than one meaning. It was an English family name that was taken from a number of place names. It is also an Old Celtic river name and comes from the Irish for 'son of the dark one'. Its Welsh meaning is 'castle dweller'. The Latin interpretation is 'much loved' and 'costly'. As a variant of Charles, Cary means 'man'.
Variants: Carey, Charles

Caspian
The British writer C S Lewis used this name for the title character of his 1951 children's novel *Prince Caspian*. The book was the second in his successful *Chronicles of Narnia* series.
   The exact meaning of the name is unclear, but it is the name of the stretch of water known as the Caspian Sea.

Cassius
Before he converted to Islam and became Muhammad Ali, the American boxer, was known as Cassius Marcellus Clay. His

Roman name has been borne by more than one personality in history. One well-known bearer was Gaius Cassius Longinus, who played an important role in the plot to assassinate Julius Caesar.

Cassius comes from the Greek for 'herb' and the Italian for 'cinnamon bark'. In Latin it means 'vain'.
Variants: Case, Casey, Cash, Casius, Cass, Cassie, Cassy, Kas

Cecil
In England the name Cecil is associated with a noble family who rose to prominence during the 16th century. It has more than one meaning, both of which are rooted in the Latin language. For example, Cecil is thought to be the English form of the Old Roman family name Caecilius, which comes from the Latin for 'blind'.

The name is also thought to be the Anglicised version of a Welsh name, Seissylt. Yet this too is merely a variation of a Latin name, this time Sextilius, which comes from Sextus meaning 'sixth'. In Roman times Sextus was bestowed upon the sixth son in a family.

Cecil gained currency as a first name during the 19th century.
Variants: Ceci, Cecile, Cecilio, Cecilius

Cedric
The exact origin of the name Cedric is unknown. One theory is that the name was invented by the Scottish writer Sir Walter Scott for a character in his novel *Ivanhoe* (1819). If that is the case, maybe Scott's inspiration was the name of the founder of Wessex, the Anglo-Saxon kingdom. Hence, sometimes, Cedric is taken to be a misspelling of Cerdic.

Nevertheless, despite this confusion a number of possible meanings for Cedric have emerged. They include 'welcome sight' in Welsh, 'generous pattern' in Celtic and 'friendly' in Old English. Later on in the 19th century the name was used by another writer, Frances Hodgson Burnett, in her work *Little Lord Fauntleroy.*
Variants: Cad, Caddaric, Ced, Cedrych, Cerdic, Ceredic, Rick, Rickie, Ricky

C

Chad

Chad is the modern variant of the Old English name Ceadda, which was borne by a 7th century saint. St Ceadda was known for being humble, holy and for his role as the Bishop of York and Lichfield. The Celtic meaning of his name is 'battle' or 'warrior'. In Old English it means 'martial'.

Chad has been popular in North America since the 1980s.

Variants: Chadd, Chaddie, Chadwick, Chaddy

Chandler

Such is the power of television that for a generation of channel hoppers Chandler will forever be associated with a character from the US sitcom *Friends*. However, the name existed long before the arrival of the fictitious Chandler Bing.

The name probably originally referred to someone's occupation for it comes from the French for 'candle maker' or 'seller of candles'.

Variants: Chan, Chaney, Cheney, Shandler

Charles

The name Charles has long been associated with royalty. Today it is the name of the future king of England, but during the Dark Ages it was also favoured by the Frankish ruling class. For example, Carolus Magnus (Charles the Great) of Charlemagne (771 to 814) founded the Holy Roman Empire.

It was the Normans who brought this Germanic name to Britain in the 11th century and during the Stuart period it became associated with more than one monarch – Charles I, who was overthrown and beheaded, and his son Charles II. Ten French kings have borne the name as have five Swedish rulers.

Charles comes from the Old German for 'man' or 'free man'.

Variants: Carl, Carlos, Carlton, Charlie, Charley, Chas, Charlton, Chaz, Chuck, Karl

Chester

Chester is both a surname and the name of an English city. When the Romans invaded England they created many fortress towns and Chester was one of them. Thus it comes from the Latin for 'fortress, castle' or 'walled town'.

Its use as a first name began during the last century.
Variants: Caster, Castor, Chesleigh, Chesley, Chet, Ches

Chip

Chip is the short form of Christopher, which comes from the Greek – 'one who carries Christ'. It also comes from the name of a Native American tribe – Chippewa.
Variants: Chipper, Christopher

Christian

To identify oneself as a Christian is to say that you are a follower of Jesus Christ. Naturally this is the meaning of the given name, which in Latin is 'Christianus'. However in Greek it means 'anointed one', a direct translation of the Hebrew term 'Messiah'.

Christian has been used as a first name since the Middle Ages.
Variants: Chris, Christiaan, Christiano, Christie, Christien, Kit, Kris, Kristian

Christobal

Christobal is a combination of two words – 'Christ' and 'ball'. Thus it means 'dance of Christ'.
Variants: Cristobal

Christopher

The 3rd century martyr St Christopher is well-known as the patron saint of travellers – and with good reason. According to tradition he acquired the name Christopher after he carried a small boy across a river. The child was unusually heavy and, when asked, explained that he was Jesus Christ who was carrying the weight of the sins of the world. Hence the name Christopher comes from the Greek for 'one who carries Christ'.
Variants: Chip, Chris, Chrissie, Christoph, Christophe, Kester, Kit, Kristofer

Cicero
In Italian this name means 'learned antiquarian' or 'guide for sightseers'. The name was borne by the Roman statesman and orator Marcus Tullius Cicero, who was assassinated in 43 BC.
Variants: Cicerone, Ciceroni, Ciro, Cyrano

Clark
For generations of children, be they comic book readers, cinemagoers or avid television viewers, Clark Kent is the alter ego of the hero Superman. During the 1930s the name was associated with the screen idol Clark Gable, but long before the arrival of the mass media Clark originated as an occupational name. A clerk was someone who earned his living by his ability to read or write. Indeed today a 'clerk' is still a secretary, someone who keeps records or a lay officer of a church.
Variants: Clarke, Claxton

Claude
This name comes from the Roman family name Claudius, which in Latin means 'limping' or 'lame'. It has existed in Britain since the time of Roman occupation. In France its popularity grew because of a 7th century saint who bore the name. (See below.)
Variants: Claudell, Claudian, Claudius, Claus

Claudius
With his limp and stutter Claudius I was an unlikely candidate for the position of Roman Emperor, but this is the role that he assumed from 41 to 54 AD. It was chosen by parents even though the name means 'limp', 'lame', 'crippled' or 'defective'.
Variants: Claude, Claudell, Claudian, Claus

Claus
As a variant of Claudius, Claus means 'limp', 'lame', 'crippled' or 'defective'. (See above.) But it is also a German form of the name Nicholas, which comes from the Greek for 'people's victory'.
Variants: Claude, Claudell, Claudian, Claudius, Klaus, Nicholas

Clay

The name Clay comes from the Old English word for 'clay' or 'fine-grained earth'. As a surname it would have been attached to someone who lived in an area of clay soil. Its use as a first name began in the 19th century.

In North America it is a short form of Clayton, which means 'town on clay land'.

Variants: Clayland, Clayton, Cle, Clea, Cletus, Klay

Clement

Clement Attlee was the name of the leader of the Labour Party who became the British Prime Minister in 1945. His name comes from the Latin for 'kind', 'gentle', 'calm' and 'merciful'.

Variants: Clem, Cleme, Clemen, Clemens, Clemmy

Clinton

In recent years the name Clinton is best known as the surname of the former President of the United States – William 'Bill' Jefferson Clinton, who lead his country from 1993 to 2001. In England the name is also associated with a noble family. Geoffrey de Clinton, who built the Castle of Kenilworth, was chamberlain and treasurer to William I. His family name comes from the Middle English for 'hilltop town'.

In North America Clinton and its variant Clint is used as a first name.

Variant: Clint

Clive

Clive comes from the Old English for 'overhanging rock face', 'cliff' or 'slope'. As a surname it was derived from a number of place names in England. Its transferred use as a first name is owed to the fame of the British soldier and statesman Robert Clive who died in 1774. He was known as Clive of India because of his part in establishing British power in India. Such was his popularity with East India Company employees that some of them named their sons Clive in his honour.

Clive was also the first name of C S Lewis, the author of the series of children's novels *The Chronicles of Narnia*.
Variants: Cleve, Cleveland, Clevey, Clevie, Cliff, Clifton

Clyde
In Scotland the River Clyde runs through the city of Glasgow, but its name has the Celtic meaning 'to wash'. It also comes from the Welsh for 'heard from far away'. As well as being a place name, it is also a surname and a first name that belonged to the 1930s American bank robber, Clyde Barrow, of 'Bonnie and Clyde' fame.
Variants: Cly, Clydesdale, Clywd

Cody
In North America and Australia the name Cody is bestowed upon both boys and girls. However, it was originally an Irish surname that meant 'descendant of a helpful or cheerful person'.
Variants: Codi, Codie

Colbert
Colbert has Old French, Latin and Germanic roots. One theory suggests that it comes from the Latin for 'neck'. Another suggests that the second half of the name is derived from the Old High German for 'bright' or 'shining', while the meaning of the first half is unknown.

Whatever its origin it was brought to Britain by the Normans in the 11th century.
Variants: Cole, Colvert, Culbert

Cole
More than one meaning is attached to the name Cole. It is derived from the Middle English for 'coal', thus the name Colby means 'coal town' and Coleman refers to a 'coal miner'. However, Cole also comes from the Welsh for 'trust'. Furthermore it can be used as pet form of Nicholas, which means 'people's victory' in Greek.

The Scottish king Coel the Adulterous, who ruled during the

6th century, is said to be the inspiration for the nursery rhyme *Old King Cole*.
Variants: Colby, Coleman, Colin, Collie, Collier, Collis, Colton, Colville, Colvin, Nicholas

Colin
As a short form of Nicholas, Colin comes from the Greek for 'people's victory'. But more than one theory exists to explain the origin of this popular name. It is thought to come from the Scottish Gaelic for 'youth' and 'puppy' and from the Irish Gaelic for 'young man'. 'Chieftain' is another Celtic meaning of Colin.

The name is common in Scotland where it is used as an Anglicisation of the Gaelic name 'Cailean' ('young').
Variants: Cailean, Colan, Cole, Collie, Collin, Collins, Colly, Colyn, Nicholas

Connor
According to Irish legend Conchobhar was the name of the King of Ulster who planned to marry Deirdre but she eloped with Naoise instead. He took revenge on his young rival by killing him. Connor is the Anglicised form of the Gaelic name Conchobhar, which means 'lover of hounds'.
Variants: Conn, Conor

Conrad
This German name was introduced to Britain during the Middle Ages. It is a combination of two Old High German words meaning 'bold', 'wise' and 'counsellor'. Thus Conrad means 'bold counsel'.
Variants: Con, Curt, Konrad, Kurt

Constantine
Until 1930, Istanbul, Turkey's largest city, was known as Constantinople. It was so-named after the first Christian Roman Emperor, Constantine I or 'the Great'. His conversion to the

faith in 312 marked the end of Christian persecution in the Roman Empire. His name comes from the Latin for 'to stand together', so it symbolises 'loyalty' and 'constancy'.

Constantine is another name that was brought to the British Isles by the Normans. Although its use in that country declined after the Reformation, it increased during the 19th century.

Variants: Con, Connie, Consta, Constant, Constantin, Costa, Konstantin

Corbin

The exact origin of Corbin is unknown. It is thought to be derived from the Old French for 'raven' or from the Anglo-Norman for 'crow'.

Variants: Corban, Corben, Corbet, Corbett, Corby, Corbyn, Korbin, Korby

Corey

In the United States Corey is bestowed upon children of both sexes, but it is especially popular for boys. Its roots stem back to the Mediterranean and to the Celtic parts of the British Isles.

The Greek meaning of Corey is 'helmet', but it is also an Irish surname that comes from the Irish and Scottish Gaelic for 'hollow dweller' or 'pool dweller'. (See also Cori in the Girls' section.)

Variants: Cori, Cory, Correy, Corry, Korey, Kori, Kory

Cornelius

During the days of the Roman Empire Cornelius was the name of a talented family. One famous bearer of the name was Gaius Cornelius Tacitus, the historian whose accounts of the first century of the Roman Empire continue to be studied by history students today. His name comes from the Latin for 'cornel tree' and 'horn' or 'hard-hearted'.

Variants: Cornell, Corney, Cornie, Cory, Neil, Neilus, Nelly

Cormac
Cormac comes from the Greek for 'tree trunk' but its popularity in Ireland is due to its association with a former king and bishop. The Irish Gaelic meaning of the name is 'defilement' and 'son'. It may also mean 'charioteer' and 'son of the raven'.
Variants: Cormack, Cormick

Count
Count comes from the Old French for 'companion' or 'colleague'.
Variant: Countee

Cosmo
St Cosmas is the patron saint of physicians, surgeons and pharmacists along with his twin brother Damian, who was also canonised by the Roman Catholic Church. Both men were early Christian martyrs who were recognised for their charitable work among the poor. They were 4th century physicians who made no charge to help the less fortunate.

The name Cosmo comes from the Greek for 'order' or 'beauty'. It was brought to Britain in the 18th century by the Scottish dukes of Gordon who had links with the ducal house of Tuscany.
Variants: Cosimo, Cosmas

Craig
Craig is the Anglicised form of the Scottish Gaelic family name meaning 'from the rocks'. It was originally given to someone who lived near a cliff, but became a first name throughout the English-speaking world in the 20th century.
Variant: Kraig

Cramer
Cramer comes from the Old English for 'to squeeze' or 'to fill up'. It was usually associated with cramming one's head with knowledge or filling the stomach with food.
Variants: Cram, Kramer

Crispin

The saints Crispin and Crispinian were early Christian martyrs and shoemakers who were brothers. Thus they are both patron saints of shoemakers, cobblers and leatherworkers. Both names were derived from the Latin for 'curly'.

Variants: Crispinian, Crispus, Krispin

Crosby

Crosby comes from the Old Norse for 'from the place with the cross' and from the Middle English for 'cross'. Therefore, it may refer to the cross that usually stood in town centres.

Variants: Crosbey, Crosbie

Curtis

Although the name Curtis is more popular in North America than it is in Europe, its meaning is very much rooted in the Old World.

This surname and first name is derived from the Latin for 'courtyard'. It is also related to the Old French for 'to be or reside at court' and 'to flatter, entice or woo' or 'be courteous'.

The Middle English meaning differs from the Latin and Old French interpretations. The English family name Curtis comes from the words for 'short stockings'.

Variants: Court, Courtenay, Courtland, Courts, Curt, Kurt, Kurtis

Cyril

In the 9th century the name Cyril was borne by one of the missionaries who took Christianity to Russia. His presence made a lasting impression on the region, not just because he brought with him the Biblical stories of Christ but because he made a valuable contribution to the Slavic languages. It was St Cyril who devised the Russian Cyrillic alphabet to translate the scriptures from Greek. His own name was derived from Greek and it meant 'lord' or 'ruler'.

Variants: Ciro, Cy, Cyrill, Syril

Cyrus

Cyrus was the name of the founder and first significant king of the Persian Empire. Known as Cyrus the Great, he is mentioned in the Bible. His name means 'sun' or 'throne'.
Variants: Ciro, Cy, Cyrie, Cyro, Kir, Russ, Sy

Dahi

Although Dahi is thought of as a variant of David, it is a Welsh name that comes from the Celtic for 'nimble'.

Dalai

Dalai Lama is the term for the Buddhist spiritual and political leader of Tibet. The name Dalai comes from the Sanskrit for 'mediator'.

Dalbert

Two Old High German words have been joined together to form the name Dalbert. It comes from 'tal', meaning 'valley' or 'hollow', and 'beraht', 'bright' and 'shining'. Thus Dalbert means 'bright valley'.
Variants: Bert, Bertie, Berty, Burt, Dal

Dale

In North America the name Dale is given to both boys and girls. It comes from the Old Norse for 'broad valley' and the Old English for 'valley'. As a surname it was probably first attached to someone who lived in a dale or valley. Dalton, a similar name, means 'valley town' and Dallin stands for 'from the vale'.
Variants: Dal, Daley, Dali, Dalton, Dayle, Delles, Dillon

Damon

Modern use of the name Damon seems to date back to the 1930s, but its roots are in the classical world. According to Greek mythology, Damon and Pythias were two friends who were devoted to each other. Legend has it that the tyrant Dionysius condemned Pythias to death, but allowed him to settle his affairs before facing his fate – as long as his friend stayed behind in his place. When Pythias stayed true to his word and returned rather than let Damon take his punishment, Dionysius, impressed by their loyalty, freed them both.

More than one meaning is attributed to the name Damon. They include the Greek for 'fate' or 'divine power' and the Old English for 'day'. It is also linked to the Latin for 'evil spirit' or 'demon'.

Variants: Dame, Damian, Damiano, Damien, Dayman

Daniel

The Biblical tale of Daniel in the lions' den was a popular one during the Middle Ages. According to the Old Testament Daniel was an Israelite slave of an Assyrian king who was favoured by his master because he could interpret dreams. Daniel's enemies conspired against him and eventually he was thrown into a den of lions. Condemned to die, it was his faith in God that saved him from what seemed an inevitable fate.

In Hebrew the name means 'God is my judge'. Deiniol, a similar Welsh name, means 'attractive' and 'charming'.

Variants: Dan, Dana, Dane, Daneil, Dani, Dano, Dannie, Danny, Deiniol

Dante

Like Daniel, the name Dante was popular during the Middle Ages. The name comes from the Italian for 'to endure, bear or be patient'. It is also the short form of the name Durante, which comes from the Latin for 'steadfast'.

Variants: Donte, Devonte, Duran, Durante, Durant

Darcy

See Darcie in the Girls' section.

Darius

Darius is a name that was borne by three kings of ancient Persia. The Persian meaning of the name is 'protector', but it also comes

from the Greek for 'wealthy' or 'rich'.
Variants: Daare, Daren, Daria, Darian, Dario, Darien, Darren

Darren
The exact meaning of this name is uncertain. As a variant of Darius, Darren is derived from the Greek for 'rich' or the Persian for 'protector'. It may also have come from an Irish family name, which has the Gaelic meaning 'great' or 'small one'.
Variants: Dar, Daren, Darien, Darin, Dario, Darius, Darnell, Daryn

Darwin
The name comes from the Old English for 'sea' or 'dear' and 'friend'. Hence it means 'lover of the sea'.
Variants: Dar, Derwin, Derwyn, Durwin

David
King David, the father of Solomon, is one of the most revered and beloved characters of the Old Testament. As a young man, armed with a sling and pebbles, he defeated the giant Goliath in single combat. He became founder and first ruler of the united kingdom of Israel and Judah. He was also a great lover and poet, writing many of the psalms, including 'The Lord is my Shepherd'. His name is favoured by both Jews and Christians alike. Its Hebrew meaning is 'beloved'.

The name David is popular among the Welsh because it was borne by their patron saint.
Variants: Dafydd, Dahi, Dai, Dave, Daveed, Davi, Davide, Davy

De Angelo
Used in North America as a first name, De Angelo comes from the Greek for 'angel' or 'messenger'.
Variants: Angel, Angelo, DeAngelo

Dean
Three theories exist to explain the origin of the name Dean. The first suggests that Dean comes from the Old English for 'valley'.

and that originally it referred to someone who lived in a valley. Another theory points to the Middle English word 'dene', which was an occupational name for someone who served as an ecclesiastical supervisor. The name may also be derived from the Greek for 'ten'. In that case 'dean' referred to someone of high rank who was responsible for ten or more people.

There is one more, fourth suggestion about the origin of Dean. Sometimes it is the Anglicisation of the Italian name Dino, which can be a short form of the longer name Bernardino. One example of this was the Italian-American actor and singer Dean Martin who was given the Christian name Dino at birth.
Variants: Dene, Denn, Dino

Declan

The exact meaning of Declan is uncertain but it may have been derived from the Irish Gaelic for 'good'. The name was borne by an early Irish saint, who was a bishop in the district of Ardmore. Declan is the Anglicised form of the Gaelic name Deaglán.
Variant: Deaglan

Delmar

Delmar comes from the Latin for 'of the sea'.
Variants: Del, Delmer, Delmore

Delvin

This name is derived from the Greek word 'delphis', which means 'dolphin'.
Variants: Del, Delwin

Demetrius

According to Greek mythology Demeter was the goddess of the earth associated with agriculture. This Mother Nature figure was responsible for mankind and its toils, including fertility and the cultivation of the soil. The name Demetrius refers to this goddess and means either 'goddess of fertility' or 'follower of Demeter'.

The name Demetrius is mentioned in the Bible more than

once and was also borne by a 17th-century saint and bishop.
Variants: Deems, Demeter, Demetre, Demetri

Dennis

Dionysus was the Greek god of wine and revelry. It is from Dionysus that the French name Denis, or Dennis, is derived. It is associated with St Dionysius of Paris, a 3rd century evangelist, who was sent from Rome to Gaul as a missionary.

The Normans brought the name to Britain, where it was used as a given name until the 1600s. Thereafter its popularity declined until its use was revived during the 20th century.
Variants: Deenys, Den, Denis, Denison, Dennison, Denny, Denys, Dion, Dionysius

Denver

In North America, Denver is a town in Colorado, but in England it was originally a family name derived from a reference to a place. In Old English Denver means 'Danes' crossing' and in Middle English it stands for 'little forested valley'. The French interpretation is 'green'.
Variants: Den, Dennie, Denny

Denzel

This is linked to the surname Denzil, which comes from the Old Cornish place name Denzell and is from the Celtic for 'stronghold' and the Old Cornish for 'high'. In the 1980s and 1990s it became associated with the actor Denzel Washington.
Variants: Denzell, Denzil

Derby

The meaning of Derby is threefold. One suggestion is that it comes from the Old English for 'deer'. Thus the town of Derby in England would mean 'farmstead where deer are kept'. Alternatively the name may be a combination of two Old English words 'dwr' and 'by', meaning 'water' and 'village, town'.

It is also used as an Anglicised form of the Irish name Dermot, which means 'without injunction' or 'without envy'. (See also Dermot.)
Variants: Dar, Darby, Dermot

Derek

The name Derek was derived from two Old High German names, both of which contain the word for 'ruler'. The first source is Hrodrick, which is a combination of two elements – 'hrod', which means 'famous', and 'richi', 'ruler', 'power' or 'wealth'. Thus, Derek means 'famous ruler'.

The name is also related to another Old High German predecessor, Theodoric. The latter, which means 'the people's ruler', was borne by the European ruler Theodoric the Great, who died in 526.

The more contemporary version, Derrick, was the name of a 17th century hangman, thus the name developed into another word for 'crane'. The French variant of Theodoric is Thierry, which developed into Terry. The Dutch interpretation is Dirk.
Variants: Del, Derrick, Derry, Dirk, Rick, Ricky, Rik, Terry, Thierry

Dermot

According to Irish legend Diarmait is a romantic figure who eloped with the Queen of Tara and faced death for his actions. Dermot is the contemporary version of his name. It means 'without injunction' or 'free from envy'. (See also Derby.)
Variants: Darby, Derby, Dermod, Dermott, Diarmid, Diarmod, Diarmuid

Derry

The Northern Irish city of Londonderry is sometimes referred to as Derry. The Gaelic meaning of Derry is 'red-headed', but it also comes from the Welsh for 'oak trees'. It is also a pet form of Derek.
Variants: Dare, Darrey, Darrie, Dary, Derek

Desmond

The Latin meaning of Desmond is 'of or from the world'. As it originates from the word 'mundus', which means 'the universe', it implies someone who is part of creation.

Desmond also has Celtic roots. In Irish Gaelic it means 'from south Munster' or 'descendent of one from south Munster'. Munster is a province in Ireland.
Variants: Des, Desi, Dezi

Devon
The name of this English county is sometimes bestowed on children of either sex. Devon is derived from the Latin name of the Celtic tribe who lived in those parts at the time of the Roman invasion.

The name can be pronounced in one of two ways – either as 'de-VON' or as 'DEV-on' with an emphasis on the first syllable. The variant Devin comes from the Celtic for 'poet'.
Variants: Devan, Deven, Devin, Devyn

Dexter
Dexter is the transferred use of a surname that comes from the Latin for 'right-sided' or 'right-handed'. It has also been derived from the Old English for 'dye'.
Variants: Decca, Deck, Dek, Dex

Dhani
A Hindu name, Dhani means 'person of wealth and riches'.

Didi
Didi is the short form of the French name Didier, which is the male version of Desirée. (See Desirée in the Girls' section.) Hence it derives its meaning from the Latin for 'ardent desire', 'deep longing' and 'wish'.

Didi is also a variant of Dodo, which means 'beloved' in Hebrew or 'stupid' and 'clumsy' in Portuguese. The latter qualities were associated with the now extinct flightless bird from Mauritius.
Variants: Didier, Didon, Didot, Dizier, Dodo

Diego
The name Diego is the Spanish form of the Biblical name James, which is itself a variant of the Old Testament name Jacob. All three come from the Hebrew for 'supplanter'.
Variants: Jacob, James

Digby
Digby is derived from a place name in Lincolnshire, England and was later attached to a notable family. The name comes from the French for 'to dig a ditch or dike' and the Old Norse for 'ditch' and 'settlement'.

Dirk
In Scotland 'dirk' is another word for 'dagger'. The name is also the Dutch and Flemish form of Derek, which comes from the Old High German for 'famous ruler' or 'the people's ruler'. (See also Derek.)
Variants: Derek, Derrick

Dominic
Dominic was the name of the Spanish saint who founded an order of monastic priests during the 13th century. Though they became known as the Order of Preachers, they are better known as the Dominican Order or, simply, the Dominicans.

Dominic's name means 'of the Lord' in Latin and traditionally was bestowed upon boys born on a Sunday. Later, Roman Catholics gave it to their sons in honour of the saint.
Variants: Dom, Domenic, Domenico, Domenyk, Domingo, Dominick, Nick, Nickie, Nicky

Donald
Donald is the Anglicised version of the Celtic name Domhnall, which means 'global or proud ruler'. It is a Scottish clan name that was borne by a number of kings of Scotland and Ireland.
Variants: Domhnall, Don, Donahue, Donal, Donaldo, Donalt, Donn, Donne, Donnie, Donovan

Donnel

St Donnan was an Irish Christian who worked with a group of monks on an island in the Inner Hebrides before he was killed by a gang of locals in 617. His name comes from the Gaelic for 'hill' or 'hill-fort'. Donnel is a variant of this name.

Another Celtic name, Donald, is related to Donnel giving it the meaning 'global or proud ruler'. (See also Donald.)

Variants: Don, Donald, Donn, Donnell, Donnelly, Donny, Dun

Donovan

Donovan was first used as a first name during the early 1900s. Its popularity soared during the 1960s following the success of the folk-rock singer of the same name. However, Donovan was, and still is, an Irish surname. In Gaelic it means 'descendant of Donndubhán'. Donndubhán was a personal name for someone who was dark in complexion. It also means 'dark warrior'.

Variants: Don, Donnie, Donny, Donavan, Van

Dorian

The Picture of Dorian Gray was the only novel written by the poet, playwright and wit, Oscar Wilde. The plot is about a handsome young man who, over the years, retains his youth and beauty while the portrait of him that hangs in his attic grows old and ugly.

Wilde is thought to have taken the name from the classical world. In Ancient Greece a Dorian was someone who came from the Doris region. Doris meant 'bountiful sea' or 'sacrificial knife'. Alternatively Dorian may come from the Greek word for 'gift', 'doron'. (See also Doris in the Girls' section.)

Variants: Doran, Dore, Dorey, Dorie, Doron, Dory

Dougal

The Irish Gaelic meaning of Dougal is 'dark stranger'. It was the nickname given to the invading Danes in contrast to Fingal, 'fair stranger', which was used for the lighter Norwegians.

Variants: Doug, Dougie, Doyle, Dug, Dugard, Duggy, Dughall

Douglas

Douglas is the name of an ancient Scottish clan who acquired the earldoms of Angus and Douglas in the 8th century. Their name is derived from two Gaelic words – 'dubh' meaning 'dark colour', and 'glas', meaning 'water'. The full meaning of the name, therefore, is 'black stream'.
Variants: Doug, Dougal, Dougie, Douglass, Dougy, Dugald, Duggie

Doyle

As a variant of Dougal, Doyle means 'dark stranger'. However, the name also comes from the Irish Gaelic for 'assembly' or 'gathering'.
Variant: Dougal

Drake

This name comes from the Greek for 'serpent' or 'dragon'. Historically dragons have not always been viewed as negative figures. Although they were considered to be evil by Christians, they have been greatly revered by the Chinese.

Dudley

The name Dudley comes from the Old English for 'Duddha's clearing or wood'. The exact meaning of Duddha is unclear but it may have been a nickname for a podgy man.
Variants: Dud, Dudd, Dudly

Duke

Duke comes from the Latin for 'leader, conductor', 'guide' or 'commander'. It is also a hereditary title of nobility like 'earl'.

It is sometimes used as a nickname for someone who has excelled in their profession, such as Edward Kennedy Ellington – the American jazz musician best known as Duke Ellington.

Duncan

Like Donald and Douglas, Duncan is a name associated with Scotland. It comes from the Scottish Gaelic words 'donn'

('greyish-brown') and 'chadh' ('warrior') and means 'dark-skinned warrior'. It is also thought to mean 'princely battle'.
Variants: Dun, Dunc, Dune, Dunkie, Dunn

Dunstan
Dunstan is derived from the Old English for 'greyish-brown' and 'stone' or 'hill'. Thus it means 'dark hill'. It was the first name of an Anglo-Saxon saint whose contribution to the British monarchy can still be felt. An adviser to the kings of Wessex in his day, he also devised the coronation service that is still used in Britain. He is the patron saint of blacksmiths and goldsmiths.
Variants: Donestan, Dunn, Dunne, Dunst

Dustin
The exact meaning of Dustin is uncertain. It could come from the German for 'warrior' or the Old Norse for 'Thor's stone'. Thor was the Viking god of thunder, after whom Thursday was named.
Variants: Dust, Dustie, Dusty

Dwayne
Dwayne derives its meaning from the Irish Gaelic for 'dark little one'. It gained popularity as a first name following the success of the American guitarist Duane Eddy whose work enjoyed popularity from the 1950s to the 1980s.
Variants: Duane, Duwayne, Dwain

Dwight
Dwight comes from the Old English for 'white, fair'.
Variants: DeWitt, Dewitt, Diot, Doyt, Wit, Wittie, Witty

Dylan
The exact origin of the Welsh name Dylan is uncertain but it may be derived from the Celtic word for 'sea'. In the first half of the 20th century the name was widely known through the work of the Welsh poet, Dylan Thomas.
Variants: Dillan, Dillon

Eamon

The Irish politician Eamon de Valera played a pivotal role in Ireland's independence from Great Britain. Born in New York City in 1882, he held the position of Taoiseach (Prime Minister) three times and the role of president once, before leaving public office aged 90.

His name is the Irish Gaelic form of Edmund and comes from the Old English for 'happiness', 'riches' and 'protector'. It is also a variant of Edward. (See also Edmund and Edward.)
Variants: Eamonn, Edmund, Edward

Earl

An earl is a British nobleman who ranks between Marquis and Viscount. The name means 'nobleman', 'chief', 'prince' or 'warrior' in Old English.

Earl is rarely used in Britain as a given name, but it was originally used as a nickname for someone who worked in the household of an earl. It is more commonly used as a Christian name in North America.
Variants: Earle, Erle

Eaton

Two Old English words combine to form this name – 'ea', meaning 'river' or 'running water', and 'tūn', 'town or village'. Thus Eaton means 'riverside town'.

Eden

Eden may be a variant of the Celtic name Aidan, which means 'little fiery one' in Irish Gaelic. Furthermore, it could come from the Old English for 'prosperity, riches' and 'bear cub'. It could also be taken from the Garden of Eden from the Book of Genesis. In North America, Eden is bestowed on baby boys and girls.
Variants: Aidan, Ed, Edan, Eddie, Eddy

Edgar

The Anglo-Saxon king Edgar the Peaceful was the grandson of

Alfred the Great. His name comes from the Old English for 'lucky spear'.
Variants: Ed, Eddie

Edmund

The Old English meaning of the name Edmund is 'happy protection'. It was borne by three English kings, one of whom was the 9th century monarch and saint, Edward the Martyr. He died at the hands of the Vikings after he refused to take up arms, preferring to follow Christ's non-violent example instead.

Another saint who bore the name was Edmund of Abingdon who held the post of Archbishop of Canterbury.

The Irish form of Edmund is Eamon. (See also Eamon.)
Variants: Eadmond, Eamon, Ed, Edmond, Eddie, Eddy, Esmund, Ned, Ted, Teddy

Edom

Edom is a pet form of the Biblical name Adam, which comes from the Hebrew for 'red earth'. In the Old Testament it is an alternative name for Jacob's brother, Esau, whose descendants lived in a land of the same name.
Variants: Adam, Idumea

Edric

Edric is another name that begins with the Old English prefix that means 'happy' or 'riches'. The second part of the name means 'ruler'. Thus, the Old English interpretation of Edric is 'happy ruler'.
Variants: Ed, Eddie, Eddy, Edred, Edrich, Edrick, Ric, Rick, Ricky

Edward

The links between Edward and the British monarchy are so strong that over the centuries England has had 10 kings bearing the name. The first was the Anglo-Saxon king of Wessex, Edward the Elder, whose father was Alfred the Great. He died in 924 and the next king with the name was eventually canonised.

Although Edward the Confessor had no children, his legacy included Westminster Abbey. Edward's death prompted the conflict over succession to the English throne. The result was William the Conqueror's defeat of Harold II at the Battle of Hastings in 1066.

Edward VIII was the most recent British monarch bearing the name. He was king briefly during 1936 before he abdicated his throne for the love of Mrs (Wallis) Simpson, a twice-divorced American woman whom he later married.

In modern times the name has been borne by the third son of Elizabeth II. Prince Edward bears a name that comes from the Old English for 'happy', 'fortunate', 'rich' and 'guardian' or 'protector'.
Variants: Eamon, Ed, Eddie, Edison, Eddy, Eduardo, Ned, Neddie, Ted, Teddy

Edwin
The Scottish city of Edinburgh is said to have been named after the first Christian king of Northumbria, St Edwin. The name comes from two Old English words – 'eadig', 'fortunate, prosperous, happy', and 'wine', 'friend'. Thus, it means 'happy friend'.
Variants: Eaduin, Ed, Edred, Edwyn, Neddie, Teddy

Egbert
This Anglo-Saxon name enjoyed a revival during the 19th century. It comes from the Old English for 'shining', 'famous' and 'sword, blade'. Egbert was borne by a 9th century king of Wessex.
Variants: Bert, Bertie, Berty

Elan
There are three meanings for the name Elan. It is said to come from the Latin for 'spirited', the Hebrew for 'tree' and the Native American for 'friendly'.
Variants: Ela, Elai

Eli
Although Eli is often used as a pet form of the names Elijah ('the

Lord is my God') and Elisha ('God is my help'), it is actually an independent name in its own right. In the Old Testament it was borne by the high priest who raised Samuel. The Hebrew meaning of his name is 'elevated', 'height' or 'Jehovah'. (See also Elijah and Elisha.)
Variants: El, Eloy, Ely, Ilie

Elijah
Elijah is a Biblical name that was favoured by the Puritan settlers in the New World of America. It was borne by an Old Testament prophet and, in Hebrew, means 'the Lord is my God'.
Variants: El, Eli, Elia, Elias, Elliott

Elisha
See Elisha in the Girls' section.

Elliott
As a variant of Elias, the Greek form of Elijah, Elliott comes from the Hebrew for 'the Lord is my God'.

Elliott is also a surname that is derived from the Old English for 'noble battle'. Another possible Hebrew meaning is 'close to God'.
Variants: Eli, Elias, Elijah, Eliot, Ellis

Ellis
The 19th century English schoolboy, William Webb Ellis, was said to be the inventor of rugby. While playing a game of football at the prestigious Rugby School he picked up the ball and ran with it.

His surname is believed to have come from the Biblical name Elijah, which means 'the Lord is my God' in Hebrew. It may equally have been derived from the Welsh for 'benevolent'.
Variants: Eli, Elias, Elie, Elis, Ellison, Elly, Elson, Elston, Ely

Elmer
To generations of children Elmer is the name of the Looney Tunes cartoon character Elmer Fudd, the enemy of Bugs Bunny. However, the history of the name stretches back centuries before

film or television were invented. Elmer comes from the Old English name Aethelmaer, which means 'noble' and 'famous'.
Variants: Ailemar, Aylmer, Edmar, Edmer, Eilemar, Elma, Elmo, Elmore

Elmo
As a variant of the name Elmer, Elmo comes from the Old English for 'noble' and 'famous'. However, Elmo is also the pet form of the name Erasmus, which was borne by the patron saint of sailors and people with intestinal diseases. It is said that St Elmo's intestines were wound out on a windlass. Thus the electrical discharge that is sometimes seen above the mast of a ship is known as St Elmo's fire and is taken to be a sign of his protection.

Erasmus comes from the Greek for 'beloved' or 'desired'. (See also Elmer.)
Variants: Elmer, Erasme, Erasmus

Elroy
Elroy comes from the Spanish and French for 'the king'.

Elton
The piano-playing singer Reginald Kenneth Dwight is better known by his stage name of Elton John. John's assumed name comes from the Old English for 'Ella's settlement' or 'noble town'. It is an English family name that was derived from a place name.
Variants: Elden, Elsdom, Elston

Elvis
Elvis Presley may be the single most important figure in American 20th century popular music. The origin of the undisputed King of Rock 'n' Roll's first name has long been disputed. It has been suggested that the Presley family, in accordance a southern tradition, made up the name.

Another possibility is that it is a variant of Elvin, which comes from the Old English for 'elf-like'.
Variants: Alby, Alvin, Elli, Elvin, Elly

Emmanuel

In the Old Testament it was predicted that the Messiah would be born to a virgin girl and that her son would bear the name of Emmanuel. The Old Testament Hebrew form of this name is Immanuel. Its New Testament version is Emmanuel. Both names mean the same thing. They come from the Hebrew for 'God is with us'. This Biblical name is popular among Spanish-speakers.
Variants: Emanuel, Emanuele, Immanuel, Mani, Manny, Manuel, Manuela

Emmett

Taken from the Hebrew for 'truth' and the Old English for 'ant', the name Emmett is sometimes bestowed on boys of Irish heritage in honour of Robert Emmet, the rebel who led an unsuccessful rebellion against the English in 1803.
Variants: Emmet, Emmit, Emmitt

Emory

This boy's name is sometimes used as a male form of Emily, which comes from the Germanic for 'industrious' and 'hard-working'. Emory is also a version of the Old German name Emmerick, which means 'powerful' and 'noble'.
Variants: Almery, Amory, Emmerick, Emerson, Emil, Emile, Emilio, Emlyn, Emmory

Emyr

This Welsh name means 'ruler, king or lord'. A 6th century Breton saint, who lived in Cornwall, bore the name.

Erasmus

Erasmus comes from the Greek for 'beloved' and 'desired'. It was also the name of Erasmus of Rotterdam, a Dutch humanist and theologian who emphasised the importance of simple Christian faith and Bible study. Erasmus died in 1536. (See also Elmo.)
Variants: Elmo, Erasme, Erasmo, Ras, Rastus

Eric

This Scandinavian name was first brought to England by the Danes before the Norman Conquest of the 11th century. Old Norse in origin, it means 'honourable ruler', 'one ruler' or 'island ruler'. The name was borne by a Norse chieftain called Eric the Red who, discovering Greenland in the 10th century, established a colony there.

Eric was increasingly given to boys during the 19th century in accordance with the Victorian trend of using Anglo-Saxon or medieval names. It has been well-known ever since.
Variants: Erik, Eryk, Euric, Ric, Rick, Rickie, Ricky

Ernest

In 1895 Oscar Wilde's comedy, *The Importance of Being Earnest*, was first performed in London. Its title was a pun upon the word and name 'Earnest', both of which mean the same thing 'intense desire' or 'seriously determined'.

The name was first brought over to Britain from Germany by the Hanoverian dynasty which succeeded the House of Stuart in 1714. Indeed Ernest comes from the Old German for 'keenness in battle' or 'seriously determined'.
Variants: Earnest, Ern, Ernie, Ernst, Erny

Eros

According to Greek mythology, Eros was the god of love. It is from his name that the word 'erotic' is derived. His name comes from the Greek for 'desire' or 'sexual love'.

Albert Gilbert's statue of Eros is a landmark that has stood in London's Piccadilly Circus since 1893. It shows the winged god poised to shoot an arrow that, according to legend, would strike instant passion into the heart of the recipient.

Errol

In the early 20th century the name Errol became inextricably linked to the swashbuckling hero of the silver screen, Errol Flynn. Unfortunately the origin of the film star's name is less certain. It

could be a German form of Earl and, if so, it is the title of a British nobleman. It may also be a Scottish family name that was taken from a Scottish place name. Alternatively Errol could be a variant of the Welsh name Eryl, which means 'watcher' or 'a lookout post', or of Harold, which comes from the Old German for 'army leader'.
Variants: Earl, Erroll, Harold, Rollo, Rolly

Erskine
Erskine is a Scottish surname and place name that was brought to Scotland by Irish settlers. It comes from the Gaelic for 'from the height of the cliff'.

Esau
In the Bible, Esau is the name of Jacob's twin brother who was the son of Isaac and Rebecca. A good hunter and farmer, Esau was his father's favourite son and was to receive his blessing as his successor. He never did because his mother deceived her blind husband by dressing his other son so that he would smell and feel like his twin. Esau's name comes from the Hebrew for 'hairy'.

Esmond
Esmond comes from the Old English for 'grace, beauty' and 'protector' and the Old Norse for 'divine protection'. Until the 19th century it was widely found as a surname.

Ethan
The Biblical name Ethan comes from the Hebrew for 'permanent' and 'assured'. It may have been used in reference to streams that flowed throughout the year without drying up through the summer months.

In North America the name may have been used in honour of Ethan Allen, a hero of the American Revolution.
Variants: Etan, Ethe

Euan
More than one theory exists to explain the origin of Euan. It is

thought to be the Welsh form of the Biblical name John, which comes from the Hebrew for 'God is gracious'. But, like Owen, it is also considered to be the Celtic version of Eugene, which is derived from the Greek for 'well-born'.
Variants: Eugene, Ewan, Ewen, Owain, Owen

Eugene
As mentioned above, Eugene comes from the Greek for 'noble' or 'well-born'.
Variants: Eugen, Eugenio, Eugenius, Ewan, Ewen, Gene, Owain, Owen

Ezekiel
Ezekiel is the name of the Old Testament prophet who is believed to be the author of the Book of Ezekiel in the Bible. His name comes from the Hebrew for 'may God strengthen'.
Variants: Ezechial, Ezell, Haskell, Hehezhel, Zeke

Ezra
Ezra is the name of another Old Testament prophet and author. It was Ezra who established Mosaic Law in Jerusalem. His name comes from the Hebrew for 'help'.
Variants: Azariah, Azur, Esdras, Ezar, Ezer, Ezera, Ezri

Fabian
Fabian comes from the Roman family name Fabianus, which is derived from the Latin for 'bean'. Quintus Fabius Maximus, who died in 203 BC, was the most famous member of the house of Fabii. His nickname was 'Cunctator' – 'the delayer' – because he defeated Hannibal's invading forces by avoiding pitched battles in favour of a war of harassment and attrition. Centuries later, in 1884, the British socialist movement, the Fabian Society, would be named after him.
Variants: Fabe, Faber, Fabiano, Fabien, Fabio, Fabius

Fadil
This name comes from the Arabic for 'virtuous' and 'distinguished'.

Boys

Fahey

Fahey comes from the Old English for 'joyful, glad' and 'happy'.

Farley

The name Farley is thought to have been derived from one of four possible sources. The name may have been taken from the Old French for 'fair', the word for 'special place and day for a market or celebration'. Farley may have also come from the Old Norse for 'beautiful or pleasing'. Alternatively it may be derived from the Old English for 'wayside'. The Middle English word for 'meadow' is another possibility.
Variants: Fair, Fairbanks, Fairleigh, Fairley, Far, Farl, Farlie, Farly

Farrell

Farrell is a variant of the Irish name Fergal, which means 'valiant man' in Gaelic. It is also a variant of Farrar, which means 'blacksmith' or 'iron' in Latin. (See also Fergal.)
Variants: Farrel, Farris, Fergal, Ferris, Ferrol

Felix

Like Leo the lion or Bruno the bear, Felix is a name now commonly associated with an animal – the cat. Borne by four popes and 67 saints the name proved to be popular with early Christians. It comes from the Latin for 'happy' or 'lucky'.
Variants: Felice, Felike

Felton

This name comes from the Old Norse for 'hill' and the Old English for 'village' or 'town'. Thus it means 'town on or near a hill'.
Variants: Fell, Felt, Feltie, Felty

Fenn

Mainly used in America the name Fenn comes from the Old English for 'town near marshland'. Originally it may have been given to someone living in a marshy area.
Variants: Fen, Fennie, Fenny

Ferdinand
This name is traditionally a favourite of the Spanish royal family. One monarch who bore it was King Ferdinand III of Castile who forced the Moors out of southern Spain in the 13th century. The name was first brought to that country in the 6th century by the Germanic Visigoths. It means either 'brave or prepared journey'. It is also thought to come from the Latin for 'wild, bold' courageous', 'warlike', 'gallant' and 'headstrong'.
Variants: Ferdi, Ferdie, Fern, Nandy

Fergal
Ferghal was the name of an 8th century king of Ireland. Fergal is its Anglicised form. The Gaelic meaning of the name is 'man of valour'. (See also Farrell.)
Variants: Farrell, Ferghal

Fergus
The fact that this name was borne by a number of Celtic saints may explain its popularity in both Scotland and Ireland. Like Fergal, Fergus could mean 'man of valour', but it is usually taken to mean 'best or manly choice' in Gaelic. An alternative meaning is 'vigorous man'.
Variants: Feargus, Fergie, Ferguson, Fergy

Fidel
Fidel Castro is the name of the Cuban ruler who was instrumental in the establishment of a Communist state in his country in 1959. His name comes from the Latin for 'faithful' and 'trust'.
Variants: Fidele, Fidelio

Finbar
Finbar is the Anglicised form of the Irish name Fionnbharr, which comes from the Gaelic for 'fair-headed'. Barry is said to be derived from this name.
Variants: Barry, Fin, Findlay, Finley, Finn

Finlay
This Scottish surname comes from the Gaelic for 'fair-haired soldier'.
Variants: Fin, Findlay, Findley, Finley, Finn

Finn
In Ireland the name is closely associated with a legendary hero called Finn mac Cumhail. This giant was a leader of the Fianna warriors and it is from him that the Fenian Brotherhood, an Irish-American revolutionary society, derived its name.

Finn comes from the Irish Gaelic for 'fair' and it is the short form of names such as Finbar and Finlay.
Variants: Finan, Finian, Finnegan, Finnian, Fion, Fionn

Fitzgerald
In Ireland Fitzgerald was the name of a powerful family from Kildare. The short form Fitz means 'son' in Old English, thus the full meaning of Fitzgerald is 'son of Gerald'. The personal name Gerald comes from the Old German for 'spear rule'.
Variant: Fitz

Flannan
This name comes from the Old French for 'flat metal' and the Old English for 'arrow'. It also has an Irish meaning, 'blood red'.
Variants: Flann, Flannery

Fletcher
Fletcher is an English family name that was originally an occupational name for someone who made arrows.
Variant: Fletch

Flint
The word 'flint' means 'hard rock' in Middle English.

Floyd
Floyd is a variant of the Welsh name Lloyd, which means 'grey'.
Variant: Lloyd

Flynn
The Gaelic meaning of this name is 'son of the red-haired man'.
Variants: Flin, Flinn

Forbes
The Greek meaning of this name is 'any plant, except grass, that grows in a field or meadow'. The Irish Gaelic interpretation is 'field owner' or 'prosperous'.
   The name is closely associated with Scotland, where it is both a surname and a place name.

Ford
The Old English meaning of Ford is 'shallow river crossing'.

Forrest
Like the vocabulary word, Forrest refers to a large area with trees and undergrowth. It is the transferred use of a surname that was originally given to someone who lived near an enclosed wood. The name also comes from the German for 'forester' or 'guardian of the forest'.
Variants: Forest, Forester, Foster

Foster
In English 'foster' means to 'promote growth or development' and in Middle English a 'foster parent' pledged to raise the child of another for a period of time. It also comes from the Middle English for 'forester', 'shearer' and 'saddle-tree maker'.
Variants: Forest, Forester, Forrest, Forrester, Forster, Foss

Francis
Although he was born Giovanni Bernardone in Italy in 1182, St Francis of Assisi was given the nickname Francesco by his friends. The name, which meant 'the little Frenchman' or 'with the airs and graces of a Frenchman', indicated that they thought he was a Francophile. Nevertheless Giovanni, who would become patron saint of animals and nature, devoted his life to God and is forever

remembered by the variant of his nickname, Francis.

In England, during the reign of Queen Elizabeth I, the name was associated with the navigator Sir Francis Drake who became the first Englishman to circumnavigate the globe.

Variants: Franc, Francesco, Francisco, Franck, Franco, Francois Frank, Frankie

Franklin

The Middle English meaning of Franklin is 'freeman'. During that period the name referred to someone who was a freeholder but not a nobleman.

However the true origin of the name is rooted in 5th century Europe when a Germanic tribe known as the Franks invaded Roman-occupied Gaul. Their new home eventually became known as France and Frank meant 'free' or someone who belonged to the Frankish tribe.

Variants: Frank, Frankie, Franklyn

Fraser

The exact origin of this Scottish surname, which later came into use as a first name, is unclear. It may be derived from the French word for 'strawberry'. Alternatively it may come from the French for 'charcoal cinders' or 'charcoal maker'.

Variants: Frasier, Frazer, Frazier

Frederick

Brought to Britain by the Normans, the name was borne by two Holy Roman Emperors, Frederick I (also known as Frederick Red Beard) and Frederick II. The name was increasingly used in England during the reigns of the Hanoverian kings when it was borne by the father and son of George III. On the Continent 10 Danish kings bore the name, as did Frederick the Great, the 18th century King of Prussia.

The name comes from the Old High German for 'peaceful ruler'.

Variants: Eric, Erick, Fred, Freddie, Freddy, Frederic, Frederik, Fridrich, Rick, Rickie

Fulbert

Brought to Britain by the Normans, this name comes from the Old German for 'very bright'.

Variants: Bert, Berty, Filbert, Fulbright, Phil, Philbert, Philibert

Fuller

Fuller was originally an occupational name for someone who shrinks and thickens cloth. It comes from the Latin for 'cloth-fuller'.

Fulton

This Scottish surname was borne by Robert Fulton (1765 – 1815), the North American engineer and inventor who designed the first commercial steamboat. His name was originally taken from a place in Ayrshire. The old English meaning of Fulton is 'town near the field'.

Gabriel

The Archangel Gabriel is the patron saint of diplomats, messengers, communication, radio, broadcasters and postal workers – and with good reason. In the Bible, Gabriel brought messages from God. In the Old Testament he appeared to Daniel. In the New Testament he told the priest Zachariah that his elderly wife Elizabeth would give birth to a son – John the Baptist. Shortly afterwards Gabriel appeared to the Virgin Mary, telling her that she too would have a son – God's child, the Messiah.

Unsurprisingly the Hebrew meaning of the name Gabriel is 'messenger of God' or 'my strength is God'.

Variants: Gab, Gabby, Gabi, Gabriele, Gabrielli, Gabriello, Gabris, Gay

Gael

A number of theories exist to explain the meaning of this name. One theory suggests that it comes from the Old French for 'gallant'. Other sources include the Old English for 'lively' and the Irish Gaelic for 'stranger'. Gael may also come from the Old Welsh for 'wild' via the name Gwyddel, which means 'Irishman'.

Gael is also used as a collective noun for the Gaelic-speaking people of Ireland, Scotland and the Isle of Man. Scottish Highlanders are also known by that name.

Finally, Gael is sometimes used as a male form of the female name Gail, which is a short form of the Hebrew name Abigail ('my father rejoices').
Variants: Gale, Gail, Gaile, Gay, Gayle

Galil
This name is a variant of Jalal, which means 'glory' or 'greatness' in Arabic.

Galvin
Galvin comes from the Gaelic for 'sparrow' or 'brilliant white'.
Variants: Gal, Galvan, Galven

Gamal
This Arabic name means 'beauty'.
Variants: Gamali, Gamli, Gil, Gilad, Gilead, Jammal

Ganesh
According to the Hindu religion the elephant-headed god Ganesh is the eldest son of the god Shiva. He is associated with prosperity and wisdom. The name Ganesh comes from the Sanskrit for 'lord of the hosts'.

Gareth
Like many of the names taken from Arthurian legend, Gareth is said to have Welsh roots. It comes from the word for 'gentle'. Garth, a pet form of the name that is used independently, comes from the northern English for 'enclosure' or 'small cultivated area'.
Variants: Garth, Gary, Garry

Garfield
In recent years this name has been associated with a cartoon character – Garfield the cat. But in the 19th century it was borne

by the 20th President of the United States – James A Garfield. His surname may have been bestowed upon North American children in his honour.

The name comes from the Old English for 'triangular piece of land', 'spears' and 'open country'. Thus Garfield may have originally been used to describe someone who lived near a triangular-shaped field.
Variants: Field, Gar, Gary

Garland
The name and vocabulary word 'garland' comes from the Old French for 'ornament of gold threads'. In the modern world a garland is a wreath of flowers or leaves presented as a prize or used as a decoration during a festival.

As a first name Garland is given to both boys and girls.
Variants: Garlen, Garlon

Garson
The Old French meaning of this name is 'to protect'.
Variant: Garrison

Gary
As a variant of Gareth, Gary comes from the Welsh for 'gentle'. It may also derive its meaning from the Old German word for 'spear', 'gar'.

Gary is also a pet form of Garfield as demonstrated by the West Indian cricketer Sir Garfield Sobers who is also known by the short form. Hence, Gary may also mean 'triangular piece of land'.
Variants: Gareth, Garfield, Gari, Garret, Garrett, Garry, Garth, Gaz

Gavin
Gavin is another Arthurian name with Welsh roots. According to legend Sir Gawain was the nephew of King Arthur who also had a seat on his Round Table. The Welsh meaning of his name is 'falcon of May' or 'hawk of the plain'.

A form of this name also featured in medieval French

literature and while Gawain fell out of favour in 16th century England, it maintained currency in Scotland, which had closer cultural ties with France than with its more immediate neighbour. Gavin is a variant of this Arthurian name.
Variants: Gauvain, Gauvin, Gav, Gawain, Gawaine, Gawen

Gene
This name is a short form of Eugene, which comes from the Greek for 'noble' or 'well-born'. (See also Eugene.)
Variant: Eugene

Geoffrey
The exact meaning of Geoffrey is not certain. As a variant of Godfrey it has the Germanic meaning 'God's peace'. It may also come from the German for 'territory' and 'stranger' or 'pledge'. A further interpretation suggests that Geoffrey comes from the Old German for 'peaceful traveller'.

First brought to England by the Normans, the name was little used by Tudor parents, but was revived in the 19th century.
Variants: Geoff, Godfrey, Jeff, Jefferies, Jefferson, Jeffery, Jeffries

George
Since George I came to the throne in 1714, the name has been associated with the British monarchy. The last king bearing the name was the father of Elizabeth II. Born Albert Frederick Arthur George in December 1895, he was not expected to succeed to the throne but was forced to do so following the abdication of his older brother, King Edward VIII, in 1936.

The name George was borne by the patron saint of England who, according to legend, slew a dragon. Thus far three Presidents of the United States have also been called George. They are George Washington, the first man to hold that position, George Bush and his son George W Bush.

Despite being associated with men of great power, the name George comes from the Greek for 'farmer'.
Variants: Geo, Georg, Georges, Georgie, Georgio, Georgy, Jorgen

Geraint

This popular Welsh name was borne by Geraint who, according to legend, sat at King Arthur's Round Table. Geraint is known for his love of Enid and their story was told a series of poems by Tennyson.

Geraint's name comes from the Greek for 'old man'. It also has links to Welsh and Old English, but retains the same meaning.

Gerald

The Germanic name Gerald was brought to England by the invading Normans. It means 'spear rule'.

Although use of the name declined in England by the 1300s, it experienced a revival in the 1800s. In the 20th century it was the first name of the American President, Gerald Ford, who took the oath of office in 1974 following the resignation of his predecessor Richard Nixon. (See also Fitzgerald and Geraldine.)
Variants: Garald, Gerard, Geralt, Geraldo, Gerry, Jarrett, Jed, Jerald, Jerry

Gerard

Like Gerald, Gerard was brought to Britain by the Normans. As a variant of Gerald it shares the Germanic meaning 'spear rule'. But separate from this similar-sounding name, Gerard means 'brave or strong spear'.
Variants: Gearad, Garrard, Gerald, Geraldo, Gerhardt, Gerry, Jarrett, Jerald, Jerrard, Jerry

Gervase

This is another name of disputed meaning. It is thought to mean 'spear' or 'armour bearer' in Old German or 'servant' in Celtic. A version of the name was borne by the 1st century martyr, St Gervasius.
Variants: Gervais, Gervaise, Gervasius, Gervis, Jarvis

Gideon

In the Bible this name was borne by an Old Testament leader of the Israelites. The Hebrew meaning of his name is 'maimed', 'stump' or 'powerful warrior'.

Gideon was another Old Testament name favoured by the 17th century Puritans.

Variant: Gid

Gil
Gil comes from the Hebrew for 'joy'. It is also the short form of Gilbert, which comes from the Old German for 'bright hostage'.

Variants: Gili, Gill, Gilli, Gilbert

Gilder
'To gild' is to cover something thinly with gold. Thus the name Gilder may have been an old occupational name for someone who did this job. A variant of the name, Gildas, was borne by a hermit and saint who lived on an island in the Bristol Channel.

Giles
According to Greek mythology Aegis was the shield of Zeus, the supreme god. It was made from animal skin and symbolised divine protection. When Zeus shook the shield, he caused a thunder-storm. The Greek word 'aegis' later became the root of the Roman name Aegidius from which Giles is derived. Thus Giles means 'kid' or 'goatskin' in Greek. It may also come from the Scottish Gaelic for 'servant'.

Variants: Gide, Gidie, Gile, Gilean, Gill, Gilles, Gyles

Gilmore
Gilmore comes from the Old Norse for 'deep glen' and the Old English for 'tree root'.

Variants: Gill, Gillie, Gillmore, Gilmour

Glen
Glen is a Scottish family name originally derived from a place name. It comes from the Gaelic word 'gleann', which means 'valley'.

Godfrey

This name is derived from two Old German predecessors – Gaufrid and Godafrid. The first meant 'district' and the second meant 'peace of God'. Godfrith was the Anglo-Saxon version of the latter, which was superseded by Godfrey, the Norman variant, in the years following their invasion of England.

Gordon

Gordon is an old Scottish name, borne by a clan originally named after the Gordon lands in Berwickshire, England. The Old English meaning of the first element 'gor' is 'marsh' and the Scottish Gaelic interpretation of the second part of the name is 'small wooded dell'.

The transferred use of the Gordon surname began in the late 19th century following the death of the British general, Charles George Gordon, who died defending Khartoum in Sudan, Africa, in 1885.

Variants: Goran, Gordan, Gorden, Gordie, Gordy, Gore

Grady

The Latin meaning of this name is 'step', 'position', 'degree' or 'grade'. It also comes from the Irish Gaelic for 'bright or exalted one'.

Variant: Gradey

Graham

In the Domesday Book the English town of Grantham in Lincolnshire was referred to as Grandham, Granham and Graham. In Old English the general meaning of those three names is 'gravel' and 'town'. It also means 'grey' or 'grant' or, in Latin, 'grain'.

In the 12th century William de Grantham, founder of the Scottish Graham clan, was given lands in Scotland by the monarch of that country, King David I.

Variants: Graeham, Graeme, Grahame, Gram, Gramm

Gram

Although the name Gram is often used as a short form of Graham it is also a pet form of Ingram. While Graham comes from the Old English for 'gravel town', Ingram is derived from the Old Norse for 'Ing's raven' – Ing being the god of peace and fertility.
Variants: Graham, Gramm, Ingram

Granger

Granger comes from the Latin for 'grain' and was used to describe either a farmhouse or granary or a person who worked on a farm. Thus it is an old occupational name.

Grant

Grant, like Gordon and Graham, is another name that was borne by a famous Scottish clan. In America its use as a first name was influenced by the 18th President and Civil War hero, General Ulysses Grant.

It is also a vocabulary word derived from the Old French 'granter', which means 'to agree, promise or bestow'.
Variants: Grantland, Grantley

Gray

In Old English the name Gray means 'bailiff' or 'grey'.
Variants: Greg, Grey, Greyson

Gregory

The Greek meaning of the name Gregory is 'watchful' or 'be vigilant'. Gregory the Great was the first of 16 popes to bear the name and was the first monk to be elected to the papal office. His many achievements during his 14 years as Pope included sending missionaries to England.

Another Roman Catholic leader bearing the name was Pope Gregory XIII who adjusted the Julian Calendar in 1582, giving us the Gregorian Calendar that is used today.
Variant: Greg

Guy

Following the 1605 attempt by Guy Fawkes to blow up the Houses of Parliament in London, the name Guy swiftly fell out of favour in England.

The exact meaning of the name is unknown but it is thought to be derived from the Old German for 'wide' or 'wood'. In Latin it is associated with the word for 'lively'.

In Britain use of the name Guy was restored in the 19th century.

Variants: Gui, Guido, Vitus, Viti

Gwyn

The name Gwyn comes from the Welsh for 'blessed, holy' and 'white'. It is the masculine equivalent of Gwen.

Variants: Gwynfor, Wyn, Wynn, Wynford

Hadrian

See Adrian.

Hal

Hal is the short form of a variety of names including Henry, Harry and Harold. These three names all come from the Old German for 'army leader'. Hal is also a variant of Hale, which means 'safe, sound, healthy and whole' in Old English.

Variants: Hal, Haley, Halford, Halley, Hollis, Holly

Hale

As mentioned above Hale comes from the Old English word 'hal', which means 'safe, sound, healthy and whole'. It was also given to someone who lived in a nook or recess.

Variants: Hal, Haley, Halford, Halley, Harley, Hollis, Holly

Ham

As well as being a short form of Abraham ('father of many'), Ham comes from the Hebrew for 'hot' or 'swarthy'. In the Old Testament the name was borne by one of Noah's sons, who accompanied him on the Ark.

The Old English meaning of Ham is 'home', 'village' or 'town'. (See also Abraham.)
Variant: Abraham

Hamal
The Arabic meaning of Hamal is 'lamb'.

Hamilton
The name Hamilton has more than one Old English meaning. It means 'home' and 'lover' or 'blunt, flat-topped hill'. The name was first brought to Scotland in the 13th century and became associated with an influential family who acquired the dukedom of Hamilton. A town near Glasgow was later named after the family.

In North America the surname was given to boys as a first name in honour of Alexander Hamilton who was Secretary of the Treasury during George Washington's presidency.
Variants: Hamel, Hamil, Hamill

Hamish
Hamish is another name that is typically Scottish. It is the Anglicised spelling of Shamus, which is the Gaelic version of James. James is the New Testament version of Jacob, which means 'supplanter' in Hebrew.
Variants: Jacob, James

Hank
In North America Hank is a pet form of the name Henry, which means 'home ruler' in Old German.
Variants: Hankin, Henry

Hans
Hans is the short form of the name Johannes, which is a German version of John. The Hebrew meaning of John is 'God has favoured', 'God is gracious' or 'God is merciful'.
Variants: Johannes, John

Harding

The Old English family name Hearding was derived from the word 'heard', which means 'hardy, brave and strong'. Hearding eventually developed into the contemporary form Harding and was borne as a surname by the American President Warren Harding. This 20th century leader may have influenced its use as a given name.

Harding may also be a variant of Hardy, which comes from the Old French for 'to grow bold'.

Variants: Harden, Hardy

Hardy

In addition to being a pet form of Harding (see above), Hardy is an independent name in its own right. It is both a given name and surname that comes from the Old French for 'to grow bold'.

Variants: Harden, Hardin, Harding

Harlan

In North America the surname Harlan was first given to boys as a first name in honour of the Republican supporter of civil rights, John Marshall Harlan. Harlan, who died in 1911, was the descendant of George Harland, an English emigrant who settled in Delaware in 1687 and went on to become its governor.

Harland's surname was derived from a variety of place names in England and comes from the Old English for 'grey or hare land'.

Variant: Harland, Harley

Harlequin

Two theories exist to explain the origin of Harlequin. One suggestion is that it comes from the Old English name Herla, which was borne by a king who led a troop of demon horsemen through the night. The second theory focuses on the Modern English and Old French meaning of 'harlequin'. Namely that it is a mute, colourfully dressed pantomime character who usually wears a black mask.

Harley

The name, which is bestowed upon children of either sex, is Old English in origin. The first element, 'har', comes from either 'haer' ('rock, heap of stones') or 'hara', which means 'hare'. The second element is derived from 'leah' – the Old English word for 'wood, meadow' or 'clearing'.

Harley also comes from the Middle Low German for 'hemp, flax'. Thus it also means 'hemp field'.

Variants: Harl, Harlan

Harper

See Harper in the Girls' section

Harold

In the 20th century the name Harold was borne by two British Prime Ministers – Harold Macmillan and Harold Wilson.

In 1066 the name was borne by King Harold, the last king of England before the Norman invasion. It was Harold whom William the Conqueror defeated at the Battle of Hastings. Harold not only lost the battle, and his kingdom; Hastings was also the scene of his death.

The name comes from the Old English for 'army ruler' and is derived from the Old German name Heriwald, which means 'army power'. Harold was probably brought to England by Danish invaders.

Variants: Hal, Haldon, Halford, Harald, Hariwald, Harlow, Harry

Harrison

Harrison means simply 'son of Harry'. And Harry is a short form of Harold, which comes from the Old English for 'army ruler'.

It is a surname that was borne by two American Presidents, William Henry Harrison and his grandson, Benjamin Harrison and may have been given to little boys as a first name in their honour. More recently, American actor, Harrison Ford, has increased its popularity.

Variants: Harold, Harry

Harte

The Old English meaning of Harte is 'hart' or 'stag'. It is also an English family name that was derived from a variety of place names in England.
Variants: Hart, Hartley, Hartman, Hartwell

Hartley

Like Harte, Hartley comes from the Old English for a 'mature male deer'. With the suffix 'ley' it also bears the meaning 'wood, meadow or clearing'. Thus Hartley means 'deer meadow'.

It is a surname that was originally the name of a number of places in England.
Variants: Hart, Harte, Hartman, Hartwell, Heartley

Harvey

When the Normans invaded England in 1066 they brought the name Harvey with them. The Breton personal name means 'battle worthy'. It was borne by a 6th century blind saint. The French version of the name is Hervé.

Harvey is also an English family name.
Variants: Ervé, Harv, Harve, Harveson, Hervé, Hervey, Hervi

Hassan

This Arabic name means 'handsome', 'good' or 'pleasant'. It was borne by the grandson of the Prophet Muhammad, who was called Hasan ibn Ali ibn Abu Talib.
Variants: Asan, Hasan

Haydn

The name was derived from the Old High German for 'heathen' and may have originally been used as a nickname. Haydn also comes from the Old English for 'hay' and 'grassy dell'. It can be given to both boys and girls.
Variants: Hayden, Haydon, Hayes, Hays, Haywood, Heywood

Heath

The Old English meaning of this name, is 'heath' or 'place where wild plants grow'.

It is an English family name originally given to someone who lived on or near a heath. It is now also used as a first name.

Hector

The name Hector comes from the Greek for 'to restrain' or 'anchor'. According to Greek mythology it was the name of the Trojan prince who fought in the Trojan War before he was slain by Achilles.

In Scotland, where the name is especially popular, Hector is the Anglicised form of the Gaelic name Eachdonn.
Variants: Eachann, Eachdonn, Ector, Ettore, Heck, Heckie, Hecky

Helmut

The Germanic name Helmut is associated with warriors, perhaps because it comes from the Old French for 'helmet' and 'strong'. It also has the Teutonic meaning 'spirited' and 'brave'.
Variants: Helm, Helmuth

Henry

When the Prince and Princess of Wales named their second son Henry (Prince Harry, as he is known, is a pet form of Henry) in 1984 they were continuing a long-held association between the name and British royalty. So far there have been eight kings of England bearing the name Henry. They include Henry I, the youngest son of William the Conqueror, and Henry V who won the Battle of Agincourt in 1415. But perhaps the best known King Henry was Henry VIII, the father of Queen Elizabeth I.

In North America the name is associated with the English navigator Henry Hudson, after whom the Hudson River, Hudson Bay and the Hudson Strait were named.
Variants: Enri, Enric, Enrico, Enrique, Hal, Hank, Harry, Heinrich, Heinz, Henri

Herbert
Herbert is an Old French name of German (Frankish) origin. It means 'bright army'. An Old English version of the name existed in England but was replaced by the Norman equivalent after the Norman Conquest of 1066.
Variants: Bert, Bertie, Herb, Herbie

Hercules
The name Hercules is associated with the son of Zeus, the supreme god of Greek mythology.

Hercules was famed for performing 12 almost impossible tasks. They included the capture of a golden horned stag and the slaying of a serpent with nine heads.
Variants: Herc, Hercule, Herk, Herkie

Herman
The Old High German meaning of Herman is 'army man' or 'soldier'. Although the Normans favoured the name Herman, its use in Britain died out by the 14th century. It was revived during the 1800s. German immigrants took the name with them to North America and in France the French form Armand is used.
Variants: Armand, Armant, Harman, Hermann, Hermie, Hermy

Hilal
Hilal means 'new moon' in Arabic.
Variant: Hilel

Hiram
In the Bible Hiram was the King of Tyre who was an ally of King David and his son King Solomon. According to the Old Testament Hiram demonstrated his friendship by sending supplies, craftsmen and money to build various buildings, including the temple at Jerusalem.

The Hebrew meaning of Hiram is 'brother of the exalted one'.

Hoffman
Hoffman is a German name that means 'courtier' or 'man of influence and flattery'. It was borne by the German romantic novelist Ernst Hoffman who died in 1822.

Holt
The Old English meaning of the name Holt is 'wooded hill' or 'copse'.

Although used as a first name it is probably better known as a surname.

Homer
The name Homer was given to a legendary poet believed to have lived in the 8th century BC, who composed the *Iliad* and the *Odyssey*. He was perhaps more a collective tradition than a single man.

In the first poem Homer detailed the Trojan War and in the second he recounted Odysseus' journey home afterwards.

In Greek the name Homer means 'being hostage or led'. The Old French interpretation of the name is 'helmet maker' and it also comes from the Old English for 'pool in a hollow'. The name has been found in Britain since the 19th century.

In recent years the name Homer has been linked to the US cartoon series, *The Simpsons,* an inescapable part of popular culture since the 1990s.
Variants: Homero, Omero

Horace
Horace comes from the Roman family name Horatius, which was borne by the celebrated 1st century BC poet Quintus Horatius Flaccus. His name comes from the Latin for 'hour'.

In Britain use of this name increased during the Renaissance when it was the vogue to choose classical names for children. Orazio is the Italian equivalent of the name.
Variants: Horacio, Horatio, Horatius, Orazio

Horatio

Horatio is a variant of the name Horace, which comes from the Latin for 'hour'. Shakespeare used the name for one of his characters in the play *Hamlet*.

Horatio was also borne by Admiral Horatio Nelson, who defeated Napoleon at the Battle of Trafalgar, a cause to which he gave his life. Horatio Nelson was killed in action in 1805.
Variants: Horace, Horacio, Horatius, Orazio

Howard

In England Howard is the surname of the family that holds the hereditary title Duke of Norfolk. A number of theories exist to explain the meaning of their name. Howard may come from the Old English for 'fence-keeper' or 'hog warden'. Thus originally it was an occupational name.

The Scandinavian meaning of Howard is 'high guardian'. It also comes from the Old German for 'heart protector' and 'bold'.
Variants: Hogg, Howey, Howie, Ward

Hubert

It is said that the 8th century Bishop of Maastricht, St Hubert, was converted to Christianity after seeing a vision of Christ's crucifixion between the antlers of a stag when he was out hunting. Hubert is the patron saint of hunters and a picture of a stag is his emblem.

The Normans first brought the name Hubert to England in the 11th century. It is an Old French name that is of Germanic (Frankish) origin. It means 'heart, mind, spirit' and 'bright, famous'.
Variants: Bert, Bertie, Berty, Bart, Hubie, Huey, Hugh, Hughie, Hugi

Hugh

Hugh is another name that was brought to England by the invading Normans of the 11th century. In medieval Europe the name was borne by the French aristocracy and in Britain Hugh was mentioned in the Domesday Book.

The Old German meaning of Hugh is 'mind, spirit', but

another Celtic name that sounds the same – Hu, Hew – means 'fire' or 'inspiration'.
Variants: Bert, Bertie, Berty, Hew, Hubert, Huey, Hughie, Hugo, Huw

Hugo
Hugo is the German version of Hugh that was frequently used in the Middle Ages. (See Hugh and Hubert.)

Humphrey
Born in 1899 Humphrey Bogart was an American actor, married to the actress Lauren Bacall, who was best known for his role in the film classic *Casablanca*, in which he starred opposite Ingrid Bergman. His name comes from the Old German for 'strength' and 'peace'.
Variants: Hum, Humfrey, Humfrid, Hump, Humph, Humphry

Hunter
Hunter was originally an occupational and family name before being given to children of both sexes as their first name. First used in Scotland, it comes from the Old English word 'huntian', which meant 'to search diligently, pursue or track down'. The Old Norse meaning of the name is 'to group'.
Variants: Huntington, Huntley, Lee, Leigh

Huxley
The Old English meaning of Huxley is 'field of ash trees'.
Variants: Haskell, Hux, Lee, Leigh

Hyam
The Jewish name Hyam comes from the Hebrew for 'life'.

Hywel
Hywel is a name that was frequently used in the Middle Ages. It comes from the Welsh for 'eminent' or 'conspicuous' and the Old English for 'swine hill'.
Variants: Howe, Howel, Howell, Howey, Howland

I

Iago
Shakespeare gave the name Iago to a key character in his play *Othello*. It is the Spanish and Welsh version of the New Testament name James, which appears in the Old Testament as Jacob.

All three names mean 'supplanter' in Hebrew. (See also Jacob and James.)
Variants: Jacob, James

Ian
Ian is the Scottish variant of the Biblical name John, which means 'God is gracious', 'God is merciful' and 'God has favoured' in Hebrew.
Variants: Iain, John

Ibrahim
This is the Arabic form of the Old Testament name Abraham, which comes from the Hebrew for 'father of many' or 'father of a multitude'. (See also Abraham.)
Variant: Abraham

Idris
According to Welsh legend, Idris the Giant was an astronomer and magician who was killed in 632. Cader Idris, a mountain in Wales, was said to be his observatory and the English translation of the place name is 'Idris's Chair'.

The name Idris comes from the Welsh for 'lord' and 'ardent, impulsive'. Although not a popular name in the 20th or 21st centuries, the name was often used during the Middle Ages and experienced a revival in the late 19th century.

Ieuan
Ieuan is a Welsh version of the name John, which means 'God is gracious', 'God is merciful' and 'God has favoured' in Hebrew.
Variants: Iefan, Ifan

Boys

I

Ignatius
The exact meaning of the name Ignatius is uncertain, although it was derived from the Old Roman family name Egnatius. It is not clear where that family name came from, but during the early Christian period the first letter 'e' was replaced with an 'i' – perhaps to associate the name with the Latin word 'ignis', which means 'fire'.

Nevertheless, the name was borne by more than one saint including St Ignatius of Loyola (born Inigo Lopez de Recalde in 1491) who founded the Society of Jesus or Jesuits.
Variants: Egnacio, Iggie, Iggy, Ignace, Ignatio, Inigo

Igor
According to Norse legend Ing was the god of fertility. The name Igor comes from the Old Norse for 'Ing's warrior'. It is also a variant of the Greek name George, which means 'farmer'.
Variants: Inge, Ingmar, Ingvar

Ike
Ike is the short form of the Hebrew name Isaac, which means 'he laughed' or 'laughter'.

One famous 20th century Ike was the former President of the United States, Dwight D Eisenhower. Eisenhower, who was in the White House from 1953 to 1961, bore the nickname even though he was not called Isaac.
Variant: Isaac

Illtyd
The Welsh name Illtyd was borne by a saint who lived during the 5th and 6th centuries. He was a well-known scholar and teacher who founded a school where a number of other Welsh saints studied. According to legend he introduced the plough to the people of Wales.

His name comes from the Welsh for 'multitude' and 'land' or 'people'.
Variant: Illtud

I

Inigo

As mentioned above, Inigo was the name of St Ignatius of Loyola. The exact meaning of the name is unknown but, as a variant of Ignatius, it may mean 'fiery'.

The name was often found in medieval Spain and is thought to be of Basque origin. Today it is little used in Spain, but in the 16th century the marriage between the English monarch, Queen Mary, and Philip of Spain may have influenced its use in England. A bearer of the name was Inigo Jones, the 16th century English architect and stage designer.
Variants: Eneco, Ignatius

Ingmar

The name Ingmar is often found in Scandinavian countries. It comes from the Norse for 'famous son'.

Ingram

According to Norse mythology Ing was the god of peace and fertility. He was known for his sword that could move by itself through the air. The name Ingram, therefore, comes from the Old Norse for 'Ing's raven'.

The name was popular throughout the Middle Ages, but fell out of favour after the Reformation. (See also Gram.)
Variants: Gram, Ingo, Ingrim

Innes

Innes, a name that can be given to both boys and girls, comes from the Gaelic for 'island'. It is also a surname.
Variant: Innis

Iolo

This Welsh name is a short form of Iorwerth, which means 'lord', 'value' and 'worth'. It is also the Welsh equivalent of Edward, which comes from the Old English for 'fortunate guardian'. (See also Edward.)
Variant: Edward

Ira
Ira is another Old Testament name that was favoured by the 17th century Puritans. In the Bible he was the captain of King David's army. The name means 'leader'.

Irvin
Irvin is the American version of the Gaelic name Irving, which may have been derived from a number of sources. One possible meaning is 'handsome or fair'. It could also come from the Welsh for 'green, fresh' or 'white water'. Irving may have also been derived from a Scottish place name that meant 'west river'.

Irving also has Old English roots meaning 'sea' or 'boar and friend'.
Variants: Irvine, Irving

Ishmael
In the Old Testament, when Sarah and Abraham could not conceive a child she encouraged her husband to have a baby with her maid Hagar. That child was called Ishmael whose name means 'God hears' or 'outcast' in Hebrew. The second meaning of his name is appropriate because after relations between Hagar and Sarah deteriorated the maid ran away. She eventually returned from her self-imposed exile in the desert and her son went on to become the father of the Arabs who were also known as the Ismailites.
Variants: Esmael, Isamel, Ismael, Ysmael

Islwyn
Islwyn is a Welsh name that is also borne by a mountain located in the county of Gwent. The name means 'below the grove'.

Isaac
According to the Bible, when God promised Abraham that he would conceive a child with his elderly wife Sarah, he laughed. As a result their son was named Isaac, which means 'he laughed' or 'laughter' in Hebrew.

Isaac was the first link in the chain that fulfilled God's promise to Abraham when he renamed him Abraham – 'father of many'. Isaac fathered the twins Esau and Jacob, and was grandfather to Jacob's 12 sons who founded the 12 tribes of Israel.
Variants: Ike, Isaacus, Isaak, Isac, Itzik, Izaak

Isaiah
In the Bible the name Isaiah was borne by one of the Old Testament prophets who lived in Judah in the 8th century BC. Isaiah, who worked as a prophet for 58 years, predicted that the Messiah would be born to a virgin.
Variants: Is, Isaias, Issa

Israel
In the Old Testament Israel was the name given to Jacob after he wrestled with an angel. In Hebrew his name means either 'may God prevail' or 'he who strives with God'. Jacob was also told that his descendants were to be known as the Israelites.

Ivan
The name Ivan was borne by six Russian leaders, including Ivan the Great and Ivan the Terrible. It is the Slavic version of the Biblical name John, which in Hebrew means 'God is gracious', 'God has favoured' and 'God is merciful'.

The name was also used by the Russian writer Leo Tolstoy in his 1886 work, *The Death of Ivan Ilyich*.
Variants: Evo, Evon, Ivo, Vanya, Yvan, Yvon

Ivor
There is more than one explanation for the origin of the name Ivor. It may come from the Latin for 'ivory' or the Welsh for 'lord' or 'archer'. Another possible source is the Old Norse for 'bow made of yew' or 'army'.
Variants: Ifor, Iomhar, Ivair, Ivar, Ive, Iver, Ivon, Yvon

Jabez

This name was a favourite among the 17ᵗʰ century Puritans. It was borne by an Old Testament character and means 'born in pain' or 'born in sorrow' in Hebrew.

Jack

As a pet form of the name John, Jack comes from the Hebrew for 'God is gracious', 'God is merciful' and 'God has favoured'. It is also sometimes used as the pet form of the name James ('supplanter'), probably under the influence of the French form of the name, which appears as Jacques.

One person who was also known by the pet form Jack was the 1961 to 1963 President of the United States, John F Kennedy. Today the name is used independently, especially in Britain where the name is popular with parents.

Variants: Jacob, Jacques, James, John

Jacob

In the Old Testament Jacob was the twin brother of Esau and the son of Isaac and Rebecca. He was also the father of 12 sons who went on to found the 12 tribes of Israel.

The name Jacob comes from the Hebrew for 'follower' or 'supplanter'. It is also said to mean 'heel grabber' because, according to the Bible, when the twins were born, Jacob was holding on to his brother's heel.

The New Testament version of the name Jacob is James and both names have spawned numerous derivatives and short forms including Jack, Jake, Iago and Jacques.

Variants: Iago, Jack, Jacobson, Jacoby, Jacques, Jago, Jaime, Jakab, Jake, Jamie

Jago

Jago is a Cornish form of the name James, which is a variant of Jacob. Jago means 'supplanter' in Hebrew. (See also Jacob and James.)

Variants: Iago, Jack, Jacobson, Jacoby, Jacques, Jaime, Jakab, Jake, James, Jamie

Jake

Although the name Jake is considered to be an independent name in its own right, it originally was used as a pet form of the names John and Jacob. As a variant of John, Jake assumes the Hebrew meaning 'God is gracious', 'God has favoured' and 'God is merciful'. As a pet form of Jacob it means 'supplanter'.
Variants: Jacob, Jacobson, Jacoby, Jacques, Jakab, James, Jamie, John

Jamal

The Arabic meaning of the name Jamal is 'handsome'. Jamelia is its feminine equivalent.
Variants: Gamal, Jahmal, Jamaal, Jamael, Jamahl, Jamall, Jameel, Jamel, Jamil

James

In Britain the name James is associated with seven kings of Scotland and two kings of England. In the Bible the name was also connected with more than one person. It was the name of two of Christ's Apostles – James the son of Zebedee and James the son of Alphaeus. James was also said to be the name of Christ's own brother.

The name is derived from the same Latin source as the Old Testament name Jacob. Like Jacob it means 'supplanter' in Hebrew.

James has been such a popular name that various cultures around the world have developed their own variants. In the Scottish Highlands James appears as Hamish and the Irish equivalent is Seamus. The pet form Jamie is also given to children of either sex. Jim is also a popular derivative.
Variants: Hamish, Jack, Jacob, Jacques, Jaime, Jamie, Jim, Jimmie, Jimmy, Seamus

Janus

In Roman mythology Janus was the double-headed god of gateways, endings and beginnings. He was often pictured looking both ways. The month of January, which signals the start of a fresh year, was derived from his name.

The Latin meaning of Janus is 'passage', 'gateway' or 'arcade'.
Variants: Januaris, Jarek

Jared

The Biblical character of Jared was blessed with longevity. He lived until the age of 962 and fathered a son comparatively early on in his life (when he was 100).

The Hebrew meaning of Jared's name was 'descent' and, given that he was a descendant of Adam, it is appropriate. The name also comes from the Greek for 'rose' and, as a variant of Gerard, boasts the Germanic meaning 'brave or strong spear'.

Although the Puritans favoured the name Jared, its use eventually went into decline before it was revived in the 1960s. It is especially popular in America and Australia.
Variants: Gerard, Jarett, Jarrad, Jarrath, Jarratt, Jarrod, Jered

Jarratt

As a variant of Jared, Jarratt means 'descent' in Hebrew and 'rose' in Greek. As a variant of Gerard it means 'brave or strong spear'. (See also Jared and Gerard.)
Variants: Garett, Gerard, Jared

Jarvis

The exact meaning of the name Jarvis is unclear. It may come from the Germanic for 'spear', as a variant of Gerard. It may equally come from the Celtic for 'servant' as a variant of the Norman given name Gervaise. (See also Gerard and Gervase.)
Variants: Gary, Gervais, Gervaise, Gervase, Jary, Jarry, Jerve, Jervis

Jason

Four different Biblical characters bore the name Jason. They include the man who was believed to have written the Book of Ecclesiastes and a relative of St Paul. It is for this reason that the name was popular among the Puritans.

As a variant of the Biblical name Joshua, Jason comes from the Hebrew 'God saves'. Its Greek meaning is 'to heal'.

Indeed, Greek mythology provides perhaps the most famous early bearer of the name – the leader of the Argonauts who undertook a quest to find the Golden Fleece. His journey took him to Colchis, where he met and fell in love with the sorceress Medea. She helped Jason in his search but he betrayed her by deserting her for another woman.
Variants: Jace, Jay, Joshua

Jasper
According to the Bible Jasper was the name of one of the three kings who brought gifts to the baby Jesus. Appropriately, the Persian meaning of the name is 'treasurer'. It also comes from the Arabic word for the semi-precious stone that is reddish-brown in colour.

Jasper has spawned a number of derivatives, including Caspar, the Germanic Gaspar and the French Gaspard.
Variants: Caspar, Casper, Gaspar, Gaspard, Kasper

Jay
As a variant of the Biblical name James, Jay comes from the Hebrew for 'supplanter' and is also related to the Old Testament name Jacob. Jay is also a short form of a wide variety of names, all beginning with the letter 'J'.

As an independent name Jay is derived from the Latin word 'gaius', which means 'a bird's harsh chirping'. Thus to give a person the nickname Jay was to say that they were a chatterbox.
Variants: Jacob, James, Jaye, Jey, Jeye

Jed
A Puritan favourite, the name Jed was originally used as a short form of Jedidiah – a name that belonged to an Old Testament character. In Hebrew Jedidiah means 'beloved of God'.
Variants: Jedd, Jedidiah

Jefferson
The name Jefferson is popular in North America where it is

associated with the third President of the United States. Born in 1743, Thomas Jefferson, who was a scientist, architect and writer, drafted the American Declaration of Independence. His surname may have been given to boys in his honour.

Jefferson simply means 'son of Jeffrey'. Jeffrey is a variant of Geoffrey, which comes from the Old German for 'God's peace' and 'peaceful traveller'. (See also Geoffrey.)

Jeffrey
See Geoffrey.

Jem
As the short form of Jeremy, Jem comes from the Biblical name Jeremiah, which means 'appointed by God' in Hebrew. As a short form of James it is a variant of Jacob, which also comes from Hebrew and means 'supplanter'. (See also Jeremy.)
Variants: Jacob, James, Jeremiah, Jeremy

Jeremy
The name Jeremy is derived from the Biblical name Jeremiah which, in Hebrew, means 'appointed or exalted by God'.

Notable bearers of the name include the English philosopher, social and legal reformer, Jeremy Bentham (1748-1832) who was associated with utilitarianism.
Variants: Gerome, Gerrie, Gerry, Jem, Jeremiah, Jerome, Jerry

Jeremiah
In the Bible the name Jeremiah was borne by the Old Testament prophet and author of the Book of Lamentations. It was Jeremiah who criticised his people for their less-than-Godly actions and was upset by the destruction of Jerusalem. The Hebrew meaning of his name is 'appointed or exalted by God'.

The name Jeremiah was used in Britain during the Middle Ages and later became popular among the Puritans of the 17th century.
Variants: Gerome, Gerrie, Gerry, Jem, Jere, Jeremia, Jeremias, Jeremy, Jerome, Jerry

J

Jermaine
Jermaine is a variant of Germaine, which comes from the Latin for 'clan brother'. The French meaning of the name is 'German'.
Variants: Germain, Germane, Germayne, Jermain, Jermayn, Jermayne, Jerri, Jerrie, Jerry

Jerome
The name Jerome has been found in Britain since the 12th century. It is a variant of Gerome, which comes from the Greek for 'holy and sacred name'.

One notable bearer of the name was St Jerome, the patron saint of archaeologists, librarians and students, who was born in 342. He was the secretary of Pope Damascus, who was involved in translating the Bible into Latin.
Variants: Gerome, Geronimus, Gerrie, Gerry, Jeromo, Jerrome, Jerry

Jesse
Jesse is an Old Testament name that found favour in Britain after the Reformation. In the Bible it was the name of King David's father. In North America the name was associated with the outlaw, Jesse James. More recently it has been linked to the politician Jesse Jackson. The Hebrew meaning of the name is 'gift'.
Variants: Jake, Jess, Jessie, Jessy

Jesus
The name Jesus is a variant of the Old Testament name Joshua, which comes from the Hebrew for 'God saves' or 'the Lord is my salvation'. Jesus is popular in Spanish-speaking countries where it is pronounced as *'Hay-soos'*.
Variants: Hesus, Jesous, Jesu, Jesuso, Jezus, Joshua

Jet
As a short form of Jethro, Jet comes from the Hebrew for 'excellence' or 'wealth'. It also means 'stone'.
Variants: Jethro, Jett

Jethro

In the Bible the name Jethro belonged to the father-in-law of Moses. As mentioned above it comes from the Hebrew for 'excellence' or 'wealth'.

In Britain the name enjoyed some currency from the 16th century and became a Puritan favourite. In particular it was the name of Jethro Tull, an English agricultural reformer born in 1674.
Variants: Jeth, Jet, Jett

Joab

The Old Testament name Joab was borne by a nephew of King David. In Hebrew it means 'God the father' and 'praise the Lord'.
Variant: Yoav

Job

To say someone has 'the patience of Job' is to say that they are able to endure great hardship or delay. This well-known saying refers to the Biblical character of Job, who patiently endured great suffering.

In the Old Testament Job was a wealthy man who fathered 10 children and was enriched with many animals and servants. He was also upright and righteous. In an attempt to prove that Job would not remain faithful to God if he underwent great tribulation, Satan afflicted him with numerous disasters. They included the deaths of his family members and a plague of boils. Throughout it all Job praised the Lord and God rewarded Job by doubling his earlier prosperity. Unsurprisingly the Hebrew meaning of Job is 'persecuted' or 'oppressed'.
Variants: Joabee, Jobey, Joabie, Jobie, Joby

Jock

Jock is often used as a nickname for a Scotsman. However, it is also the Scottish variant of the names Jack and John, both of which come from the Hebrew for 'God is gracious', 'God is merciful' and 'God has favoured'.
Variants: Jack, John

J

Joel

The Hebrew meaning of Joel is 'Jehovah is God' and 'God is willing'. The name was a favourite among Puritans and Christian fundamentalists.

The book of Joel is in the Old Testament and is considered a 'literary jewel'.

Variant: Yoel

John

Of all the names found in the Bible and favoured by Christians, John has been a source of inspiration for parents for centuries, spawning variants and short forms around the world. Numerous saints and popes have borne the name. In the New Testament it belonged to three important characters – namely John the Baptist (the prophet, preacher and cousin of Jesus), John the Apostle (a fisherman and brother of James) and John the Evangelist (the author of the Gospel of St John, three Epistles and the Book of Revelation).

The name these three men shared also had a holy meaning that would have appealed to Christian parents. It comes from the Hebrew for 'God is gracious', 'God is merciful' and 'God has favoured'.

Unsurprisingly numerous men from history have borne the name. They include the British poets John Milton and John Keats, the English painter John Constable, the former American President, John F Kennedy and the British-born musician and former Beatle, John Lennon. The name John has also produced the short forms and variants Jack, Jock, Ian, Johannes, Sean, Ivan and Juan, among others.

Variants: Ian, Ivan, Jack, Jock, Johannes, Jonnie, Jonny, Juan, Owen, Zane

Jonah

The Biblical story of Jonah and the whale was a popular tale in the Middle Ages. Miracle plays were performed that recounted Jonah's disobedience of God. Refusing to preach in Nineveh, defiant Jonah boarded a ship and sailed in the opposite direction. God responded by creating a storm that threatened the safety of the vessel. Jonah was thrown overboard and swallowed by a 'great fish' that deposited him at the shores of Nineveh.

Jonah's name comes from the Hebrew for 'dove' or 'pigeon'. *Variants: Jonas, Yona, Yonah*

Jonathan
In the Old Testament the name Jonathan was borne by King Saul's son who was also a friend of King David. The Hebrew meaning of the name is 'God's gift'.
Variants: Johnathan, Johnathon, Jon, Jonathon, Jonnie, Jonny, Jonty, Yonatan

Jordan
The River Jordan plays an important role in the New Testament story of Jesus Christ. It was there that John the Baptist baptised his cousin Jesus, the Messiah. It is for this reason that medieval pilgrims who travelled to the Holy Land returned with a flask of water from the River Jordan to baptise their own offspring, some of whom would have been called Jordan as a result.

The Hebrew meaning of Jordan is 'to flow down'. The name, which is given to boys and girls, is also associated with Jordan, the Middle Eastern country.
Variants: Jared, Jarrod, Jerad, Jordain, Jori, Jory, Judd

Joseph
The name Joseph was borne by two prominent characters in the Bible. In the Old Testament it was the name of the first of Jacob and Rachel's two sons. Although Jacob had 10 more sons Joseph was his favourite and he demonstrated this by giving him an elaborate coat of many colours. In the New Testament Joseph was the name of the earthly father of Jesus, the Virgin Mary's husband. The Hebrew meaning of the name is 'God will add (another son)'.
Variants: Jo, Joe, Joey, Jojo, José, Josephe, Yousef

J

Joshua

In the Old Testament Joshua was the successor of Moses who led the Israelites into the Promised Land. The Hebrew meaning of his name is 'the Lord saves'.

Jason is the Greek form of the name and Jesus is the version that is used in the New Testament.

Variants: Hosea, Jason, Jesous, Jesus, Josh

Joubert

Joubert comes from the Old English for 'bright, shining'. It is a derivative of the Old English name Godbeorht, which meant 'God's radiance'.

Variant: Jovett

Juan

Juan is the Spanish version of John, which means 'God is gracious', 'God is merciful' and 'God has favoured' in Hebrew. (See also John.)

Variants: DeJuan, John

Judd

As a variant of Jordan, Judd comes from the Hebrew for 'to flow down', but as a short form of Judah it means 'praise'. It is also a surname. (See also Jordan.)

Variants: Jordan, Judah, Jude

Jude

Of the 12 Apostles of Christ, two bore the name Judas – Judas Iscariot and Judas Thaddaeus.

The first Judas was infamous for his betrayal of Jesus with a kiss. The second Judas is also known as St Jude who wrote the Epistle of Jude and is the patron saint of lost causes and desperate situations.

Like Judd, Jude is derived from Judah, which means 'praise' in Hebrew. The name has been a source of inspiration for more than one artist.

In the 19ᵗʰ century British novelist Thomas Hardy wrote *Jude the Obscure.*
Variants: Jud, Juda, Judah, Judas, Judd, Judson, Yehudi

Jules

Jules is the short form of the name Julian, which means 'fair-skinned' in Latin. (See Julian and Julius.)
Variants: Julian, Julius

Julian

Julian is taken from the name of the Roman clan, the Julii, who claimed to be direct descendents of Aphrodite, the goddess of love. The exact meaning of their name is somewhat unclear, but it is thought to come from the Latin for 'fair-skinned'.
Variants: Giuliano, Iola, Jolin, Jolyon, Jule, Jules, Julianus, Julius, Julyan

Julius

Since the days of Ancient Rome the name Julius has been inextricably linked to Julius Caesar. The name Julius Caesar was borne by more than one leader of Rome. They include the military and political leader who had an affair with Cleopatra, the Queen of Egypt, and is the subject of a Shakespearean play. His adopted son, Gaius Julius Caesar Octavianus, became the first emperor of Rome.
Variants: Jule, Jules, Julian, Julianus

Jun

The Chinese meaning of Jun is 'truth', and in Japan it means 'obedience'.

Justin

The name Justin was borne by a 2ⁿᵈ century saint who refused to sacrifice to the gods. His name comes from the Latin for 'just'.

Iestyn and Iestin, the Welsh equivalents of the name, have been in use since the 6ᵗʰ century.
Variants: Iestin, Iestyn, Justinian, Justis, Justus, Jut

Justus
Justus is a variant of Justin, which comes from the Latin for 'just' or 'fair'.
Variant: Justin

Kalil
The name Kalil has more than one meaning. It comes from the Arabic for 'good friend', the Greek for 'beautiful' and the Hebrew for 'wealth' or 'crown'.
Variants: Kahil, Kahlil, Kailil, Kal, Kallie, Khaleel, Khalil

Kalle
The Scandinavian meaning of this name is 'strong' and 'manly'.

Kamal
Kamal comes from the Arabic for 'perfection'. In India it is the name for the lotus flower and comes from the Sanskrit for 'pale red'.

Kamil
Like Kamal, Kamil means 'perfection' or 'complete' in Arabic. In the Koran it is listed as one of the 99 qualities of Allah.
Variant: Kameel

Kane
More than one theory exists to explain the meaning of Kane. It is the Anglicised form of the Irish Gaelic name Cathan, which means 'warrior'. It also comes from the Celtic for 'tribute', 'battler' and 'dark'. The Welsh meaning of Kane is 'lovely'. In Japan it means 'golden' and the Hawaiian interpretation is 'man'.

Kane may also come from the Old French for 'battlefield'. As well as being an Irish surname it was also the family name of someone from the French town of Caen. Kane was especially popular in 1960s Australia.
Variants: Kain, Kaine, Kayne

Karim

Karim comes from the Arabic for 'generous' and 'noble'. Like Kamil it appears in the Koran as one of the many names or qualities of Allah.
Variants: Kareem, Kario

Kasimir

The Slavonic meaning of Kasimir is 'commands peace', 'proclamation of peace' or, alternatively, 'to spoil peace'. It is also a name that was popular among supporters of Polish independence. Immigrants of Polish descent took the name with them to North America.

Kasper

Kasper is the German form of the name Jasper, which was borne by one of the three wise men who visited the baby Jesus. Thus it bears the Persian meaning of that name, 'treasurer'.
Variants: Kaspa, Caspar, Casper, Gaspar, Gaspard, Jasper

Keane

The Irish Gaelic meaning of Keane is 'warrior's son'. In Old English, the name means 'wise, clever' or 'brave and strong'. It is also the Anglicised form of the Gaelic name Cian, which means 'ancient'.
Variants: Kane, Kani, Kayne, Kean, Keen, Keenan, Kene, Keene, Kian, Kienan

Keegan

Keegan is the Anglicised form of the Gaelic surname MacAodhagáin.

Keir

The Irish Gaelic meaning of Keir is 'dark-skinned' or 'spear', although it also has an Old Norse meaning – 'marshland containing brushwood'. Keir is also a Scottish surname.
Variant: Kerr

Keith

The Scottish surname Keith was originally derived from a number of place names. The Scottish Gaelic meaning of the name is 'wood', while in Irish Gaelic it stands for 'battlefield'. It was not used as a first name until the 20th century.

Kelly

See Kelly in the Girls' section.

Kelsey

Kelsey has more than one Old English meaning. It means 'ship's keel' or 'ship' and 'victory'. It also comes from the Irish Gaelic for 'warrior'. It is given to both boys and girls.
Variants: Kelcey, Kelley, Kelsee, Kelsie, Kelson, Kelton

Kelvin

First used as a given name in the 1920s, Kelvin is the name of a river that runs through Glasgow in Scotland. The Old English meaning of Kelvin is 'ship's keel' or 'friend'. It also means 'narrow stream' in Gaelic.
Variants: Kelvan, Kelven, Kelwin

Kendall

In North America the name Kendall is given to both boys and girls. However, the name was originally taken from two place names in Britain – one in Cumbria and the other in Humberside.

The Old English meaning of the name is 'royal valley'. It also boasts the Celtic meaning 'high, exalted' and 'image, effigy'.
Variants: Ken, Kendal, Kendell, Kenn, Kennie, Kenny, Kendahl, Kendale, Kendyl, Kyndal

Kennedy

The Kennedy name comes from the Irish Gaelic for 'head' and 'ugly'. It also comes from the Old English for 'ruler'. As a first name it is given to both boys and girls.

In North America the name Kennedy is associated with the

powerful political family who are of Irish descent. The Kennedys rose to prominence during the 20th century, under the guidance of the patriarch Joseph Kennedy. Joseph's second son with his wife Rose, was John Fitzgerald Kennedy who was President of the United States in the early 1960s, before he was assassinated in 1963. Their third son, Robert F Kennedy, met the same fate in 1968 when he was on the campaign trail to the White House.
Variants: Ken, Kenman, Kenn, Kennard, Kennie, Kenny, Kent, Kenton, Kenyan

Kenelm

The Old English meaning of the name Kenelm is 'brave helmet'. The name was popular in the Middle Ages because of the fame of a 9th-century Mercian prince who was a saint and a martyr. The name was later borne by the 17th century diplomat, scholar and writer, Sir Kenelm Digby.
Variants: Ken, Kennie, Kenny

Kenneth

Two kings of Scotland bore the name Kenneth, including Kenneth I who defeated the Picts and was the first to rule both the Picts and the Scots.

The Gaelic meaning of the name is either 'born of fire' or 'handsome'. The Old English meaning is 'royal oath'.
Variants: Cainnech, Ken, Kene, Kenn, Kennie, Kenny, Kent, Kenton, Kenward

Kent

In England Kent is a southern county. It is also a family name, which shares the Old English meaning 'white', 'border' or 'coastal district'. Kent is also a short form of the name Kenton, which may come from the Old English for 'royal manor'.

As a variant of Kennedy it means 'ugly head' and as a derivative of Kenneth it means 'born of fire', 'handsome' or 'royal oath'. (See also Kennedy and Kenneth.)
Variant: Ken, Kennedy, Kenneth, Kenton, Kenyon

Kern
The Old Irish meaning of Kern is 'band of infantry'.
Variants: Kearney, Kearny

Kerr
As a variant of Keir, Kerr comes from the Irish Gaelic for 'dark-skinned' and 'spear'. It also comes from the Old Norse for 'marshland containing brushwood'. The name was originally given to someone who lived near wet ground.
Variant: Keir

Kerry
See Kerry in the Girls' section.

Kevin
Before the 1920s, use of the name Kevin was largely confined to Ireland, where it is associated with the patron saint of Dublin who died in 618. St Kevin's name comes from an Old Irish name that means 'handsome birth'.
Variants: Coemgen, Kev, Kevan, Keven, Kerrie, Kerry

Kieran
Like the girl's name Kiera, Kieran comes from the Irish word 'ciar', which means 'black'. Thus the name Kieran means 'dark one'.

Several Irish saints bore the name, which may explain its popularity.
Variants: Ciaran, Ciaren, Kiaran, Kyron

Killian
Killian is another name that is closely linked to Ireland. It was borne by an Irish saint who was martyred during a mission to Germany in the 7th century. Killian's name is thought to come from the Irish word for 'strife', but it also derives its meaning from the Gaelic for 'church' or 'little warrior'.
Variants: Cilian, Cillian, Killie, Killy, Kilmer

Kim

In 1901, British writer Rudyard Kipling published his book *Kim*, which told the story of a little boy who lived in India. Kim, the title character's name, was a short form of Kimball, which is derived from more than one source. The Greek meaning of the name is 'hollow vessel', but it also comes from the Old English for 'kin' or 'royal' and 'bold'. In Welsh the name means 'chief' and 'war'.

Kimball may also be a contemporary version of a name borne by an Old English ruler called Cymbeline. Cymbeline, who died in 42, ruled the area that is now Hertfordshire. His name meant 'high' and 'mighty'.

At the same time that Kipling's book was published, Britain was involved in the Boer War in South Africa and a number of soldiers were stationed at a garrison in the town of Kimberley. As a result many of them named their children – boys and girls – Kimberley. Kim is its short form.
Variants: Kimball, Kimberley, Kimberly

Kingsley

The Old English meaning of this name is 'king's clearing' or 'king's wood'. It is an English family name derived from a number of English place names.
Variants: King, Kingsleigh, Kingsly, Kingston, Kinsey

Kipp

Kipp comes from the Old English for 'pointed hill'.
Variants: Kip, Kipper, Kippie, Kippy

Kirk

The name Kirk has roots in Old English, Scottish and Scandinavian. In all three languages Kirk has the same meaning, 'church'. In England the name was originally given to someone who lived near a church. The actor, Kirk Douglas increased the name's popularity in North America.
Variants: Kerk, Kirby, Kirke, Kirklan, Kirkland, Kirtland, Kyrk

Klaus
See Claus and Nicholas.

Kumar
Kumar comes from the Sanskrit for 'prince' or 'son'.

Kushal
Kushal is an Indian name that means 'clever'.

Kurt
As the short form of Conrad, Kurt comes from the German for 'brave advice' or 'bold, wise counsellor'.
Variants: Conrad, Curt, Curtis, Kurtis

Kyle
Kyle is both a surname and a Scottish place name. It comes from the Gaelic for 'narrow strait'.
Variants: Kile, Ky

Lachlan
In Scotland Lachlan was the Gaelic name given to someone from Norway. It means 'from the land of the lakes' or 'warlike'. Over time Lachlan became a family name and produced the surname MacLachlan. In Australia Lachlan is associated with a 19th century governor of New South Wales, General Lachlan Macquarie.
Variants: Lachann, Lachie, Lachlann

Lal
Lal comes from the Sanskrit for 'caress' and the Hindi for 'beloved'.

Lamar
A surname and a first name, Lamar comes from the French for 'the pond'.

Lambert
The name Lambert was borne by St Lambert of Maastricht, who

is the patron saint of children. His name comes from the Old High German for 'bright or shining land'. It also means 'pride of the nation'.

The invading Normans first brought the name to Britain.

Variants: Bert, Bertie, Berty, Lamberto, Lammie, Landbert

Lamont
Mainly used in North America, the name Lamont comes from the Norse for 'law man' and the Scottish Gaelic for 'law giver'. It also comes from the French term 'la mont', which means 'the mountain'.

Variants: Lammond, Lamond, LaMont, Lemont, Monty

Lance
A lance is a sharp spear used in battle by the cavalry in charging at the enemy. It comes from Lancelot, which comes from the Latin for 'lance'.

According to Arthurian legend, Sir Lancelot was a Knight of the Round Table who fell in love with King Arthur's wife, Guinevere.

The name also has the German meaning 'god'.

Variants: Lancelot, Lancing, Lansing, Launce, Launcelot

Lane
The name – which comes from the Old English for 'narrow pathway between hedges or banks' – was originally given to someone who lived in or near a lane. It also has the Old Frisian meaning 'to move'. In North America the name Lane is given to both boys and girls.

Variants: Lanie, Leney

Lawrence
The Latin meaning of Lawrence is 'from Laurentum' – Laurentum being the Roman name of an Italian town. The French form of the name is Laurent, the Scottish version is Lowrie and the Italian variant is Lorenzo.

Throughout history the name has been borne by a number of

notable men, including three saints. The first was a Roman martyr and deacon of Rome who lived in the 3rd century. The second was Laurence of Canterbury who accompanied St Augustine on his mission to southern England and Lawrence O'Toole, the 13th century bishop of Dublin, was the third.
Variants: Larrance, Larry, Lars, Larse, Larson, Laurel, Laurence, Laurent, Lorenzo, Lowrie

Leander
Leander is derived from two Greek words 'leon', which means 'lion', and 'andros', which means 'man'. Thus it means 'man with the strength of a lion' or 'lion man'.

According to Greek mythology Leander was the handsome lover of Hero, a priestess of Venus. He was so devoted to her that every night he swam across the Hellespont to see her. One night he drowned during a storm and the distraught Hero threw herself into the sea to join him.
Variants: Ander, Andor, Lea, Leandre, Leandro, Lee, Leo, Leon, Maclean

Lee
This name is derived from the Old English word 'leah', which means 'wood, clearing' or 'meadow'. In 19th-century North America, the name was often bestowed on children of either sex in honour of the Confederate General Robert E Lee who died in 1870.

Lee, which can be given to children of either sex, also comes from the Old English word for 'shelter' or 'cover'.
Variants: Lea, Leigh

Leeland
Leeland comes from the Old English word 'hleo', which means 'shelter' or 'cover'.
Variants: Layland, Layton, Leighland, Leighton, Leland

Lennox
Lennox was originally a place name of a Scottish district, once

known as The Levenach. It comes from the Scottish Gaelic for 'elms' and 'water'.

Now widely used as a first name, Lennox is also a Scottish surname and has been made famous lately by British boxer Lennox Lewis.

Leo
The name Leo comes from the Latin for 'lion'. It is also one of the signs of the zodiac. The name has been popular throughout history, primarily because of its association with powerful characters. It was the name of six Byzantine emperors, several saints and 13 popes.

One such bearer of the name was Pope Leo I, who was also known as Leo the Great. He lived in the 5th century and twice saved Rome from attack. The success of actor Leo Di Caprio has helped to popularise the name since the late 1990s.
Variants: Leander, Lee, Leon, Leonardo, Leopold, Lonnie

Leonard
Leonard comes from the Old High German for 'strong as a lion' or 'lion' and 'hard'. The name was borne by more than one saint, including the patron saint of prisoners and the patron saint of parish missions.
Variants: Lenard, Lennard, Lenn, Lenny, Leo, Leon, Leonardo, Lionardo, Lonnie

Leopold
The conquering Normans first brought the name Leopold to England when they invaded the country in 1066. Use of the name eventually died out, although it was restored during the reign of Queen Victoria in the 19th century. The British monarch bestowed the name on one of her sons in honour of her Uncle Leopold, who was king of Belgium: the name was borne by more than one Belgian king and two Holy Roman emperors. The name comes from the Old German for 'bold or brave people'.
Variants: Leo, Leopoldo, Leupold, Pold, Poldo

Leroy

A popular African-American name, Leroy comes from the French for 'the king'. It was originally a surname that was given to servants of the king of France.
Variants: Elroy, Lee, Lee Roy, Roy

Leslie

See Lesley in the Girls' section.

Lester

The name Lester is a contracted form of Leicester, which is the name of a town in England. The Old English meaning of Leicester is 'Roman clearing' or 'Roman fort'.
Variants: Leicester, Les, Letcher, Leycester

Levi

In the Old Testament Levi was the name of Jacob and Leah's third son. The Hebrew meaning of his name is 'attached' or 'pledged'. His mother gave him the name in the hope that her husband would be more attached to her because that she had borne him three sons.

Like his brothers, Levi became the patriarch of one of the 12 tribes of Israel. His descendants, the Levites, were a Jewish priestly caste.
Variants: Lavey, Lavi, Lavy, Leavitt, Lev, Levey, Levy

Lewis

The Old Germanic meaning of Lewis is 'famous warrior' or 'famous battle'. In the 19th century it was the pen name of the British writer, Lewis Carroll, who wrote *Alice in Wonderland*. Carroll's real name was Charles Lutwidge Dodgson.
Variant: Lew, Lewie, Louis, Ludwig

Lex

As a variant of Alexander, Lex comes from the Greek for 'defender of men' or 'warrior'. Interestingly, it may also be

derived from another Classical source as the Latin word for 'law'.
Variants: Alexander, Laxton, Lexie, Lexton

Liam
Liam is the short form of the Gaelic version of William, which means 'resolute protection'. It also comes from the French for 'to bind' or 'protect'.
Variants: Lyam, William

Linden
The Old English meaning of Linden is 'lime tree' or 'the hill with linden trees'. It was originally an English place name that became a surname.
   In North America, as a first name, it was associated with the Democratic President Lyndon Baines Johnson, who assumed the office in November 1963 following the assassination of John F Kennedy.
Variants: Lin, Lindon, Lindy, Lyn, Lynden, Lyndon, Lynn

Lindsay
See Lindsey in the Girls' section.

Lionel
Lionel is another name connected with Arthurian legend. The French meaning of the name is 'little lion'.
Variants: Len, Lennie, Lenny, Leo, Leon, Leonel, Lionell, Lonnell

Llewellyn
The name Llewellyn means 'leader', 'lion' and 'resemblance'. It was borne by two Welsh princes – although with a slightly different spelling. The first was Llywelyn the Great who was born in 1173. The second Welsh prince bearing the name was Llywelyn the Last, who died in battle with Edward I of England, which resulted in the loss of Welsh independence.
Variants: Fluellen, Lywelyn, Llywellwyn, Lyn

L

Lloyd

Lloyd comes from the Welsh for 'brown, grey' – the implication being that the bearer is of a dark complexion.
Variants: Floyd, Llwyd, Loy, Loyd

Logan

The surname Logan was derived from a Scottish and Irish place name that means 'little hollow' in Gaelic. Logan also comes from the Middle English word 'logge', which means 'record or journal of performance'.

Lorenzo

Lorenzo is the Italian and Spanish form of Lawrence, which means 'from Laurentum'. (See also Lawrence.)
Variants: Laurence, Lawrence, Loren

Lorimer

The Latin meaning of Lorimer is 'harness maker'.
Variants: Lori, Lorrie, Lorry

Louis

The name Louis is closely linked to the history of France. When the Germanic tribe, the Franks, invaded Gaul in the Middle Ages they brought with them the name Hludowig or Chlodowig, which became Clovis. It is from Clovis that the name Louis was derived and, like its English derivative Lewis, it means 'famous battle or warrior'.

Eighteen kings of France bore the name including Louis XVI who was executed during the French Revolution.
Variants: Aloysius, Clovis, Elois, Lewie, Lewis, Ludwig, Ludvig, Luis

Lucas

Lucas comes from the Greek for 'from Luciana'. Luciana is a region in southern Italy.
Variants: Luc, Lucais, Luka, Lukas, Luke

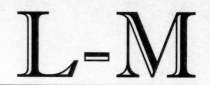

Ludovic

More than one theory exists to explain the origin of the name Ludovic. Introduced to Scotland in the 17th century, the name comes from the Gaelic for 'devotee of the Lord'.

But, like Lewis and Louis, it also comes from the German for 'famed warrior' or 'famous battle'.

Variants: Lewis, Louis, Ludo, Ludovick, Ludwig

Ludwig

A variant of Louis and Lewis, Ludwig comes from the German for 'famed warrior' or 'famous battle'. It was borne by the German composer Ludwig von Beethoven and three kings of Bavaria.

Variants: Clovis, Lewis, Lothar, Louis, Ludovic, Ludwik

Luke

Like Lucas, Luke comes from the Greek for 'from Luciana'. It was the name of the author of the Gospel of St Luke, who is the patron saint of doctors and painters.

Variants: Luc, Lucais, Luka, Lukas

Luther

The name Luther was borne by the founding father of the Lutheran church, Martin Luther, who was born in 1483. This Augustinian monk, who disapproved of papal indulgence, launched the Protestant Reformation in 1520.

Centuries later the name was associated with the African-American Civil Rights leader, Martin Luther King.

Luther comes from the Old German for 'people' and 'army'.

Variants: Lothar, Lothario, Lother, Lother, Lutero

Macabee

The Hebrew meaning of Macabee is 'hammer'. The name was associated with the Jewish dynasty of kings, high priests and patriots of the 2nd to 1st century BC.

Variant: Maccabee

Mace

Mace is of Latin origin and refers to the aromatic spice of the same name, which is used in perfumes and cooking.
Variants: Maceo, Macey, Mack, Mackey, Macy

Maddox

The name Maddox is both Celtic and English in origin. It means 'son of the Lord' and 'beneficent'.

Madison

In North America the name Madison is bestowed upon children of either sex. Originally a surname it comes from the Old English for 'son of Maud', 'son of Matthew' or 'son of Magdalene'.

In the United States the name is associated with James Madison who was President during the War of 1812.
Variants: Maddi, Maddie, Maddison, Maddy

Magnus

The Frankish king, Charlemagne, was commonly known by the Latin name Carolus Magnus, which in English means 'Charles the Great'. The byname Magnus was subsequently borne by a number of Norwegian kings and early saints. They include the 11th century ruler of Norway, Magnus the Good, and the 13th century king, Magnus the Law Mender.

The name was later imported to Scotland and, in Britain, was borne by the Scottish broadcaster Magnus Magnusson.
Variant: Manus

Malachai

The Hebrew meaning of Malachai is 'my messenger' or 'my angel'. In the Old Testament it was borne by the last of the 12 minor prophets who predicted the coming of Christ.

Malachy is the Irish version of the name that belonged to two kings of Ireland and one saint. The saint, who lived in the 11th and 12th centuries, was the abbot of Banger, Armagh and Derry.

One of the kings who bore the name Malachy defeated the Norse invaders.
Variants: Mal, Malachy

Malcolm
Generations of parents have named their children after saints or holy people. However, in the Middle Ages, it was thought to be presumptuous to do so without first using a prefix. Thus, boys who were named after the Irish monk, St Columba, were called Malcolm or 'devotee or servant of Columba'.

The name Malcolm is connected with Scotland because St Columba was the 6th century missionary who founded a monastery in Iona in 563. It was from this base that he set about converting the Scottish people.

Later, four kings of Scotland bore the name Malcolm including, it is said, Macbeth's father. In the 20th century the name was associated with the African-American activist Malcolm X, who was born Malcolm Little.
Variants: Colm, Colum, Mal, Maolcolm

Malik
Malik means 'master' in Arabic.
Variants: Mal, Mali

Manford
The Old English meaning of Manford is 'ford', which is the shallow part of the river that can be crossed by wading through it. People who lived near a ford were usually given the name.

Manfred
Brought to Britain by the Normans, the name Manfred comes from the Old German for 'man of peace'. It was also the title of an 1817 poem written by Lord Byron.
Variants: Fred, Freddie, Freddy, Manifred, Mannie, Manny, Mannye

Mansur
The Arabic meaning of the name Mansur is 'divinely helped' or 'helped by God'.

Mark
A number of historical figures have borne the name Mark. They include St Mark, the author of the second gospel in the New Testament, who is the patron saint of lions, prisoners, lawyers and notaries. The name also belonged to Marcus Antonius (Mark Antony), the Roman political and military leader who was a follower of Julius Caesar and the lover of Cleopatra.

In North America, Mark Twain was the pen name of the writer Samuel Langhorne Clemens who produced the literary classics *The Adventures of Tom Sawyer* and *The Adventures of Huckleberry Finn*. The Venetian explorer Marco Polo bore the Italian version of the name.

Unfortunately, the exact meaning of Mark is unknown. It may come from the Latin for 'martial' as a derivative of the name Mars, the god of war.
Variants: Marc, Marcel, Marcello, Marco, Marcus, Marques, Marquis, Mars

Marley
Charles Dickens gave the name to one of the characters in his story *A Christmas Carol.* Jacob Marley was the business partner of Ebeneezer Scrooge who returned in a ghostly form to visit his friend. The name Marley means 'field near water'.

Marlon
The exact meaning of Marlon is unknown. As a variant of Marlow it may come from the Old English for 'pond', 'sea' and 'remnant'. But it may equally be derived from the Welsh for 'sea' and 'hill' or 'fort' as a variant of Merlin.
Variants: Mar, Mario, Marle, Marlen, Marlin, Marlo, Marlow, Marlowe, Merlin

Marlow

Marlow comes from the Old English for 'pond', 'sea' and 'remnant'.
Variants: Marle, Marlin, Marlis, Marlon

Marshall

Marshall is the transferred use of a surname that was originally an Old French occupational name. Historically a 'marshall' was either someone who looked after horses or a high-ranking official in the royal household.
Variants: Marsh, Marshal, Marshe

Martin

The exact meaning of the name Martin is unknown. Like Mark it is thought to come from the Latin for 'martial' as a derivative of the name Mars, which belonged to the Roman god of war.

Martin Luther (1483-1546), professor of theology at Wittenberg was a leading figure in the Reformation. After him was named the African-American Civil Rights leader, Martin Luther King. The name was also borne by the son of a Roman soldier who became a pacifist and, later, a missionary and bishop, the 4th century saint, Martin of Tours. It was after this Martin that the London church, St Martin-in-the-Fields, was named.
Variants: Mart, Martainn, Martel, Marten, Martie, Martyn

Marvin

The Old English meaning of the name Marvin is 'famous friend'. As a variant of Mervyn it means 'sea fort'.

In the 20th century the name was borne by legendary soul singer Marvin Gaye who died in 1984.
Variants: Marv, Marve, Marven, Marvine, Marvyn, Mervyn, Merwin, Merwyn

Maskil

The Hebrew meaning of Maskil is 'educated' or 'learned'.

Mason
Mason is an occupational name for someone who works with stone. The Old French meaning of the name is 'to make'.

Matthew
St Matthew was the author of a gospel in the New Testament. He was also one of Christ's Apostles who used to collect tax for the Romans. Thus he is the patron saint of tax collectors, bankers, accountants and bookkeepers. The Hebrew meaning of Matthew is 'gift of God'.
Variants: Macey, Mat, Mate, Mateus, Matiah, Matias, Matt, Mattie, Matty

Maurice
A Moor is a member of the Muslim people from North Africa. The Latin name used for this race of people was 'Maurus', which developed into the French name Maurice.

The name was borne by an early Byzantine emperor and by a Roman soldier who was martyred in Switzerland in 286.
Variants: Maryse, Maur, Maurie, Morey, Morie, Morry, Morris, Morus

Max
As the short form of the Roman name Maximilianus, Max is derived from the Latin for 'great'. In the 15th century Emperor Frederick III bestowed a variant of the name on his first-born son Maximilian I.

As a diminutive of Maxwell, Max comes from the Scottish surname that means 'Mac's well'.
Variants: Mac, Mack, Maks, Massimo, Maxey, Maxie, Maxim, Maximilian, Maxwell

Maxwell
As mentioned above Maxwell is the transferred use of the Scottish surname that means 'Mac's well'.
Variants: Mac, Mack, Maks, Max, Maxie, Maxim, Maxime, Maxy

Maynard
Keynes's middle name comes from the Old German for 'strong' and 'powerful'.

Mel
See Melvin.

Melvin
The exact meaning of Melvin is uncertain. It may come from the Old English for 'council' and 'friend' or the German for 'Amalo's settlement'. As a variant of Melville, it has the Old French meaning 'bad town'.
Variants: Mel, Melville, Melvyn

Michael
In the Old Testament the archangel Michael was seen as a messenger. In the New Testament Michael is portrayed as the leader in the war against Satan and the weigher of souls at the Last Judgement.

In Hebrew his name means 'who is like God?'.
Variants: Michele, Mick, Mickey, Miguel, Mikael, Mike, Misha, Mitchell, Mychal

Milan
A Czech name that means 'grace', Milan may also be a given as name after the Italian city.

Miles
The exact meaning of the name Miles is unclear. What is known is that the name was moderately popular shortly after the Norman Conquest. One suggestion is that it is a variant of the Biblical name Michael, which means 'who is like God?' in Hebrew. It may also come from the Latin for 'mils' of a thousand (mills) paces, or the Old German for 'beloved' or 'gentle'.
Variants: Michael, Milan, Mills, Milo, Myles

Milo
Milo comes from the Old Slavic for 'grace' and the Germanic for 'merciful'.
Variants: Miles, Myles

Milton
The Old English meaning of the name Milton is 'mill town' or 'middle settlement'. It is best known as the surname of the 17th century English poet John Milton who wrote *Paradise Lost* and *Paradise Regained*.
Variants: Millard, Miller, Mills, Milt, Miltie, Milty, Mull, Muller

Mitchell
Mitchell is a surname and variant of the Biblical name Michael. Thus, it means 'who is like God?' in Hebrew.
Variants: Michael, Mitch, Mitchel

Montgomery
Montgomery is a French baronial name of Old French and German origin. It is the combination of the French for 'mountain' and a German personal name that means 'power of man'.

Montgomery is also a variant of Montague, which comes from the French and Latin for 'pointed mountain or big hill'.
Variants: Montague, Monte, Montgomerie, Monty

Morgan
See Morgan in the Girls' section.

Mortimer
The aristocratic surname Mortimer is taken from the French place name 'mort mer', which means 'dead sea'.
Variants: Mort, Mortie, Morty

Moses
Moses is one of the most significant characters in the Old Testament and an important figure for both Jews and Christians.

Though he never reached the Promised Land, the prophet Moses led the Israelites out of enslavement in Egypt. With God's help he performed numerous miracles including the parting of the Red Sea. God also entrusted Moses with the Ten Commandments. The Hebrew meaning of the name is 'saved from the water'. It is a fitting name for a man who, as a baby, was left in a basket among the bullrushes of the River Nile.
Variants: Moe, Moke, Mosheh, Moss, Moy, Moyes, Moyse

Muhammad
Muhammad was the name of the prophet who founded the Islamic religion. Born in 570, Muhammad was a rich merchant and member of the ruling tribe in Mecca. His life was changed when he had a vision directing him to teach the true religion. He went on to conquer Mecca in 630, which is now a holy site and place of pilgrimage for millions of Muslims around the world.

The Arabic meaning of Muhammad is 'praised' or 'glorified'.

In the 1960s when the African-American boxer Cassius Clay announced he was changing his name to Muhammad Ali, it signified that he had converted to the Muslim faith.
Variants: Mahamet, Mohamad, Mohammad, Mohamed, Mohammed

Murdoch
Murdoch comes from the Irish and Scottish Gaelic for 'sailor' or 'seaman'.
Variants: Murdo, Murdock, Murtagh, Murtaugh

Murray
The northern Scottish district of Moray derived its name from the Old Celtic for 'settlement by the sea'. The name Murray comes from this place name.
Variants: Murrie, Murry

Naaman
Naaman comes from the Hebrew for 'beautiful, pleasant'. In Arabic it means 'good fortune'.

Nahum

In the Old Testament Nahum was a prophet who foretold the downfall of Nineveh. A Jewish name, it has been used by Christians since the Reformation.

It comes from the Hebrew for 'comforting' and was borne by the Restoration dramatist Nahum Tate who re-wrote Shakespeare's *King Lear* with a happy ending.
Variant: Nemo

Naim

Naim is derived from the Arabic for 'comfortable' or 'contented'.
Variant: Naeem

Namid

According to Native American legend there once existed a coyote that wanted to dance with the stars. The name Namid refers to this tale and means 'star dancer'.

Namir

The Arabic meaning of Namir is 'leopard'.

Naphtali

In the Old Testament Naphtali was one of Jacob's 12 sons. His mother was Bilhah, the handmaid of Jacob's co-wife Rachel.

The Hebrew meaning of the name is 'wrestler'.
Variants: Naftali, Naftalie, Naphthali

Napoleon

The most famous bearer of this name was the great French commander and emporer, Napoleon Bonaparte. His name comes from the Greek for 'new town'.
Variants: Leon, Nap

Naresh

Naresh comes from the Sanskrit for 'lord' or 'king'.

Nassar
The Arabic meaning of Nassar is 'victorious'. It is listed in the Koran as one of the 99 names for God.

Nathan
In the Bible, when King David committed adultery with Bathsheba, it was the prophet Nathan who told him that God was not happy with his actions.

In Hebrew Nathan means 'gift'. It is also a short form of Jonathan and Nathaniel, both of which mean 'God's gift'.
Variants: Jonathan, Jonathon, Nat, Nata, Natan, Nate, Nathaniel

Nathaniel
In the New Testament Nathaniel was one of Christ's Apostles who was also known as Bartholomew. His name was derived from the Hebrew for 'he gave' or 'God's gift'. Nathan is its short form.
Variants: Nat, Nata, Natal, Natan, Natanael, Natale, Nathan

Nav
This English gypsy name means exactly that, 'name'.
Variants: Nev

Ned
As the short form of Edward, Ned is derived from the Old English for 'happiness, riches' and 'guardian'. As a diminutive of Edmund it means 'happiness, riches' and 'friend'.

Ted is now a more common short form of both these names. (See also Edward and Edmund.)
Variants: Edmund, Edward, Neddie, Neddy, Ted, Teddie, Teddy

Neil
Although it is now widely used in the English-speaking world, before the 20th century Neil was primarily associated with Ireland and Scotland. This is because it is the Anglicised form of the Gaelic name Niall, which means 'cloud', 'passionate' and 'champion'.

Notable bearers of the name include the North American playwright, Neil Simon and the astronaut, Neil Armstrong and the popular singer, Neil Diamond.

Variants: Neal, Neale, Neall, Nealson, Neely, Neill, Nelson, Niall, Nyles

Nelson

In the 19th century the name Nelson was often bestowed upon boys in honour of the British military hero Horatio Nelson, who defeated the powerful French navy at the Battle of Trafalgar in 1805.

In the 20th century the name became associated with the first black African President of South Africa, Nelson Mandela.

The name that both these powerful leaders shared was derived from the Old English for 'son of Neil' or 'son of Nell'. As mentioned above Neil means 'cloud, passionate or champion' in Irish Gaelic.

Variants: Nealson, Neaton, Neil, Nils, Nilsen, Nilson

Nemo

As a short form of Nahum, Nemo comes from the Hebrew for 'comforting'. Its Greek meaning is 'from the glen'.

Variant: Nahum

Neville

As a surname Neville was brought to England by a Norman baronial family. The French meaning of the name is 'new town or settlement'.

Variants: Nev, Nevil, Nevile, Nevill

Newton

Like Neville, Newton means 'new town or settlement'. But the meaning of this name is derived from the Old English language. It is an English family name that was originally taken from a variety of locations in England.

Variants: Newgate, Newland, Newman, Newt

Niall

The Irish and Scottish Gaelic form of Neil is Niall. It means 'cloud', 'passionate' and 'champion'. (See also Neil and Nelson.)
Variants: Neil, Nelson

Nicholas

The name Nicholas comes from the Greek for 'victorious people'. The most well-known bearer of the name is the 4th- century saint, St Nicholas, who inpired the modern figure of Santa Claus, because of his generosity to others.
Variants: Claus, Klaas, Klaus, Nic, Nicolai, Niccolo, Nick, Nicky

Nigel

As a Latinised form of the Irish Gaelic name Neil, Nigel means 'champion', 'passionate' and 'cloud'. However, a more likely source is the Old Latin for 'dark, night'. The Normans introduced the name to Britain.
Variants: Neil, Nidge, Nigi, Nige, Niguel, Nye

Nir

Nir comes from the Hebrew for 'ploughed field' and is associated with industry and fruitfulness.
Variants: Niral, Niria, Nirel

Noam

This Jewish name comes from the Hebrew for 'joy, delight and pleasantness'.

Noble

Noble comes from the Latin word 'nobilis' which means 'renowned, famous' or 'born into nobility'. It is mainly used in North America.

Noel

This Old French word for 'birthday of the Lord' is traditionally given to babies born at Christmas.
Variants: Noël, Noëlle, Noelle

Nolan
Nolan is an Irish family name that comes from the Irish Gaelic for 'famous noble' or 'son of the famous one'.
Variant: Noland

Norman
The Old English meaning of the name Norman was 'man from the north'. It was used in England before the arrival of the invading forces from northern France. Henceforth it came to mean 'Viking' or 'Norseman'.
Variants: Norm, Normand, Normann, Normie

Norton
Norton is a surname and first name that comes from the Old English for 'north settlement'.
Variants: Nort, Nortie, Norty

Nye
Born in 1897, Aneurin Bevan was a Welsh member of the Labour Party who helped to establish the National Health Service in post-war Britain. Nye is the pet form of his first name, which comes from the Welsh for 'little one of pure gold'.

Nye, however, also boasts Latin and Middle English roots. In Latin it means 'man of honour'. The Middle English interpretation is 'islander or island'.
Variants: Aneurin, Ny, Nyle

Obediah
From the Hebrew 'servant', the implication being that the bearer of the name is a 'servant of God.' Obediah was one of the 12 minor prophets in the Bible.

The name was also used in Anthony Trollope's 1857 novel *Barchester Towers*, the second in the series of novels known as the *Chronicles of Barsetshire*. It was popular in the 17th and 18th centuries.
Variants: Abdias, Obadiah, Obadias, Obe, Obed, Obie, Oby

Oberon
A variant of Auberon, the name is thought to be of German Frankish origin to mean 'noble' and 'bear'. The name was given by Shakespeare to the King of the Fairies in *A Midsummer Night's Dream*. (See also Auberon.)

Octavius
A Roman family name, Octavius is Latin for 'eighth' and was traditionally given to the eighth son of a family. It was also the name of the first Roman Emperor, Augustus Caesar.
Variants: Octave, Octavio, Otavio, Octavian

Oliver
An old Norse name, taken from the French for 'olive tree', Oliver was introduced into Britain by the Normans. It became popular in the Middle Ages thanks to the *Song of Roland*, about a heroic commander under Charlemagne; Oliver was the name of the hero's friend.

The name's popularity declined after the ousting of Oliver Cromwell, but it enjoyed something of a 19th century revival after the publication of Charles Dickens' 1838 novel *Oliver Twist*.
Variants: Olivier, Ollie, Olivero

Olaf
From the Old Norse meaning 'ancestor' or 'remains', Olaf was brought to Britain by the Danes. Five Norwegian kings have been named Olaf, including Olaf I (995-1030), who was canonized.
Variants: Olav, Olave, Ole, Olen, Olif

Omar
Arabic in origin, Omar has the meaning 'long life', 'flourishing', 'first-born son' and 'follower of the Prophet'. The name appears in the book of Genesis in the Bible.
Variants: Omri, Oner

Orpheus
Derived from the Greek for 'ear' or perhaps 'darkness', the name Orpheus is associated with the Greek mythological poet whose music was so beautiful that it charmed wild beasts and moved trees and rivers to come and listen to him.

Orrin
From the Hebrew word for 'tree', the name Orrin is mostly found in the southern states of North America. It probably has origins in the Irish name Oran, meaning 'grey-brown' or 'dark'. Oran was also the brother of St. Columba.
Variants: Oren, Orin, Orren

Orson
The male form of Ursula, Orson comes from the old French for 'bear cub', Orson being a character in a medieval story who was raised by a bear in the woods.
Variants: Sonnie, Sonny, Urson

Orville
A made-up name, Orville was created by novelist Fanny Burney for her 1778 work *Evelina*, which features as its hero one Lord Orville.
Variant: Orval

Osbert
Taken from Old English, Osbert's meaning is 'bright' and 'gold'.
Variants: Oz, Ozzie, Ozzy

Oscar
An old Norse name, Oscar means 'divine spear'. The name is a favourite with Swedish royalty, with two kings of Sweden and of Norway bearing the name.

Another notable Oscar is novelist and playwright, Oscar Wilde (1854 -1900), whose plays include: *The Importance of Being Earnest* (1895) and *An ideal Husband* (1895).
Variants: Ossie, Ossy, Oke

Osmond

An English family name, Osmond derives from the old Norse for 'god' and 'protector', making the bearer of the name 'protected by God'. Saint Osmond is the protector against paralysis, toothache and insanity.

Variants: Esmand, Osman, Osmand, Osmant, Osmen, Osmon, Osmont, Osmund, Osmundo, Oswin, Oz, Ozzie, Ozzy

Ossian

Originating in the Irish name meaning 'little deer', Ossian has links to Irish mythology, as Ossian was the son of Finn MacCool, who was one of the most popular heroes of Irish folklore, an Ulster tribal chieftan sometimes referred to as 'the Irish King Arthur'. According to folklore, he went on a series of adventures and bore his son Oisin (Ossian) with the goddess Sadb.

Oswald

Oswald comes from the old English and Norse words for 'god and ruler' and 'power of wood'. The name's most positive associations were with Oswald of Winchester, a 10th century bishop of Worcester and Oswald of Northumbria, who was a close friend of St. Aidan.

Variants: Ossie, Osvald, Oswal, Oswaldo, Oswall, Oswold, Oz, Ozzie, Ozzy, Waldo, Waldy

Othello

Originally from the Greek, meaning 'prosperous', the name is best-known from Shakespeare's play *Othello*, in which Othello blinded by jealousy, kills his innocent wife, Desdemona.

Otis

Otis' origins are in the Greek for ear, as in having 'a good ear for music'/giving and taking good advice. The name was borne by James Otis, a Boston lawyer who played an integral part at the start of the American Revolution.

Variants: Otes, Otto

Otto
With its origins in the German for 'wealth' and 'prosperity', Otto arrived in Britain with the Normans as Odo, the name of William the Conqueror's brother. It was also the name of a 12th century saint and of four Roman Emperors.
Variants: Odo, Osman, Othello, Othman, Othmar

Overton
Derived from the Middle English for 'higher' or 'above' and 'town' or 'village', Overton means either 'higher of two towns' or 'hillside town'.

Ovid
The name Ovid is taken from the Latin for 'egg', which is seen as a symbol for life.

Owen
The Welsh form of 'Eugene', Owen is derived from the Greek for 'well-born' or 'lucky'.
Variants: Bowen, Bowie, Eoghan, Eugene, Euan, Evan, Ewen, Owain, Owayne, Ovin

Pablo
Pablo is the Spanish version of the name Paul, and is dervied from the Greek for 'small'. (See also Paul.)

Paddy
The 19th century generic name for an Irish man, Paddy is also a pet form of Patrick. (See also Patrick.)

Paolo
Paolo is the the Italian version of Paul and as such comes from the Greek for 'small'. (See also Paul.)

Paris
While Paris immediately suggests the capital of France, the

original meaning of the name Paris is uncertain. It probably derives from 'marshes of the Parisii', this being the Latin name for the Gaulish Celtic tribe. It was also the name of the Trojan prince who abducted Helen of Troy and caused the Trojan War.

Parker
Taking its meaning from the old French for 'park-keeper', Parker as a first name is derived from an English family name, and enjoys popularity in North America.

Parley
This name is derived from the Latin word for 'discourse'.

Parnell
Possibly sharing 'Peter's' roots in the Greek word for 'rock', Parnell is thought to be a diminutive of Petronella, which in turn comes from the Roman family name Petronius. Parnell is also an English family name.
Variants: Parnall, Parnel, Parnell, Pernel, Pernell

Pascal
Pascal is derived from the Old French word for Easter.
Variants: Pasco, Pasqual, Pascoe, Pesach

Patrick
From the Latin meaning 'patrician' or a 'member of the Roman nobility', Patrick was not widely used until the 17th century due to Saint Patrick being so revered. Captured and taken to Ireland by pirates, Deacon's son Patrick became a slave herdsman, but studied religion and eventually escaped to Gaul. Training as a Bishop, he returned to Ireland as a missionary, spreading the gospel there. Patrick is the patron saint of Ireland, engineers and those who fear snakes.
Variants: Pad, Paddie, Paddy, Padriac, Pat, Patraic, Patric, Paxton

Paul

Derived from the Greek for 'small', the name Paul was borne by numerous saints, the most famous being the author of Epistles in the New Testament. Originally named Saul, he was a Jewish citizen of Rome who persecuted Christians. Saul was converted after seeing a vision of Christ on the road to Damascus, changing his name to Paul to reflect his new-found humility.

Variants: Pablo, Pal, Paolo, Pasha, Paulie, Paulino, Paulinus, Paulis, Paulo, Pol

Paxton

The name Paxton derives from two Latin words, 'pax', meaning peace and 'tūn', meaning 'town', hence the meaning 'town of peace'.

Penn

Meaning 'hill' in old English, 'commander' in ancient German and 'pen' or 'quill' in Latin, Penn first appeared as an Old English surname given to someone who lived near a sheep pen.

It was popularised in North America by Sir William Penn, founder of Pennsylvania.

Variants: Pennie, Penny, Penrod

Percival

Originally a Norman baronial name, Perci, the name means 'to pierce the veil'. Percival increased greatly in popularity thanks to the poet Percy Bysshe Shelley (1792-1822).

Variants: Percy, Perceval, Perseus

Perry

Derived from numerous sources, Perry is either from an Old English family name, whereby it means 'pear tree', a pet form of Peregrine (meaning foreigner or stranger) or a diminutive of Peter.

Variant: Perigrine

Peter
This name is taken from the Greek for 'rock'. Saint Peter was the most prominent of the disciples during the ministry of Jesus and was charged with spreading the gospel and founding a universal church.

The name was popularised by JM Barrie's classic children's tale *Peter Pan* with its hero who never grows up.

Variants: Pete, Perry, Pierre, Piers, Rock, Rocky

Philip
The name originally derives from the Greek for 'loving horses'. It was the name of Philip of Macedonia, the father of Alexander the Great.

Variants: Felip, Phillip, Phil, Pip, Philipot, Philippe

Philmore
Philmore is aquatic, and its roots can be found both in Greek, where it means 'loving', and Welsh where it has the meaning 'lover of the sea'.

Phoebus
First appearing in Britain in the 16th century, Phoebus comes from the Greek for 'bright' or 'shining'.

Variants: Feibush, Feivel, Feiwel

Phoenix
See Phoenix in Girls' section.

Piers
This name is a French version of Peter. (See also Peter.)

Pip
A diminutive of Philip, the name Pip came to prominence thanks to Charles Dickens novel *Great Expectations* (1861), where the hero was named Pip.

Plato
Derived from the Greek word for 'broad' or 'flat', Plato is best known as the name of the celebrated Greek philosopher (428-347 BC).
Variant: Platon

Poco
This is an Italian name meaning 'little'.

Porter
Taken from French meaning 'to carry', the name Porter was initially bestowed upon someone who guarded a gate.

Powell
This name is a derivation of Howell, taken from the Old English meaning 'wild boar/domestic swine' and 'hill'.

Pravin
A Hindu name, meaning 'skilful' or 'able'.

Preston
Initially a surname, Preston probably derives from the old English for a priest's enclosure, or a village which had a priest, or a village that was built on church land.
Variant: Prescott

Priestley
Deriving its meaning from both Latin and Old English, Priestly means 'elder' or 'elder of the church'.

Purnal
Taken from the Latin, meaning 'pear', the purnal is a long-living tree, and a symbol of longevity in China.

Purvis
Purvis is derived from the Latin for 'forsee', 'look after' or 'provide'.

Putnam
Taken from the Latin for 'pruner' or 'one who prunes trees',
Putnam was originally an English surname and place name, and
means 'Putta's homestead' in Old English.

Quentin
Quentin comes from the Latin name Quintus, which means
'fifth'. It was traditionally bestowed upon the fifth son in a
family.
 In France the name is associated with a 3rd century martyr
and missionary.
Variants: Quent, Quenton, Quincy, Quinn, Quint, Quintus

Quincy
In North America the name Quincy was borne by a former
President of the United States, John Quincy Adams. It is also the
name of a place in Massachusetts.
 In France, the name is associated with a noble family from
Normandy. Like Quentin, Quincy comes from the Latin for
'fifth'.
Variants: Quentin, Quincey, Quintus

Quinn
The Irish meaning of Quinn is 'descendant of Conn' – Conn
being a word that meant 'leader' or 'chief'.
Variants: Quentin, Quincy

Rabi
Arabic in origin, this name means 'fragrant breeze.' It is the male
form of Rabia.

Rafferty
Deriving from Gaelic and German roots, Rafferty means 'rich
and prosperous.' It is also a surname. The name is popular in
North America.
Variants: Rafe, Raff, Rafer, Raffer

Raja
This name is Arabic for 'anticipated' or 'hoped for'. Raja is the male version of Rani and means 'prince'.
Variant: Raj

Raleigh
This is an Old English name that comes from 'Ra', or 'roe deer' and 'leah' or 'grassy clearing'. It is also a surname, most famously that of Sir Walter Raleigh (1554-1618), the noted Elizabethan courtier and explorer.

Ralph
Taken from the German 'rand', meaning 'advice' or 'might' and 'wulf', meaning 'wolf', Ralph means 'fearless advisor'.
Variants: Raaf, Rafe, Raff, Raffy, Randolph, Ranulf, Rauf, Rauffe, Rolf

Ramsey
Ramsey, and its variant, Ramsay, have their origins in the Old English 'ram' (male sheep), and 'sey', which has the literal meaning 'land of the rams'. It is also a surname: James Ramsay MacDonald (1866-1937) was the first Labour Prime Minister of Great Britain, holding the post from 1924 to 1927 and again from 1929 to 1935.
Variant: Ramsay

Randall
A version of Randolph, which is also a surname. (See Randolph.)
Variants: Randal, Randel, Randle, Rand, Rands, Randl

Randolph
Randolph's origins are in the Old English for 'shield' and 'wolf', which come from the Norse words 'rand', meaning 'rim' or 'shield', and 'ulfr' meaning 'wolf'. Famous Randolphs include Randolph Churchill (1849-1895), father of Sir Winston Churchill.
Variants: Dolph, Rand, Rands, Randolf, Ranulf, Randall, Randy, Randal, Rand, Randle

Raphael
The name of an archangel in the Bible, Raphael comes from the Hebrew for 'God has healed'. Besides the archangel, it was also the name of one of the best-known Renaissance painters.
Variants: Raf, Rafael, Rafaelle, Rafe, Rafel, Raffael, Raphel

Rashad
Of Arabic origin, Rashad means 'to have good sense' or 'integrity'.

Raul
Raul originates in the old Germanic for 'counsel' or 'might' (as in strength) and 'wolf', where it is a variant of Ralph.
Variants: Ralph, Raolin, Raoul

Raven
This name means 'black bird'. Raven is a variant of the Old English 'hraefn'.

Ravi
Ravi means 'sun', and also has origins in Hindi myth, where it was the name of the sun god. In popular culture, it is associated with Indian musician Ravi Shankar.

Ravid
A Hebrew-derived name meaning 'jewellery' or 'adornment'.

Ravinder
Taken from the Old French 'rapine', meaning a 'mountain stream' or 'rush of water', this name is insinuative of the power of rushing water as boundless energy and enthusiasm for life.

Raymond
With its origins in Old German, Raymond derives from the words 'ragen' for 'wisdom', and 'mund' meaning 'guardian'; literally 'advisor and protector'. There are numerous saints with

the name, including St. Raymond of Toulouse.
Variants: Monchi, Mondo, Mundo, Raimond, Ramond, Ramone, Raynard, Redmond, Rai, Ray

Raynor
Raynor has Old German/Flemish roots, coming from the Flemish words 'ragan' meaning 'wisdom' or 'advice', and 'harja' meaning 'army' or 'people'.
The derivative Rainier is popular with the Grimaldis, who are the royal family of Monaco.
Variants: Ragnar, Rainer, Ray, Rayner, Rain, Raines, Rainier, Rains, Lee, Leigh, Rally, Rawleigh, Rawley

Regan
Derived from Hebrew and Old German roots, meaning 'wise', Regan and its variants are also surnames, especially in North America, where the name is associated with former US President Ronald Reagan (1911-2004).
Variants: Reagan, Reagen

Redford
This name is taken from the Old English words 'red', meaning 'reedy', and 'ford', a shallow river crossing.
Variants: Ford, Red, Redd

Reeves
An occupational name, Reeves is derived from the Old English for a bailiff, overseer or chief magistrate.
Variants: Reeve, Reave

Reginald
This first name is derived from the Old English for 'powerful warrior'. The British singer, composer, and pianist, Sir Elton John's original name is Reginald Kenneth Dwight.
Variants: Reg, Reggie, Rex, Ronald, Reginauld, Reinhold, Reinold, Reinwald, Renardo, Reynold, Rinardo, Nardo

René
This is a French name meaning 'reborn'. In France, the name is associated with René Descartes (1596-1650), the noted French philosopher and mathematician.
Variants: Renato, Renatus, Reni

Reuben
Reuben is a Biblical Hebrew name, meaning 'behold, a son'.
Variants: Rube, Ruben

Reuel
Derived from Hebrew, Reuel means 'friend of God'.

Rex
This name is a diminutive of Reginald and Reynold, and is Latin for 'ruler' or 'leader'.
   The name was borne by British actor Rex Harrison (1908-1990), who changed his name from Reginald Carey.
Variants: Regino, Regis, Rexer, Rexford, Reynaud, Reyner, Ray, Rayner

Reynard
Reynard has roots in Flemish and French. In Flemish, it derives from 'ragin', or 'advice' and "nard', meaning 'hardy' or 'strong'. It is also the French word for fox.
Variants: Rainardo, Ray, Raynard, Ragnard, Reinhard, Renaud, Rey

Rhodric
An Anglicised version of the Spanish Rodrigo, Rhodric comes from the Old German meaning 'famous ruler', 'hrod' meaning 'fame' and 'ric' meaning 'ruler'.
Variants: Rouven, Revie, Ribbans, Rouvin, Rube, Ruben, Rubens, Rubin, Ruby, Ruvane, Ruvim, Rod, Rodd, Roddie, Rodrich, Roddy, Roderick, Roderich, Roderigo, Rodrique, Rofi, Rory, Rurih, Ruy

Rider
A Middle English name, derived from the word 'ridde', meaning 'to clear' or 'to make space', Rider was often applied to someone who would clear land.

The name is associated with the British writer, Sir Henry Rider Haggard (1856-1925), who wrote the classics *King Solomon's Mines* (1885) and *She* (1887).
Variants: Rid, Riddle, Ridgeley, Ridley, Ryder, Ryerson

Riordan
Of German and Gaelic origins, Riordan is derived from the words for 'royal' and 'poet'.
Variants: Rearden, Riorden

Ripley
Another occupational name, Ripley is related to the Old English for 'one who would clear wooded areas'.
Variants: Lee, Leigh, Rip, Ripp

Rockwell
The literal meaning is 'a well with rocks'. Rockwell comes from the Old English words 'roche' for 'rock' and 'wella' for 'well'.
Variants: Roache, Rocco, Roch, Rocher, Rochie, Roche, Rochy

Roger
Roger has its roots in Old German and Old English. The English lineage derives from the word 'hodge', meaning 'a peasant labourer'. The German origin comes from 'hrod', or 'fame' and 'ger' or spear, hence a 'famous spear-carrier'.

British actor Roger Moore, of *The Saint* and James Bond fame, is a popular icon who boasts this name.
Variants: Rog, Roggie, Rodge, Rodger, Dodge, Hodge, Rogello, Rogerio, Rogers, Roj, Rugero, Ruggerio, Rutger

Rollo
A variant of Roland and diminutive of Raoul, Rollo is believed

to be the Old French version of Rolf.
Variants: Rolf, Rolly, Rolan, Roul, Rudolf, Rudolph

Romain
With its literal meaning 'a citizen of Rome', Romain is essentially French for 'Roman'.
Variants: Roman, Romano, Romeo, Romulus

Roone
An Old English name taken from 'rune', Roone means 'secret consultation, magic or mystery'.

Roswell
Roswell, derived from the Old German, means 'a skilled fighting horseman'.

Rouel
Rouel is a Hebrew name, meaning 'friend of God'.
Variant: Ruel

Rowan
Of Gaelic origins, Rowan means 'red haired' or 'rugged'.
Variants: Rouan, Rooney, Rowen, Rowney, Rowan, Rowanne

Rhys
Rhys is derived from the Welsh word for 'ardour', and was the name of several Welsh rulers during the Middle Ages. It is also a Welsh surname.
Variants: Reece, Ray, Rees, Reese, Rey, Rhett, Rice, Royce

Richard
Taken from the Germanic words meaning 'he who rules' and 'hard', the enduring popularity of the name Richard was carried by many famous men throughout history. Among them are three kings of England, including Richard the Lionheart (Richard I), who lead the third Crusade. The

composer Richard Wagner is another well-known personality with this name.
Variants: Dic, Dick, Dickie, Dicky, Ric, Ricard, Ricardo, Riccardo, Richie, Richey, Ritchie

Riley
Taken from the Old English 'ryge', meaning 'rye' and 'loan',' meaning 'clearing' or 'meadow', Riley means 'rye meadow'.
Variants: Reilly, Ryley, Royley

Robbie
This name is a pet form and diminutive of Robert. (See Robert.)
Variants: Rob, Robo, Rabbie

Robert
Derived from the ancient German for 'bright' and 'famous', Robert is the name of many famous men. These include Robert the Bruce (1274-1329) who freed Scotland from British domination, two other Scottish kings and Robert Peel (1788-1850) who established the police force. More recently, it is associated with actor, Robert Redford.
Variants: Bob, Bobbie, Hobson, Robb, Robbie, Robby, Roberto, Rory, Bert, Bertie, Robertson

Robin
Robin is the original French version of Robert. Notable Robins include Robin Hood and also Christopher Robin, a character in A.A. Milne's literary works.
Variants: Rob, Robyn

Rodney
Rodney derives from the Old English, meaning 'island of reeds'.
Variants: Rod, Rodd, Roddie, Roddy

Roland
With its origins in the Old German words for 'fame' and 'land',

Roland was widely popularised by the French *Song of Roland*, the tale of a famous warrior in Charlemagne's army, who fought valiantly after being betrayed by his stepfather.
Variants Roly, Rowles, Rollie, Rolly, Rory, Orlando

Rolf
German in origin, Rolf combines the old German words for 'hroth', meaning 'fame' and 'wulf', meaning 'wolf'. The name itself is defined as meaning 'renowned for bravery' and/or 'courage'.
Variants: Ralf, Rolfe, Rollo, Rolph, Rolphe, Roul, Roulf, Rudolf, Rudolph

Romeo
Coming from the Italian name Romolo, Romeo is Latin for 'Citizen of Rome', and the male version of Roma. It is, of course, most famously used as the hero's name in Shakespeare's *Romeo and Juliet*.
Variants: Romallus, Romanus, Roman

Rory
Originally a nickname, Rory is the Anglicised version of a Gaelic name meaning 'red-haired one'. It has the same source as Roy.
Variants: Roderick, Rurik, Rorie

Ross
Ross is a Gaelic name meaning 'headland' and is popular as a Scottish surname. It is also the male form of Rose.

The name was made popular in the 1990s in Northern America by the US sitcom *Friends*, which featured a lead character named Ross.

Roy
With its origins in Gaelic, Roy means 'red', deriving from 'Ruadh', the word for the colour. It is also a Scottish surname, carried famously by Rob Roy. The name was popularised in the

US by actor/singer Roy Rogers, who starred in many western movies.

Variants: Delroy, Elroy, Leroy, Loe, Ray, Rey, Roi, Royce, Royle, Royston

Rufus
Rufus is of Latin derivation, Rufus it means the 'red-haired one'.

Rudy
Rudy is a Germanic diminutive form of Rudolph and Rolf. (See Rolf.)

Rudyard
An Old English name, Rudyard means 'red gate'. The name is associated with British writer, Joseph Rudyard Kipling (1865-1936).

Rupert
A development of the German name Rupprecht, meaning 'bright' and 'fame', this name was borne by Prince Rupert of the Rhine, a nephew of King Charles I.

Variants: Robert, Rubert, Ruberto, Rudbert, Rupe, Ruperto, Ruprecht

Russell
Russell is derived from the Old French for 'red-haired' or 'red-faced', the French noun rousel literally meaning 'little red one'.

Variants: Rosario, Rus, Russ, Russel, Rustie, Rustin, Rusty

Ryan
The name Ryan has Gaelic origins, and means 'little king'.

Samir
Samir is Arabic for 'entertainment'.

Variants: Zamir, Sameer

Samson
Taken from the Hebrew meaning 'bright as the sun', the most

famous use of the name occurs in the Bible where strong-man Samson is betrayed by Delilah, and destroys the temple of the Philistines.
Variants: Sam, Sammy, Sampson, Shimson

Samuel
A Biblical name of Hebrew origin, Samuel means 'asked of God' and may be a derivative of Saul.
Variants: Sam, Sammie, Sammy, Shmuel

Sancho
A derivative of the Spanish for 'sincere' and 'thoughtful', as well as the Latin 'San Etus' meaning 'holy' and/or 'pure', Sancho is the male form of Sancha.

It was popularised by Miguel De Cervantes' novel, *Don Quixote* (1605-1615) where Sancho Panza was the faithful servant of the deluded title character.
Variant: Sanchez

Sanford
Sanford originates in Old English, meaning 'he who dwells at a sandy river crossing' (a ford).
Variant: Sandy

Sasha
Originating in Old French, Sasha means 'defender' or 'helper' as in the 'helper of mankind'. French singer Sacha Distel made the name popular in the 1960s and 70s.
Variant: Sacha

Saul
Saul translates from the Hebrew for 'asked/prayed for', as in a prayed-for child. The name is also Biblical: St Paul was originally named Saul, and it was also the name of the first King of Israel.
Variants: Shaul, Sol, Sollie, Solly, Saulo, Shane, Paul

Saville
Also a surname, Saville drives from the French words, 'Sa' and 'ville', literally meaning 'his' and 'town'.

Sawyer
Sawyer has its origins in Middle English, and is occupational in derivation, meaning 'someone who saws'. It is also a surname, Sawyer was popularised by Mark Twain's 1876 novel *Tom Sawyer*.
Variants: Saw, Sawyere.

Scott
Of Old English derivation, Scott translates very simply as meaning 'one of Scottish origin'.
Variant: Scot

Sean
Sean is Gaelic in origin. As the Irish version of John it shares the meaning 'God is gracious'. (See John.)
Variants: Shaughan, Shaun, Shane

Sear
This name comes from an Old English word for 'battle'.
Variants: Searle, Sears, Serle, Serlo

Sebastian
Derived from the Greek for 'venerable', Sebasta was also a town in Asia Minor (now called Siva). It is also a saint's name: Saint Sebastian was a Roman soldier who was martyred when he was shot with numerous arrows, inspiring many religious paintings.
Variants: Seb, Sebbie, Bastian, Bart, Bartiana, Barties, Sebastianus

Seth
Given to the third son of Adam and Eve in the Bible, Seth is a Hebrew name meaning 'the appointed one'. In Sanskrit it also means 'bridge'.

Seymour

In France, Seymour is derived from the old French place name of Saint-Maur, Maur meaning 'Moorish' or 'African'. In Old English, meanwhile, the name is a combination of 'sae', meaning 'sea' and 'mor' meaning marshland or moor.
Variant: Seymore

Shaanan

This name is derived from the Hebrew word for 'peaceful'.
Variants: Shanen, Shannon, Shanon

Shamir

Shamir's origins are in the Hebrew for 'flint'. There is a Jewish legend in which the Shamir were worms capable of cutting through the hardest substances on earth, and as such were used to cut the stones for King Solomon's temple.

Shem

Shem's origins are Hebrew and Biblical, where Shem was one of Noah's sons, the older brother of Ham and Japeth. The Biblical Shem was supposedly born to Noah when Noah was 500 years old.
Variants: Shammas, Shemuel

Shelley

Originating in the Old English for 'wood near a ledge clearing or meadow', Shelley is also an old English surname.
Variants: Shell, Shelly

Sheridan

The name Sheridan is thought to be a Gaelic name meaning 'wild' or 'untamed', a development of 'Siridran'. It is also a surname, belonging to US Unionist Commander General Philip Henry Sheridan (1831-1888).
Variants: Sheridon, Sherry

Sidney
Sidney has origins in Old English, where it translates as 'of a riverside meadow', and in the Old French meaning 'of St. Denis'.
Variants: Sid, Syd, Sydney

Silas
Silas' origins are in the Greek word for 'wood', Sylvanus or Silvanus. The name became popular in the 19th century after the publication of George Eliot's novel *Silas Marner*.

Simon
Simon is derived from the Greek for 'snub-nosed' and the Hebrew words for 'God has heard', 'listening' and, oddly enough, 'little hyena'. The name occurs several times in the Bible, where it was the original name of St Peter. The Old Testament also features Simeon, the second son of Jacob and Leah, while the New Testament gives us no less than six Simeons.
Variants: Cimon, Imon, Sameir, Semon, Shimone, Si, Silas, Sim, Simao, Samer, Simeon, Simi, Simion, Simkin, Simone, Simp, Simpson, Sims, Sy, Symon

Sinclair
Sinclair is a contraction of Saint-Clair, the French place name borne by a Norman martyr. Clair in Old English also means 'clear', 'bright' or 'famous'. The name is also a Scottish surname.
Variations: Clarence, Sinclaire, Sinclar

Sol
Meaning 'sun' in Latin, Sol is a short form of Solomon. (See Solomon.)

Solomon
Derived from the Hebrew word for 'peace', 'Shalom', Solomon was most famously the name of temple-building Biblical King Solomon, who died in 980BC.

Variants: Sol, Salaman, Salamon, Salo, Salman, Saloman, Salome, Salomo, Shelomo, Solmon.

Somerby
Somerby is derived from the Middle English for 'over' and 'village or town', meaning 'town across the fields' or 'nearby town'.

Spencer
Derived from the Old French, it means 'dispenser of provisions' or 'administrator'.
Variants: Spence, Spenser

Spike
Taken from the Latin 'spika', meaning a spiky point, or an ear of corn, Spike's origins are given as Old English.

Stacey
A short form of Eustace, Stacy is derived from the Greek, meaning 'rich in corn', 'fruitful' or a 'good harvest'. Eustace is also the male form of Anastasia.
Variants: Stacy, Stacie

Stanhope
Derived from the Old English for 'stone' and 'hope', a Stanhope was a high stone one would stand on to get a good view. It was also the name of a light, open, horse-drawn carriage invented by the British clergyman Reverend Fitzroy Stanhope (1787-1864).
Variants: Ford, Hope, Stan, Stancliff, Stanford

Stanley
Taken from the old German for a 'stony clearing', where 'stan' is 'stone' and 'leah' is 'meadow' or 'grassland', Stanley is also an English surname.
Variants: Stan, Stanford, Stanleigh, Stanly, Stanton

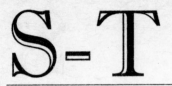

Stockton
Stockton is derived from the Old English words 'stoc' and 'tūn', meaning 'trees' and 'town' respectively. Hence Stockton's meaning is 'town near felled trees'.

Sven
Mostly used in Sweden and Norway, Sven is Norse for 'boy'.
Variants: Svarne, Svend, Swen

Sweeney
Sweeney is derived from the Gaelic word meaning 'little hero'. The name is probably best known by association with the murderous barber Sweeney Todd.

Tad
As the Anglicised form of the Gaelic name Tadhg, Tad comes from the byname that means 'poet' or 'philosopher'.

However, it is also the short form of the name Thaddeus, which was used in the Bible to distinguish between two of Christ's Apostles, both of whom were called Judas, Judas Thaddeus and Judas Iscariot.

The exact meaning of Thaddeus is unclear but it may come from the Aramaic for 'praise, desired' or the Greek for 'gift of God'.
Variants: Tadhg, Thaddeus, Theodore

Tariq
The Arabic meaning of Tariq is 'visitor'. In Hindi it means 'morning star'.

Tarquin
Tarquin was the name of two early kings of Rome – Tarquin the Proud and Tarquin the Old.

The Roman family name, Tarquinus, was originally given to those who came from Tarquinii, an ancient town of Rome.
Variants: Quin, Tarq

Tate
The Middle English meaning of this name is 'cheerful' or 'spirited'. It is also a surname.
Variant: Tait

Terence
The exact meaning of Terence is unknown. As a derivative of the Roman family name Terentius, it may come from the Latin for 'to wear out' or 'to polish'. Terentius was the name of the North African slave and playwright who adopted the name of his former master when he became a free man.

Terence is also the Anglicised form of the Irish Gaelic for 'initiator of an idea'.
Variants: Tel, Telly, Terencio, Terrance, Terry, Terryal

Thatcher
In the late 20th century, Thatcher was the surname of the first woman to hold the position of Prime Minister in Britain.

The family name Thatcher can also be used as a first name, but it was originally an occupational name. It comes from the Old English for 'thatch'.
Variants: Thacher, Thatch

Theobald
Theobald is an Old French name that is of Germanic (Frankish) origin. It means 'bold people'. An Old English version of the name, Theodbeald, was already in existence in England before the arrival of the Normans prompted the use of the German variant.
Variants: Tebald, Ted, Tedd, Teddie, Thebault, Theo, Thibaud, Thibault, Tibald, Tibold

Theodore
The name Theodore comes from the Greek for 'gift of God'.
Variants: Tad, Tadd, Taddeus, Ted, Teddie, Teddy, Thadeus, Theo, Theophilus

T

Thomas
In the Bible Thomas was one of Christ's Apostles. He is known as 'doubting Thomas' because he would not believe that Jesus had risen from the dead until he could touch his wounds with his own hands. Thomas comes from the Aramaic and Greek for 'twin' and has been borne by numerous saints.
Variants: Tamas, Tom, Tomas, Tome, Tomm, Tommie, Tommy

Thornton
The Old English meaning of Thornton is 'thorn' and 'town', thus it was often used to refer to a town or village located near thornbushes or hawthorn trees.
Variants: Thorn, Thorndike, Thornie

Timothy
Timothy is derived from a Greek name that means 'honouring God'. In the New Testament it was borne by a young man from Asia Minor who was converted to Christianity by St Paul. He later became the Bishop of Ephesus.
Variants: Tim, Timmie, Timofey

Toby
Toby is a short form of the Biblical name Tobias. In the Old Testament Tobias was the son of Tobit who left his home and went travelling with the archangel Raphael as his companion. When he returned Tobias was wealthy, married and possessed a cure to restore his father's eyesight.

Tobias comes from the Hebrew for 'God is good'.
Variants: Tobe, Tobey, Tobiah, Tobie, Tobin, Tobit, Tobye, Tobyn

Todd
The transferred use of the surname Todd comes from the Middle English for 'fox'. As a nickname it was used for someone who either had red hair, or was known for being cunning.
Variants: Tad, Tod, Toddie, Toddy

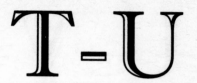

Travis
Travis is an English family name that comes from the Old French for 'a crossing', given to someone who lived near a ford or crossroads. Alternatively original bearers of the name gathered tolls at a crossing, gate or bridge.
Variants: Travers, Travus, Travon, Trevon

Trey
Originally Trey was a nickname given to a boy who bore a name that had been in his family for three generations. It comes from the Latin for 'three'. As a variant of Tremaine, it has the Cornish meaning 'the house on the rock'.
Variant: Tremaine

Tyler
Tyler was an Old English occupational name given to someone who tiled roofs or made tiles.
Variants: Tiler, Ty, Tye

Tyrone
The name Tyrone is derived from a Northern Irish county. Its Gaelic meaning is 'Owen's country'. Owen is the Celtic form of Eugene, which means 'well born' in Greek.
Variants: Ty, Tye, Tyron

Tyson
Tyson comes from the French for 'firebrand' and was originally given to a bad-tempered person as a nickname.
Variant: Tie, Ty, Tye, Tysen, Tysone

Uri
In the Bible Uriah was the name of the husband of Bathsheba, the woman with whom King David committed adultery. His name comes from the Hebrew for 'God is my light' and Uri is its short form.
Variants: Uriah, Urie, Yuri

Ulysses

Ulysses was the name of the hero of the epic poem *The Odyssey*, attributed to the Greek poet Homer.

The exact meaning of the name is unknown but it is thought to come from the Greek for 'to hate'. In North America Ulysses was the first name of the American Civil War hero and President of the United States, Ulysses S Grant.

Variants: Odysseus, Uileos, Ulick, Ulises

Valentine

See Valentina in the Girls' section.

Vaughan

Vaughan comes from the Old Welsh for 'little' and the Celtic for 'small'.

Variants: Vaughn, Vaune, Vawn, Vawne, Van, Vonn

Vernon

Richard de Vernon was one of the Norman conquerors of England. His name comes from the Gaulish word for 'where alders grow'. Vernon also comes from the Latin for 'belonging to the spring'.

Variants: Vern, Verna, Verne

Victor

Victor, the masculine equivalent of Victoria, comes from the Latin for 'victory'. It was a popular name among early Christians who used it as a reference to Christ's victory over death and sin. In Britain use of the name was revived during the reign of Queen Victoria.

Variants: Vic, Vick, Victoir, Viktor, Vito, Vitor

Vincent

Vincent derives its meaning from the Latin for 'conquering'. The name was borne by several early saints, including Vincent de Paul who founded a charitable order to help the poor.

Variants: Vince, Vincente, Vine, Vinnie, Vinny, Vinson

Virgil
The name Virgil has traditionally been given to children in honour of the Roman poet who lived during the 1st century BC. The name comes from the Latin for 'stick' and is thought to imply 'staff-bearer'.
Variants: Verge, Vergit, Virge, Virgie, Virgilio

Vivian
See Vivian in the Girls' section.

Walker
The Old English meaning of Walker is 'to tread'. It is a former occupational name used for 'a fuller of cloth'.
Variant: Wal

Warner
Warner is a medieval name that was brought to Britain by the Normans. It comes from the Old German for 'guard' and 'army'.
Variants: Garnier, Warren, Werner, Wernher

Warren
As a derivative of the French town name La Varenne, Warren means 'game preserve', 'wasteland' or 'sandy soil'. It was first brought to England by the Normans as Guarin or Warin.
Variants: Varner, Ware, Waring, Warner, Warrener

Webster
This is an Old English occupational name for a 'weaver'. The name is associated with the lexicographer Noah Webster after whom the Webster series of dictionaries derive their name.
Variants: Web, Webb

Wesley
The Old English meaning of Wesley is 'western wood, meadow or clearing'.
Variants: Lee, Leigh, Wellesley, Wes, Wesleigh, Wesly, Wezley

W - X

Boys

Wilbur

The exact origin of the name Wilbur is uncertain, but a number of theories exist. It may come from the German and Old English for 'will' and 'defence, fortress'. It may also be derived from the Old English for 'wild boar'.

As a variant of Wilbert, Wilbur could come from the German and Old English for 'will' and 'bright'. Or it could have the Germanic meaning 'pledge or hostage' and 'bright'. Wilbur could equally mean 'servant of St Gilbert' in Scottish Gaelic.
Variants: Gilbert, Wilbert, Wilburh, Wilburn, Wiley, Wilgburh, Willard, Willmer, Wylie

William

William I of England is known as William the Conqueror, after he defeated King Harold in 1066 at the Battle of Hastings. Other monarchs bearing the name include William III (William of Orange). It is also the name of the future British king, Prince William. The name means 'will, desire' and 'helmet, protection'.
Variants: Bill, Billy, Guillaume, Liam, Wil, Wilem, Wilhelm, Williamson, Willie, Willy

Winston

Sir Winston Churchill was perhaps the most beloved British Prime Minister of the 20th century. The family name comes from the Old English for 'joy' and 'stone'. It also has the Old English meaning 'to win, defeat or conquer' and 'town'.
Variants: Win, Winnie, Winton, Wynston, Wyston

Wycliffe

Wycliffe comes from the Old Norse for 'village near the cliff'. It was the surname of the 14th century religious reformer John Wycliffe who produced the first English translation of the Bible.
Variants: Wyche, Wyck, Wycke

Xavier

In the 16th century the Spanish soldier, St Francis Xavier, spread

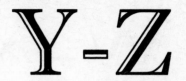

the Christian faith to lands in the Far East, including China and Japan. The patron saint of missionaries, he was also a founding member of the Jesuits. The Arabic meaning of the name is 'bright'.
Variants: Javier, Zever

Yosef
Yosef is a variant of the Biblical name Joseph, which comes from the Hebrew for 'God will add (another son)'. (See also Joseph.)
Variant: Joseph

Zachary
Zachary is a variant of the Biblical name Zachariah, which was borne by the elderly father of John the Baptist who was husband to Elizabeth. The Hebrew meaning of the name is 'remembrance of God'.
Variants: Zachariah, Zack, Zechariah

Zakkai
This name comes from the Hebrew for 'pure, innocent'.

Zamir
Zamir comes from the Hebrew for 'song'.

Zeus
In Greek mythology Zeus was the supreme god who ruled the heavens. He was also the god of weather, maintained law and order and protected earthly kings. His name comes from the Greek for 'shining', 'bright' and 'bright sky'.
Variants: Zeno, Zenon, Zenos

Zion
Zion is a name that is used in connection with Israel, Judaism, the Christian church and heaven. Rastafarians believe that it is also the name of the Promised Land.

Zion is a variant of Sion, which is the name of the hill on which the city of Jerusalem was built in King David's time.

African names

In African culture, names are of paramount importance, and a lot of work goes into their choosing. Current events, astrology and the aspirations of parents are all taken into account, as it is generally felt that whatever name is picked, it will influence the child's life and reflect on the family. The following is a list of the more popular African names.

FEMALE

	Halima	Oni
	Horera	Pili
Adia	Imani	Pulika
Aisha	Imara	Rabia
Aliya	Ina	Rafiya
Ama	Jamala	Rashida
Amira	Jamila	Rayha
Asya	Jirani	Rehani
Azalee	Kali	Saada
Bashira	Kesi	Sabiha
Bebi	Kinah	Saburi
Bishara	Kioja	Safi
Chaniya	Kisima	Salaam
Chiku	Laini	Salima
Dafina	Latifah	Shani
Dalila	Lela	Suma
Dene	Lisha	Tabita
Eidi	Malaika	Talha
Eshe	Malia	Tamasha
Etana	Marjani	Tumaini
Fahima	Matima	Ujamaa
Faiza	Muna	Uzima
Fatima	Nadra	Wanja
Freya	Naima	Wema
Gasira	Nasra	Wesesa
Gerda	Neema	Yasmin
Gimbya	Njema	Yetunde
Hadiya	Noni	Yusra
Hafsa	Omolara	Zaina

MALE

Abdul
Ahmed
Akram
Amar
Asim
Aziz
Badru
Bakari
Chandu
Chiké
Dajan
Damu
Daraja
Elimu
Eze
Ezenachi
Fahim
Fakhri
Faqihi
Fidel
Gahiji
Ghalib
Haamid
Habib
Hakim
Harun
Hasan
Hashim
Ibrahim
Iman
Islam
Ismael
Jaafar
Jafari

Jalil
Jamal
Jamil
Kadhi
Kamil
Kasim
Khalil
Kwame
Lali
Latif
Lutalo
Maalik
Mahmud
Maliki
Mandala
Mkamba
Muhammed
Mwangi
Naadir
Naeem
Nemsi
Nizam
Njama
Obaseki
Ojore
Okello
Oman
Omar
Ouma
Pandu
Petiri
Pili
Quaashie
Rafiki
Rahim
Rashaad

Rashid
Rehani
Ruhiu
Saalim
Saeed
Salaam
Salim
Sefu
Simba
Sudi
Suhuba
Taalib
Taji
Tajiri
Talib
Tarik
Ubora
Ufanisi
Umar
Usiku
Waitimu
Warui
Waziri
Weke
Wemusa
Yahya
Yasini
Yoofi
Yusuf
Zahir
Zahran
Zaid
Zende
Zuber
Zuka
Zuri

Celtic names

There is much speculation about where exactly the Celts originated, but it is generally believed that they came from the region that is now Germany or Switzerland, and spread across Europe, settling as far afield as Ireland, Britain, Brittany, Spain, Hungary, Bohemia and Asia Minor. The original Celtic language split into two separate languages, known as Goidelic and Brythonic. Celtic names originate in both these languages, as well as in the original Celtic language, or in Celtic mythology. Following are some examples.

FEMALE

	Colleen	Kathleen
	Cordelia	Keelin
Africa	Dana	Kendall
Aileen	Dawn	Lorna
Aine	Dee	Melvina
Aislinn	Devnet	Meredith
Alanna	Deirdre	Moira
Alvina	Edith	Morgance
Annabelle	Eilis	Morgandy
Arden	Enid	Nola
Arleen	Erin	Piper
Arlene	Erlina	Pixie
Bevin	Etain	Rae
Birkita	Evelyn	Raelin
Brenna	Fainche	Rhonda
Bretta	Fallon	Seanna
Briana	Fiona	Shayla
Bridget	Fionn	Shea
Brietta	Fionnula	Shela
Brites	Gilda	Shylah
Brooke	Gwen	Tara
Caitlin	Gwendolyn	Treasa
Cara	Gwynne	Treva
Cary	Isolde	Ula
Casey	Kaie	Wilona
Cerdwin	Kaitlyn	Wynne

Celtic names

MALE

Abenzio
Ahearn
Ainsley
Alan
Angus
Arland
Arthur
Beacan
Bevin
Boyd
Bram
Briac
Brian
Brice
Brody
Bryant
Caedmon
Camlin
Carden
Carney
Carroll
Cary
Casey
Chadwick
Clancy
Clyde
Coalan
Cody
Colin
Con
Conan
Condon
Conner
Corey

Craig
Cullen
Dale
Dane
Davis
Dermot
Derry
Desmond
Donnelly
Driscoll
Duff
Duncan
Dunn
Edan
Egan
Erin
Evan
Farrell
Fergus
Ferguson
Ferris
Finlay
Fionn
Flynn
Frazer
Galen
Gallagher
Gilroy
Greg
Irving
Kane
Kearney
Keary
Kegan
Keir
Keith

Kelvin
Kendall
Kerwin
Maddox
Malvin
Melvin
Mannix
Marmaduke
Marvin
Melvin
Merlin
Monroe
Murray
Nevin
Palmer
Perth
Regan
Ronan
Scully
Sean
Sheridan
Sloane
Tadc
Teague
Tegan
Tiernan
Tierney
Torin
Torrance
Torrey
Trevor
Tuathal
Ultan
Urien
Varney
Vaughan

Muslim names

In Islam, it is taught that the Prophet Mohammad requested that his followers should avoid naming their offsping with meaningless names, and should choose a name with care. The following are a selection of Muslim names.

FEMALE

	Jamila	Shahla
	Khadija	Shahnaz
Alisha	Kulsum	Shahrazad
Aamira	Leila	Shaliza
Aarifa	Lubna	Shalizar
Afsana	Mahjabeen	Sayeeda
Amani	Maimun	Shabab
Ameena	Malika	Shabnam
Azra	Marjaan	Shagufta
Ayesha	Mehrnaz	Shaheen
Aziza	Mumina	Shakeela
Basheera	Nadira	Shakira
Benazir	Nafisa	Shamina
Bushra	Naima	Shamshad
Bibi	Nargis	Shirin/Shireen
Darya	Nazia	Suhaila
Dilbar	Nazima	Suraiya/Soraya
Dilruba	Nazmoon	Taslima
Faiza	Niloufar	Wafa
Farida	Nusrat	Waheeda
Farah	Parvin	Yasmeen
Fatima	Rabia	Zahira
Firuza	Raisa	Zarin
Gulshan	Rashida	Zarina
Gulzar	Razia	Zeba
Habeeba	Rehana	Zeb-un-Nisa
Halima	Sadika	Zeenat
Haseena	Sakeena	Zenia
Husna	Salena	Zohra
Ismat	Salima	Zubaida
Jahanara	Sanaz	Zulekha

Muslim names

MALE

Abdul
Abdullah
Abed
Ahsan
Akbar
Alam
Ali
Amir
Amzad
Aslam
Azaad
Aziz
Babur
Basheer
Basit
Bilal
Chaghatai
Chengiz
Dara
Dilbar
Dilshad
Eijaz
Faiz
Farhad
Farookh
Fayyad
Fazil
Firouz
Ghalib
Gulzar
Habeeb
Hamid
Hassan
Hussain

Ibrahim
Ifran
Imran
Iqbal
Irshad
Ishrat
Izhar
Izmet
Jalal
Jalil
Jansher
Javed
Kamal
Karim
Khadim
Khalid
Khan
Latif
Liaqat
Mahtab
Mahmood
Majid
Mohammad
Moshin
Mustafa
Nabeel
Nadeem
Naseem
Nasser
Nadir
Nizam
Omar
Ossama
Pasha
Qasim
Raamiz

Rafi
Rahim
Rashad
Rashid
Raza
Rehman
Sadik
Salman
Selim
Sayeed
Shahab
Shahrukh
Shakir
Shahbaz
Sharif
Shamshad
Sherally
Suhail
Sultan
Talal
Taj
Tazim
Talat
Talib
Tariq
Timur
Usman
Wahab
Wajid
Wasim
Wazir
Yasin
Yasir
Yusuf
Zafar
Zahid

Native American names

Native American names have meanings that are usually derived from nature and/or relate to the family of the child. In many cases, the family themselves would not name a child, but rather this would be left to an important member of the tribe – often someone said to have been born with the 'gift' to be able to name children. The following are a selection of Native American names.

FEMALE

Ahanu
Ahiga
Ahiliya
Anoki
Ashkii
Awan
Bidziil
Bimisi
Chesmu
Chunta
Ciqala
Delsin
Dustu
Dyami
Elan
Elki
Elsu
Etu
Ezhno
Gosheven
Guyapi
Hahnee
Hakan
Hania
Helki
Honani

Istaqa
Istu
Iye
Jacy
Jolon
Kajika
Kele
Keme
Kitchi
Kohana
Kono
Kwahu
Lansa
Lanu
Leyati
Lokni
Lonato
Manipi
Moki
Molimo
Mona
Muata
Muraco
Nahele
Nayati
Neka
Nikiti
Ohanko

Ouray
Oya
Pahana
Patwin
Payat
Paytah
Sakima
Shiye
Sike
Siwili
Songan
Sucki
Taima
Takoda
Tse
Tupi
Uzumati
Viho
Wahkan
Waquini
Wicasa
Wuyi
Wynono
Yahto
Yancy
Yanisin
Yiska
Yuma

Native American names

MALE

Abetzi
Aiyana
Alawa
Anaba
Ankti
Ayashe
Ayita
Bena
Bly
Catori
Chenoa
Chepi
Chilaili
Chumani
Cocheta
Dena
Dyani
Ehawee
Enola
Fala
Flo
Galilahi
Haloke
Halona
Huyana
Imala
Istas
Ituha
Kachina
Kai
Kaya
Leotie
Liseli
Macawi

Mahu
Mai
Maka
Manaba
Mansi
Maralah
Mausi
Memdi
Mika
Minal
Mituna
Nahimana
Namid
Nara
Niabi
Nituna
Nova
Olathe
Onawa
Onida
Pakuna
Papina
Pavati
Powaqa
Pules
Sahkyo
Salali
Sanuye
Satinka
Shada
Shadi
Shima
Sihu
Sitala
Sitsi
Sunki

Tablita
Tadewi
Tadita
Taigi
Taini
Taipa
Takala
Takhi
Tala
Tama
Tansy
Tayanita
Tehya
Tiponi
Tiva
Tolinka
Tuwa
Una
Urika
Utina
Wachiwi
Wakanda
Waki
Waneta
Wauna
Weeko
Winema
Wuti
Wyanet
Yamka
Yazhi
Yepa
Yoki
Zaltana
Zihna
Zitkala

Index

Index – Girls

(v) = variant

Index – Girls

Index – Girls

Index – Girls

(v) = variant

Index – Girls

Index – Girls

(v) = variant

Index – Girls

Index – Girls

(v) = variant

Index – Boys

(v) = variant

Index – Boys

Index – Boys

Index – Boys

Index – Boys

Index – Boys

Index – Boys

Index – Boys

Index – Boys

(v) = variant